COMPARATIVE POLITICAL FINANCE

D0757839

DATE DUE

DE 18 '96			
AP 18 '97			
MY 21 '01			
JE 7 '06			

Advances in Political Science

Comparative Political Finance in the 1980s

This book, the first from Cambridge in the series *Advances in Political Science*, concerns the financing of politics, political parties, candidates and elections in eleven countries. It contains case studies of individual countries, various country-by-country comparisons, and a conceptual framework enabling the reader to understand the context of financial sources and implications of funding sources. All the chapters demonstrate the problems common to democracies seeking to regulate uses and abuses of money in politics in pluralistic societies in which there are numerous openings for political disbursements; many present themes emphasizing forms of public funding (alternatively called state aid in some countries) in which governments assist parties or candidates to subsist and compete. Professor Alexander has assembled a distinguished international team of contributors to present this first major appraisal of such a vital aspect of democratic practice for nearly twenty years.

Advances in Political Science: An International Series reflects the aims and intellectual traditions of the International Political Science Association: the generation and dissemination of rigorous political inquiry free of any subdisciplinarity or other orthodoxy. Along with its quarterly companion publication, the *International Political Science Review*, the series seeks to present the best work being done today (1) on the central and critical controversial themes of politics and/or (2) in new areas of inquiry where political scientists, alone or in conjunction with other scholars, are shaping innovative concepts and methodologies of political science.

Political science as an intellectual discipline has burgeoned in recent decades. With the enormous growth in the number of publications and papers and their increasing sophistication, however, has also come a tendency toward parochialism along national, subdisciplinary, and other lines. It was to counteract these tendencies that political scientists from a handful of countries created IPSA in 1949. Through roundtables organized by its research committees and study groups, at its triennial world congresses (the next of which takes place in summer 1991 in Buenos Aires, Argentina), and through its organizational work, IPSA has sought to encourage the creation of both an international-minded science of politics and a body of scholars from many nations (now from more than 40 regional associations), who approach their research and interactions with other scholars from an international perspective.

Comparative Political Finance in the 1980s, edited by Herbert E. Alexander, is the seventh volume in *Advances in Political Science: An International Series*. Like its predecessors, it comprises original papers which focus in an integrated manner on a single important topic – in this case, how eleven countries finance their politics, political parties, candidates, and elections. Originally presented at meetings of the IPSA Research Committee on Political Finance and Political Corruption, the volume taps the vast intellectual resources of political scientists linked to the International Political Science Association.

Richard L. Merritt, Editor, *Advances in Political Science*

Comparative Political Finance in the 1980s

EDITED BY

HERBERT E. ALEXANDER

Citizens' Research Foundation
University of Southern California

WITH THE ASSISTANCE OF

JOEL FEDERMAN

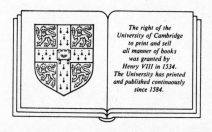

The right of the
University of Cambridge
to print and sell
all manner of books
was granted by
Henry VIII in 1534.
The University has printed
and published continuously
since 1584.

CAMBRIDGE UNIVERSITY PRESS

Cambridge
New York   Port Chester   Melbourne   Sydney

Published by the Press Syndicate of the University of Cambridge
The Pitt Building, Trumpington Street, Cambridge CB2 1RP
40 West 20th Street, New York, NY 10011, USA
10 Stamford Road, Oakleigh, Melbourne 3166, Australia

First published 1989

Printed in Great Britain by the University Press, Cambridge

British Library cataloguing in publication data

Comparative political finance in the 1980s.
–(Advances in political science).
1. Western world. Political parties.
Financing
I. Alexander, Herbert E. (Herbert Ephraim)
1927 – II. Federman, Joel III. Series
324.2′1′091812

Library of Congress cataloguing in publication data

Comparative political finance in the 1980s/edited by Herbert E.
Alexander with the assistance of Joel Federman.
p. cm. – (Advances in political science)
Includes index.
ISBN 0 521 36464 7
1. Campaign funds. 2. Comparative government. I. Alexander,
Herbert E. II. Federman, Joel. III. series.
JF2112.C28C64 1989
324.7′8–dc19 88–29938 CIP

ISBN 0 521 36464 7

VN

Dedicated to the memory of Khayyam Zev Paltiel,
a respected and beloved student of political finance,
who gave selflessly to the work of the Research Committee
on Political Finance and Political Corruption,
and to the development of this book.

Contents

Preface and acknowledgements   *page* ix
List of contributors   xi
Introduction   1

1   Money and politics: rethinking a conceptual framework   9
HERBERT E. ALEXANDER

2   Trends in British political funding, 1979–84   24
MICHAEL PINTO-DUSCHINSKY

3   Canadian election expense legislation, 1963–85: a critical appraisal or was the effort worth it?   51
KHAYYAM ZEV PALTIEL

4   Public funding of elections in Australia   76
ERNEST A. CHAPLES

5   American presidential elections since public funding, 1976–84   95
HERBERT E. ALEXANDER

6   Party financing in Israel: experience and experimentation, 1968–85   124
JONATHAN MENDILOW

7   Public financing of parties in Italy   153
GIAN FRANCO CIAURRO

8   Financing of Spanish political parties   172
PILAR DEL CASTILLO

9   The "modesty" of Dutch party finance   200
RUUD KOOLE

10 The new German system of party funding: the
    Presidential committe report of 1983 and its
    realization   220
        HANS-PETER SCHNEIDER

11 Structure and impact of public subsidies to political
    parties in Europe: the examples of Austria, Italy,
    Sweden and West Germany   236
        KARL-HEINZ NASSMACHER

    Index   268

Preface and acknowledgements

This book emerged as a product of several meetings of the Research Committee on Political Finance and Political Corruption of the International Political Science Association (IPSA), including those at Moscow, Rio de Janeiro, Oxford, and the 1985 IPSA Convention in Paris. The Research Committee is a network of scholars interested in aspects of the financing of politics in their own countries, countries they study, and on a comparative basis. The Committee is similarly interested in political corruption in all its manifestations. While this text deals only with issues of political finance, the Committee hopes to publish a volume on political corruption in the near future.

Many people contributed their talents and energies to the creation of this volume. Among them, I am happy to give special acknowledgement to Joel Federman, Research Assistant at the Citizens' Research Foundation and a graduate student in the Department of Political Science at the University of Southern California. Joel managed the project from its inception, contributed greatly to the editing of each chapter, drafted the introduction and, not least, suggested the title for the volume. His invaluable contribution is also given recognition on the title page.

I am grateful to each of the chapter authors, who met every deadline with aplomb despite the often-great disadvantages of distance. Also greatly appreciated is the patience and cooperation of the IPSA series editors, Richard Merritt, John Trent and Jean A. Laponce, and of Michael Holdsworth, our editor at Cambridge University Press.

Several people contributed information for the public financing inception dates table in Chapter one. Particularly helpful were Mr. Wang at the Consulate General of Brazil in Los Angeles; Mr. Hazar at the Turkish Embassy in Washington, D.C.; Mrs. Morris at the Colombian Embassy in Washington, D.C.; Roy Pierce at the University of Michigan with information concerning French public financing and Henry Wells with information about Costa Rican and Venezuelan public funding.

Klauss Klott, a graduate student in the German Department at USC, helped to edit the footnotes in the Schneider and Nassmacher chapters.

Barbara Sanchez typed the first draft and early revisions to the text and Annie Tran typed the final changes to the manuscript; each did their part quickly, ably and with a smile.

Gloria Cornette, CRF's assistant director, coordinated the transfer of the text onto computer files and provided technical expertise and moral support at every stage of the manuscript's development. For all who worked on the project, Gloria's encouragement has been especially appreciated.

None of those who were so helpful is responsible for errors of omission or commission; for those, as for interpretations, I bear sole responsibility.

I always appreciate the cooperation and encouragement received from officers and members of the board of trustees of the Citizens' Research Foundation and of my colleagues at the University of Southern California, but the presentation is mine and does not reflect their views.

Without the contributions of numerous supporters of the Citizens' Research Foundation, this study would not have been possible.

Contributors

HERBERT E. ALEXANDER is Professor of Political Science at the University of Southern California and Director of the Citizens' Research Foundation. He has taught at Princeton University, Yale University, and the University of Pennsylvania. In 1961–1962 he was executive director of the President's Commission on Campaign Costs and has been a consultant to various levels of government in the United States.

PILAR DEL CASTILLO is Profesora Titular of Constitutional Law at the Universidad a Distancia (UNED) in Madrid. She studied Political Science at Ohio State University sponsored by a Fulbright scholarship. She is the author of *La Financiacion de Partidos y Candidatos en las democracias occidentales*, as well as of several articles on Spanish political parties finance in Spanish journals.

ERNEST A. CHAPLES is Senior Lecturer in Government at the University of Sydney. He is co-author of *The Wran Model, Case Studies in New South Wales Electoral Politics*, and a wide variety of articles concerning Australian, American and Scandinavian politics. He is a regular commentator on Australian network radio.

GIAN FRANCO CIAURRO is Associate Professor of Constitutional and Parliamentary Law at the University of Rome. He is Recording Secretary of the Italian Chamber of Deputies, Director of the quarterly review, *Nuovi Studi Politici*, and the National Secretary of the Italian Association of Political and Social Science. He is the author of several volumes concerning Italian parliamentary democracy and political finance.

JOEL FEDERMAN is a doctoral candidate at the University of Southern California and Research Assistant at the Citizens' Research Foundation. His fields of interest are political philosophy, international relations and comparative politics. His dissertation will concern the theory of nonviolence and conflict resolution.

RUUD A. KOOLE is Director of the Documentation Centre on Dutch Political Parties of the University of Groningen and lecturer in political science at the University of Leiden. He has published various articles on party organization, party finance and on the defense policies of political parties. He has edited several Yearbooks of the Documentation Centre and two other volumes on political parties and parliament.

JONATHAN MENDILOW is Associate Professor of Political Science at Rider College in Lawrenceville, New Jersey. He has published widely in British and American journals on Israeli politics, comparative politics and political theory.

KARL-HEINZ NASSMACHER is Professor of Political Science and Director of the Institute of Comparative Politics (ICP) at the University of Oldenburg (West Germany). Since 1981 his comparative study of party finance has included field research in Canada, the United States, Austria, Italy and Sweden, and resulted in several articles on public funding published in German and Austrian periodicals.

KHAYYAM Z. PALTIEL was Professor and former Chairman of the Department of Political Science at Carleton University, Ottawa, Canada. He was the author of *Political Party Financing in Canada* and many studies on the control of election expenses, party finance, political broadcasting, corporatism, and Israeli politics. He served as consultant to numerous public bodies in Canada and abroad. Professor Paltiel passed away on April 17, 1988, during the process of publishing this volume.

MICHAEL PINTO-DUSCHINSKY is Senior Lecturer in Government at Brunel University. He is co-executive secretary of the International Political Science Association's research committee on political finance and political corruption. He is the author (with David Butler) of *The British General Election of 1970* and of *British Political Finance*. He contributed to *Britain at the Polls, 1974* and *Britain at the Polls, 1979*.

HANS-PETER SCHNEIDER is Professor of Public Law, Philosophy of Law and Ecclesiastical Law at the University of Hannover. He is the author of *Judge Made Law, The Parliamentary Opposition in the Constitutional Law of the Federal Republic of Germany*, as well as numerous related articles. In 1982–83, he was a member of the President's Committee on Party Funding.

Introduction

The complexion of political finance in the mature democratic nations has undergone significant changes in the last two decades. Spurred in some cases by scandal, in others by the rapidly escalating costs of politics, many governments have enacted new laws to regulate or to alter their national systems of political finance. Among these reforms are laws governing disclosure, transparency, expenditure and contribution limits, as well as direct forms of public subsidies to parties and candidates.

Concurrently, while scholarship concerning reforms in individual countries has flourished, there has been a paucity of literature addressing itself to comparative themes: the two most recent book-length texts on the subject were *Comparative Political Finance: A Symposium*, edited by Richard Rose and Arnold J. Heidenheimer as a special issue of the *Journal of Politics* in 1963; and a book, edited by Arnold J. Heidenheimer, *Comparative Political Finance: The Financing of Party Organizations and Election Campaigns* (Lexington, Massachusetts: D. C. Heath and Company, 1970). The present volume seeks to address this gap in the comparative literature on political finance.

The two chapters which frame this book – written by myself and Karl-Heinz Nassmacher – deal with comparative themes. The other eight chapters are case studies of political finance in individual countries. This is a representative group of countries and authors: Michael Pinto-Duschinsky writes on British political funding, Khayyam Zev Paltiel on Canada, Ernest A. Chaples on Australia, myself on the United States, Jonathan Mendilow on Israel, Hans-Peter Schneider on the Federal Republic of Germany, Pilar del Castillo on Spain, Gian Franco Ciaurro on Italy, and Ruud Koole on the Netherlands. All chapters investigate the problems common to democracies seeking to regulate uses of money in election campaigns. The topic has been the subject of national commissions in the United States, Canada, Australia, Great Britain and West Germany,

1

among others. This is an indication of the extent of concern about political financing, in presidential as well as parliamentary systems, in both strong and weak party systems.

Though the broader theme of comparative political finance is the intended subject of this volume, the particular issue of the role of public funding has emerged as a salient feature. Seven of the country studies deal substantially with the effects of public funding on the political system; Britain is an exception because its system of public funding only indirectly subsidizes its parties through availability of free television time and its candidates through free mailing. Thus it is appropriate that the chapters which address comparative themes focus also on the subject of public financing.

In the first chapter, I note that the effects of public money on political systems have not received sufficient attention in the analysis of political finance. Public funding has an impact upon political parties, individual and group contributors, and on government itself. Some of these effects may be intended by the sponsors of the various legislations, while others may arise as unintended consequences. The chapter attempts a preliminary revision of previous political finance theory to include government as a constituent element of its formulation. It goes on to discuss the role of public funding in comparative perspective, noting the numerous forms and effects of such funding. The design of public funding programs should include consideration of the mechanisms by which the money is raised, who should receive the subsidy, and how and when it should be made. The chapter addresses the possibility that funding mechanisms can be used unfairly and suggests measures to avoid the establishment of programs which may do damage to the ideal of equality of opportunity. I conclude that policy makers in each country must strike their own balance between the competing forces of public and private monies, attempting policy tradeoffs in which the greater good outweighs the occasional hurts.

Michael Pinto-Duschinsky reports on the continuing British political debate over the funding of parties, including skirmishes over proposals to provide direct public funding. He reviews the finances of the Conservative and Labor Parties, as well as those of the Alliance between the Liberal and Social Democratic Parties. Pinto-Duschinsky examines trade union donations to the Labor Party in particular detail, noting that, despite declining union membership, the party has managed to receive increased funding from unions between 1979 and 1983 due to increases in the political levy assessed from each union member. In fact, union donations to the Labor Party have exceeded business donations to the Conservatives since 1979. Pinto-Duschinsky notes two salient features of British political finance in the mid 1980s. The first is the emergence of the Alliance, which has been the most successful third party since the First World War in terms of collecting both small and large individual contributions. Secondly, the Conservative Party, which has achieved great political success, has nonetheless lagged in its fund raising. This, Pinto-Duschinsky suggests, may be partially the result of its failure to employ direct mail solicitation methods.

Responding both to scandals and to rising campaign costs, Canadian lawmakers have devoted considerable attention to the area of political finance since 1963. But the reforms which have resulted from this attention, writes the late Khayyam Z. Paltiel, have generally worked to the advantage of the established parties and have run counter to the principle of equality of opportunity. The Canadian federal registration law for parties, for example, requires at least twelve sitting Members of Parliament or the sponsorship of fifty candidates, thereby severely handicapping those who would attempt to establish regional groupings outside the two large central Canadian provinces. Canadian federal law, Paltiel notes, "appears to opt for less rather than greater public participation, except through established parties." A similar situation exists below the federal level, where public subsidy programs are in place in eight out of ten provinces. In Quebec, for example, only those parties which obtain the first and second largest number of votes in each constituency are assured of reimbursements. Citing these and other instances, such as Bill C-169, which was promulgated clearly for the convenience of the major parties and which had several of its provisions struck down in a court challenge concerning their constitutionality, Paltiel argues that fundamental reform of the federal Election Expenses Act is in order. Specifically, he calls for changes in the regulatory administration of the law, including the creation of an agency along the lines of the formal Commission on Election Contributions and Expenses of Ontario. Such a body would avoid the "colonization of the regulators by the regulated," assuring "input from others than incumbents." Paltiel observes that Canadian public funding, by enabling less affluent candidates to borrow funds, has granted some groups, such as women, a greater degree of access to the political process. Overall, however, the two major parties have been the principal beneficiaries of the extant public funding system.

As Ernest A. Chaples observes, public financing in Australia emerged as a partisan issue of the Labor Party. Responding to the combined pressures of spiraling campaign costs in the television era and its inability to compete adequately with the conservative parties in raising funds, Labor has long been an advocate of public funding measures. Amid strong conservative opposition, public funding was enacted in New South Wales in 1981. It was only after the successful application of the law in New South Wales in 1981, combined with growing conservative acceptance of the funds (which they had originally boycotted), that legislation on a national scale was brought forward and passed with little controversy in 1983. Though Chaples reports widespread non-compliance with campaign expenditure limits and disclosure laws, he finds that there may be an emerging consensus in Australia concerning public funding legislation. Conservative parties are much more opposed to disclosure of contributions than to a minimal public funding program. Chaples predicts that now that public financing has taken hold at the federal level in Australia it will probably be enacted also in the states of Victoria, South Australia and Western Australia.

In my chapter on American presidential elections, I provide an overview of campaign fund raising and spending in the 1984 election, including the pre-nomination, convention and general election periods. I also review the effects on three presidential elections of the dramatic changes made to the laws regulating federal election campaign finances in the 1970s. Mainly in the wake of Watergate, public funding, contribution limits, expenditure limits and disclosure requirements were enacted with the intention of minimizing opportunities for undue financial influence on officeholders and to make the election process more open and competitive. The new laws have accomplished some of their aims, but they also have had some unintended, and not always salutary, consequences. Public matching funds have had the effect of helping to establish candidates, such as Jimmy Carter, George Bush, Gary Hart, John Anderson and Jesse Jackson, who lacked early access to traditional sources of contributions. But the laws also have led candidates seeking their parties' presidential nominations and those who support them to alter traditional campaign strategies and tactics. For example, by prohibiting candidates from gathering seed money for their campaigns through large contributions, the contribution limit has given an advantage to well-known candidates who have already achieved significant name recognition and has forced less well-known candidates to begin fund raising for their campaigns as much as a year and a half before the nominating convention. The law has exchanged the big giver for the big solicitor: contribution limits have forced many campaigns to rely on those who specialize in direct mail solicitations and on "elite solicitors" who can tap into networks of individuals capable of contributing up to the maximum allowed. The degree to which the laws have failed to achieve their intended effects testifies at least as much to the inventiveness of political actors in circumventing the laws and to the intractability of election campaign finance in a pluralistic society as to the deficiencies of the laws themselves.

Jonathan Mendilow's chapter on Israeli political finance presents a summary of the political conditions surrounding the extremely heavy spending by Israeli parties in 1965 which resulted in a call by parties across the political spectrum for political finance reform. The result was the Law for the Elections to the Knesset and to the Local Authorities, 1969, which initiated the public funding of electoral expenses, expenditure limits and the auditing of campaign finances. Public financing represented a fundamental change in the way parties were viewed, since Israeli parties were by tradition totalistic in nature, tracing back to the pre-1949 period when parties were state-like entities, performing educational, health, housing, welfare and cultural functions. By contrast, the principle of state financing of parties is "based on the recognition of the right to disagree and on the desirability of party competition." Certain public funding issues are unique to Israel, such as the controversy concerning public monies granted to certain religious organizations which are connected to major political parties. Mendilow's chapter also covers major alterations made to the public funding program in 1973 and traces the changing degrees to which the parties have complied with the law in the years since its enactment. He notes major breaches of the spending limits by the major parties in the 1985 elections and suggests a series of measures which might help prevent further abuses.

Gian Franco Ciaurro notes that public financing in Italy emerged as a response to public displeasure concerning a situation in which political parties obtained funds in a variety of questionable ways, including the illegal diversion of public monies directly to party coffers. The public funding system which came into effect in 1974 subsidizes the national, regional and European parliamentary electoral expenses of parties, as well as their ongoing daily expenses. As a transparency measure, the law requires the publication each year of the parties' financial balance sheets for the previous year. Ciaurro examines these documents, noting several factors which point to their unreliability as clear indicators of Italian party finance. For example, since the law requires only that the parties publish their national balances, the substantial sums raised and spent by local and peripheral party organizations are not accounted for officially. Ciaurro estimates that actual party spending amounts to more than double the figures declared in the official balance sheets. In addition, the amounts reported for certain party activities are far below what one might logically expect such activities to cost. "In some instances," Ciaurro comments, "the reported figures stretch the limits of the observer's credulity." Further, the undependability of the official accounts is highlighted by numerous recent court cases involving ongoing illegal campaign contributions and "kickbacks" to party treasuries. Despite these limitations, Ciaurro argues, the balance sheets do provide some useful data. He finds that membership dues play a relatively minor role in party income, in contrast to that supplied by public funding. Only the Communist and Socialist parties were able to consistently declare that public funding accounted for less than half their income; though the Christian Democrats appear to be relying less on public funds over time, all of the other Italian parties declared public funding to be their sole or predominant source of income. Ciaurro also notes that the parties spend a large portion of their funds propping up deficit-ridden party newspapers, which have little influence with the electorate but are too much an element of party honor to be abandoned. Reflecting on the first twelve years of Italian public financing, Ciaurro concludes that the system has had little impact on closing off questionable fund-raising efforts by the parties. He argues that the system sometimes acts as an incentive for parties to increase their overall expenditure levels, and, in addition, has encouraged a concentration of power in the central executives of the parties. He suggests that the system of cash grants to parties might well be wholly or partially replaced by the provision of certain free services to the parties.

Pilar del Castillo opens her chapter with a description of the party system which began to develop in Spain after the death of General Franco in 1975. The lack of a stable party system, she points out, hampers methodic analysis of the parties and, in turn, of party finances. Such difficulties are aggravated by the lack of an effective system of legal control and by the failure of the parties to disclose their financial accounts. Castillo reviews the consequences of the laws establishing public financing of Spanish political parties, noting that, while both extra-parliamentary and minor parliamentary parties are marginalized by the compensation structure, such parties have thus far neglected to protest this discrimination in the courts. Castillo reviews existing prohibitions on contributions, expenditure limits and disclosure laws, remarking that, until 1985, party compliance with the latter laws has been deficient due to an understaffed and underfinanced Junta Electoral Central (the Spanish election commission) and a system of fines that are too small to be meaningful deterrents to non-compliance. The deficiency of disclosure was exacerbated by the negligence of the Junta Electoral Central, which did not even publish reports for the 1979 and 1982 elections and has refused reporters and investigators the right to inspect the financial accounts presented by the parties. "The financing of political parties between 1977 and 1985," Castillo writes, "has lacked practically all legal control." The Electoral Law of 1985 addresses some of the deficiencies in the disclosure laws, increasing the penalties for non-compliance with the disclosure regulations and requiring disclosure of individual contributions. The effectiveness of the new regulations, however, remains to be seen. Given these limitations, Castillo attempts an outline of party finance in Spain, working from data gathered in interviews with party managers, published party reports and news accounts. As Castillo concludes, without a normalization of the party system and, especially, without adequate disclosure, a complete and accurate picture of Spanish political finance will continue to be extremely difficult to construct.

Ruud Koole sets the background for his study of Dutch political finance by describing the decline, since the 1960s, of the "pillarized," or consociational party system that had been in place since the 1920s. This system was characterized by several societies, or "pillars," organized around political, cultural, religious and ideological identification, which existed side-by-side in Dutch society; the principal pillars were Catholic, Protestant, socialist and liberal societies. It is this lingering system of pillarization that, in Koole's view, has hindered the development of public funding of Dutch political parties. Political parties in the Netherlands have traditionally relied heavily on membership dues and on other small contributions from individual members. The financing of parties by the business sector, so prevalent in other democracies, is relatively taboo. Each individual pillar has found its own justifications for echoing the Christian Democrat's appeal for "sovereignty within one's own circle." Thus, public funding had been "accepted only very reluctantly and always on the condition that the dependence of a party or foundation on its rank-and-file membership would not be endangered." In addition, the total amount of money needed to finance Dutch politics is relatively small when compared with other mature democratic nations. Limited public funding, the near absence of business donations and a relatively inexpensive party system contribute to Koole's overall assessment of the "modesty" of Dutch political finance.

Hans-Peter Schneider's chapter documents the deliberations, in 1982–3, of the West German Presidential Committee of Experts on Party Funding, of which Schneider was a member. Schneider's article provides a unique perspective in that it shows, from the viewpoint of a participant, the actual lines of reasoning employed in the promulgation of political finance regulations. The recommendations issued by the panel covered a wide range of political finance issues, including public funding of parties, transparency, the legality of foreign contributions, and related tax laws. The Committee's overall intent, Schneider writes, was to "shift the emphasis of party funding in Germany away from the state and toward the individual citizen." Schneider also reports on the Bundestag's response to the Committee's proposals, as well as on the public response to the Bundestag's eventual revision of federal election law. Schneider notes that portions of the new law were successfully challenged in the courts by the Green Party on grounds that provisions dealing with tax deductibility of contributions gave greater advantages to parties supported by the wealthy. These provisions were struck down in 1986 by the Federal Constitutional Court in Karlsruhe, which found them to be in conflict with equality of opportunity.

In the closing chapter of the volume, Karl-Heinz Nassmacher studies public funding programs in Western Europe, focusing on the cases of Austria, Italy, Sweden and West Germany. The chapter presents a comparison of the legal framework and impact of subsidies in these nations, evaluating differing techniques of subsidization, their impact on internal party structure and competition, related controls on income and expenditure and procedures to cope with inflation. It is important to note, as Nassmacher does, the fundamental differences between North American and European political finance. In the "campaign- and candidate-oriented political cultures of North America," he writes, "political finance heavily connotes campaign finance pointing at money spent in order to influence the outcome of an election. In Europe, the term political finance can appropriately be used as a synonym for party finance." In each of the four countries studied, public funding provides considerable support for party activities, though West Germany provides greater support than Austria and Sweden with Italy lagging even further behind. Nassmacher looks at the issue of whether public funding contributes to the "petrification" of party systems, that is, whether it reinforces the relative political strength of the established parties and whether it allows for the entry of new parties into the system. In general, he finds, public subsidies have neither kept the governing party in power nor excluded new parties from competing successfully. Another concern related to public funding is that subsidies often foster centralization of power and bureaucratization within parties. Noting European evidence which substantiates such worries, Nassmacher suggests that direct public subsidies are less likely to alleviate this problem than tax incentives for individual political donations. "In this respect," he adds, "the European countries should learn a lesson from North American experience." Nassmacher also notes that, in each of the four countries he studied, regulations regarding disclosure limitations on expenditures and contributions are inadequate and thus the financial accountability of the parties is limited. The "underregulation" of political finance which is prevalent in Western Europe, he concludes, is not "the optimum for public policy."

1

Money and politics: rethinking a conceptual framework

HERBERT E. ALEXANDER

The effort to understand the relationships between money and politics is an enterprise as old as the development of political theory. From Aristotle on, many political philosophers have regarded property or economic power as the fundamental element in politics. According to some, the attempt to reconcile economic inequalities lies at the base of the problem of money in politics. In this view, broadly based political power, such as that effected through universal suffrage, has helped mitigate the political effects of disparities in economic resources. The wealth of one group with small membership thus may be matched by the human resources or voting power of another. I myself have written in this vein.[1]

Now in the latter part of the twentieth century, another factor, not included in earlier analyses, needs explication. I refer to the power of government to set the rules of electoral competition and especially to provide public funds for use in the electoral process. The intent of this essay is to analyze the governmental factor and relate it to traditional theory in order to make the contemporary role of money in the political process, and the articles that follow in this volume, better understood.

In the context of political donations made by individuals or groups, I wrote elsewhere that, in virtually all societies, money serves as a significant medium by which command over both energies and resources can be achieved.[2] The distinguishing characteristics of money are that it is transferable and convertible without necessarily revealing its original source. The convertibility of money is of particular advantage in politics. Money can buy goods, skills and services. Other resources, in turn, can be converted into political money through an incumbent's advantages of public office (for example, in awarding contracts and jobs), in controlling the flow of information, and in making decisions. Skillful use of ideology, issues, and the perquisites or promises of office attracts financial support to political actors – in legitimate forms as contributions or dues, or in unethical or illegitimate forms such as personal bribes.

The convertibility of money, then, makes the financing of politics a significant component of the governing processes of all but the most primitive societies. But money is symbolic. The deeper competition is for power, prestige or other values. In this sense, money is instrumental, and its importance lies in the ways it is used by people to try to gain influence, to convert into other resources, or to use in combination with other resources to achieve political power.

Power is distributed unequally in society. It does not vary directly with wealth, status, skill, or any other single characteristic; rather, the degree of power is determined by many such factors, not one of which stands alone and not one of which has meaning unless related to the purposes of the individual and the environment in which he or she acts. Money, therefore, is but one element in the equation of political power. But it is the common denominator in the shaping of many of the factors comprising political power because it buys what is not or cannot be volunteered. Giving money permits numbers of citizens to share in the energy that must go into politics. In affluent societies, many individuals find it easier to show their support for a candidate or their loyalty to a party by writing a check than by devoting time to campaign or other political work. Of course, many citizens have no special talent or taste for politics, or they will not give their time, so that money is a happy substitute and at the same time a means of participation in a democracy.

If money is considered as a substitute for service, however, it does not require so firm a commitment; for example, one might give money to both parties, but one is less likely to give time to both. Yet money has one advantage over service in that it is not loaded down with the personality or idiosyncracies of the giver. Because of its universality, money is a tracer element in the study of political power. Light thrown upon transactions involving money illuminates political processes and behavior and improves our understanding of the flows of influence and power.

This conventional analysis, however, does not focus on the role or impact of money when its source is government or public funds. In this case, the source is well-known, directly the government, indirectly the taxpayers. Is money neutral when it comes from government sources? Does the piper call the tune when the government is the source? What are the influences at work when the source is the government? How is government power utilized in the electoral and political arenas? Does government funding lead to more or less competition? Is equality of opportunity enhanced or diminished? What is the extent to which voter turnout or party participation are enhanced or diminished due to public funding?

These are questions that have rarely been asked, and attempts to seek answers have been rarer still. While much has been written about the roles of money emanating from the private sector, little has been said about its roles when derived from the public sector.

Both human and material resources are necessary to acquire, retain and nurture political power. These resources can be purchased or volunteered and to be used effectively must be organized, patterned and channeled in varying combinations.[3] Political power is built upon three constituencies: the electoral, the financial, and the organizational. These in turn are composed of three sources of political power: numbers of people, resources, and social organizations.[4] Thus numbers of persons, situated in electoral constituencies, find political expression through their elected representatives who are grouped according to political party. The power of social organizations, or interest groups, stems from the combination of two factors, people and resources. And resources are brought to bear upon the political process in many ways, through many available channels.

When wealthy persons seek to translate their economic power into political power, one of their tools may be money contributions. The translation of individual or group demands into public policy occurs in various ways, mediated in part by ideological references and by group or class alignments. Since policy preferences are in competition with conflicting claims for political action, individuals or groups use wealth to achieve policy goals by promoting nominations or elections of candidates and parties with views congenial to theirs. Between and during election campaigns they cultivate the sympathies of public officials and the public through lobbying and other means, and through party activity.

Coincident with the extension of the franchise and the democratization of the institutional framework, the economic element that makes for political power – wealth – has been increasingly concentrated. The great industrial, financial, labor, and other interests not only vie to dominate economic life but they also seek to master the political environment. They do this in many direct and indirect ways – directly through lobbies, party influence and the contribution of money, indirectly through access to the public in both election and non-election activities.

Government fits into this three-constituency formulation by virtue of it comprising both the organizational and resource components. Government power stems from the combination of the two but it embodies several characteristics that distinguish it from the private-sector elements that make for power. First, government sets the rules by which the three constituencies operate. It controls elections and sets the parameters on the use of aggregations of people, resources, and social organizations. Secondly, government can exercise sanctions, or the threat thereof, which the private sector does not have available, namely, the ability to enforce laws. When government imposes contribution or expenditure limitations, or prohibits contributions from certain sources, or provides direct or indirect assistance, the equations change. In these senses, government is not necessarily a neutral factor but becomes a player that might help or hurt certain other players.

In the three constituency context, one can argue that the central one is money, and that the financial dominates the other two, the electoral and the organizational.[5] However, one might also argue that government, with its powerful control of the political arena, its ability to impose sanctions, and its tax-supported capacity to provide significant funds for parties or candidates, has supplanted money as a central factor, or at the least has reinforced money as a crucial factor by means of its ample supply. However, government often is controlled or influenced by monied interests, so the two may be synonymous.

PUBLIC FINANCING IN COMPARATIVE PERSPECTIVE

The principle of government funding of political parties or candidates or election campaign activities is well-established across the democratic world. Historically, of course, government financing of the political process has often been conducted in secret or indirectly to benefit the party or parties in power; use of state-controlled radio and television is just one example. Partly in response to abuses of such state instrumentalities, attempts have been made by many countries to formulate systems of public funding of elections that are open and fair. At least twenty-one countries have forms of public funding; included in this tally are Argentina, Australia, Austria, Brazil, Canada, Costa Rica, Denmark, Finland, France, Israel, Italy, Japan, Mexico, Netherlands, Norway, Spain, Sweden, Turkey, United States, Venezuela and West Germany (See Table 1).[6] In addition, Puerto Rico, New South Wales, the German and Austrian laender, eight Canadian provinces and twelve American states have forms of public funding; in the United States, three localities, Seattle, Washington and Tucson, Arizona, and Sacramento County in California, provide public funding for local elections (See Table 2).[7] Sweden pioneered the concept of subsidies to regional and local party organizations provided by provincial and local authorities. And public funding has been provided in numerous countries for the European parliamentary elections.

Where direct aid is not provided, some forms of indirect assistance may be made available, such as free television or radio time, free mailings, free poster space, free transportation, or tax incentives for political contributions. Some additional countries, such as Great Britain, are examples within this latter category. And nine U.S. states permit utilization of their tax systems to enable tax payers to add-on limited political contributions to their tax payments.[8]

In most of the nations with subsidies, governments fund the parties annually, not only at election time. Historically, at first, most of the subsidies were given in small amounts to supplement private resources already available to the political process, and later increased when the system adjusted to the infusion of new funds.

Particularly in parliamentary systems, political parties underwent growth and development that led to important transformations. Parties were no longer campaign organizations that were election oriented. Because elections were not fixed but could occur whenever a vote of confidence was lost, the parties became large and permanent organizations, with education and research appendages, party presses, and even party foundations.[9] Because such party organizations are so large, they need constant support, and so fund raising occurs on an on-going basis. Money becomes so important that subtle changes occur in the system. Instead of only raising money for campaigns, money is needed to maintain the party organization. This in turn affects the government in parliamentary systems because incumbents are enlisted to adopt public policy positions that will benefit the party. As a result, government and parliamentary leaders are involved day by day in helping to sustain the parties. Thus permanent campaigning occurs, triggering permanent fund raising and pressuring incumbents to work more and more for money for the party. There have been suggestions, for example, that the attendant increases in public funding may have been a factor in the shortening of periods between elections in West Germany from four to three years. This type of outcome has implications for theories of representation if parties compete with constituents as a main focus of interest of elected representatives.

Moreover, as Nassmacher points out, public funding may transform parties from voluntary associations to political institutions, shifting the balance of power to a party bureaucracy, and possibly centralizing the locus of power within the party.[10] These developments also may be relevant to political party theory, to the extent that parties move from closed membership to open voter parties, as illustrated by Otto Kirscheimer's "catch-all parties"; this increases costs by requiring new techniques in which political consultants apply their skills to seek new voters.[11]

The United States represents an interesting case. Throughout most of its history, federal and state laws relating to political finance were predominantly negative. Their purpose was to prohibit, limit and restrict ways of

Table 1. *Nations with public financing, 1988*[a]

Country	Effective date[b]	Country	Effective date[b]
Argentina	1955	Japan	1976
Australia	1984	Mexico	1978
Austria	1963	Netherlands	1972
Brazil	1971	Norway	1970
Canada	1974	Spain[c]	1977
Costa Rica	1954	Sweden	1966
Denmark[c]	1969	Turkey	1983
Finland[d]	1967	United States	1976
France[c]	1965	Venezuela	1978
Israel	1969	West Germany[c]	1959
Italy[c]	1974		

[a] Not including free use of electronic media.
[b] Where reference sources were specific, the year listed is the one in which the subsidies were first distributed. In some cases, however, the year listed may be the one in which the public financing legislation was enacted.
[c] Also provides funding for election to the European Parliament. The European Parliament provides some public funding for the information activities of those political parties in member countries that are already represented in Parliament; it also provides funds to promote participation in the European Parliamentary election process.
[d] It should be noted that, in Finland, some Communes and municipalities assist financially certain cultural and issue organizations, some of which are close to or allied with political parties; in effect, there is some indirect public financing of parties at these levels.

getting, giving and spending. In the 1970s, a shift occurred from negative to more positive laws, with public funding devised as a means of helping to fill the gaps left by restrictions on sources or amounts. Hence presidential public financing was enacted at the federal level, and various forms of public funding or income tax add-ons in twenty-one states. At the presidential level, the money is given to candidates' campaign committees, and to the parties only to hold their national nominating conventions. In the pre-nomination period the public funding is based on a matching formula, but in the general election period both major party candidates receive flat grants in equal amounts. These procedures differ from public funding in other systems in which parties receive funding proportional to their parliamentary strength. In the U.S., too, the money is derived in a unique fashion, through a tax checkoff on federal income tax returns. The funding is available for payouts only in the presidential election year, although the checkoff to accumulate the funds is provided on the tax forms every year.

Table 2. *States, laender, provinces, territories, and localities with public funding,*
1988[a,b]

Territory	Effective date	Territory	Effective date[d]
Puerto Rico	1957	*German laender*	
		Baden-Wurttemberg	1967
Canadian provinces		Bavaria	1968
Alberta	1978	Berlin	1978
Manitoba	1984	Bremen	1971
New Brunswick	1978	Hamburg	1972
Nova Scotia	1969	Hesse	1972
Ontario	1975	Lower Saxony	1967
Prince Edward Island	1983	North Rhine-Westphalia	1967
Quebec	1963	Rhineland-Palatinate	1969
Saskatchewan	1974	Saarland	1973
		Schleswig-Holstein	1967
United States[c]			
Florida	1990	*Austrian laender[d]*	
Hawaii	1980	Burgenland	1962
Idaho	1976	Carinthia	1962
Iowa	1974	Lower Austria	1967
Kentucky	1977	Salzburg	1962
Michigan	1978	Styria	1962
Minnesota	1976	Tyrol	1962
New Jersey	1977	Upper Austria	1961
North Carolina	1977	Vienna	1963
Rhode Island	1974	Voralberg	1960
Utah	1975		
Wisconsin	1978	*American localities*	
		Seattle	1979
Australian state		Tucson	1985
New South Wales	1981	Sacramento County	1988

[a] Where reference sources were specific, the year listed is the one in which the subsidies were first distributed. In some cases, however, the year listed may be the one in which the public financing legislation was enacted.
[b] The territorial, provincial, state and city governments included here provide autonomous aid to candidates or parties. A number of countries, including Italy, France, Spain, and Sweden, subsidize sub-national elections or parties at the national government level.
[c] These include states with checkoff systems or legislative appropriation of public funds. Nine additional states have add-on procedures.
[d] In Austria, the public funding by the laender totals five times as much as federal public funding.

As Khayyam Z. Paltiel observed, rationales for public financing plans often obscure the real public issues involved in their enactment:

Whether the motive for change was financial stringency, the reduction of the burden of rising election costs, or the desire to escape the taint of corruption, or a mixture of these, efforts were made to justify these reforms in terms of liberal democratic ideology. Democracy, it was argued, required a fair chance for competitors in the electoral process. The allocation of public funds to parties and candidates was necessary to assure equality of opportunity and access to the electorate whose support was being sought. Such assistance would further reinforce the voters' right to know and to be informed of the policy alternatives and the candidates and parties competing for their favor. Furthermore, public subsidies would reduce the dependence of parties and candidates on large contributions from powerful sectoral interests and free politicians from the temptation to resort to questionable sources of funds, thus rendering the electoral process more transparent and pure.[12]

Such rationales are important but do not address a central question: Is money from government different in intent and consequence than is money from private sources?

Scant attention has been paid to the implications of the various public funding plans for the political system. Questions of fairness, cost, administration and enforcement need to be asked, assumptions challenged, and understanding developed of the conditions that are required when subsidies are provided. It is simplistic to believe that fundamental changes in the political structure of electoral processes will not result. Some critics have argued that the state is not obligated to help meet the financial needs of parties and that it should not relieve parties of the risk of failure and the responsibility that goes along with it.[13]

By protecting parties from the failure which results from a lack of public enthusiasm for their platforms, public financing may make it less necessary for parties to respond to the real political issues of the day, thereby interfering with the effectiveness and responsiveness of the political system as a whole. Other critics have charged that in most democracies private donations cannot be completely prohibited by law and are not necessarily morally wrong. In contrast, they argue, private donations are a form of political participation to be encouraged. Further, as Michael Pinto-Duschinsky has noted, public financing tends to supplant individual contributions to political campaigns rather than those of large corporations and labor unions, often the original target of such legislation.[14] When public financing programs are enacted, some individuals may feel that government has assumed primary responsibility for the financing of politics and therefore they need no longer give. However, organized interests, whose donations are more closely tied to their lobbying activities, continue to contribute regardless.

While public financing may strengthen the position of party professionals by assuring their livelihood, conversely it may weaken parties in other ways. For example, government subsidies may create a distance between the parties and the electorate by seeming to relieve the parties of the necessity to solicit individual contributions. "Once party professionals are released from the need to raise money from the ordinary members," writes Pinto-Duschinsky, "a major incentive for recruitment is lost."[15] Evidence offered in this book suggests that this is the case in at least Israel, West Germany and the United States. In this context, limitations on private giving raise still more constitutional and public policy questions, and these must be considered part of the subsidy question.

The main design difficulties in public funding are who should receive the subsidy, and how and when it should be made. Presumably, the goal of government subsidization is to help serious contestants, yet retain enough flexibility to permit opportunity to challenge those in power without supporting with significant tax funds parties or candidates merely seeking free publicity and without attracting so many candidates or parties that the electoral process is degraded. Accordingly, the most difficult problems in working out fair subsidies are definitional, that is, how to define major and minor parties, and in the U.S. system, distinguish serious from frivolous candidates seeking nomination. Any standards must be arbitrary, and certain protections should be provided to ensure that unpopular voices are heard. Certain screening devices can be used, based upon past vote, numbers of petitions, posting of money bonds, or other means. Some of these means require "start-up" funds or masses of volunteers to get petitions signed, and other plans, such as matching funds or matching incentives, require popular appeal that can best be achieved through incumbency or years of exposure which also costs money.

A useful point for inquiry is whether a subsidy program should be linked to the tax system as in the U.S., or be optional for candidates to choose at their discretion, again as in the U.S.

Policy makers also must ensure that public financing plans do not do violence to equality of opportunity. An ill-advised – or ill-intended – formula might do damage to that principle. The German system of public financing, for example, was originally designed with the intention of making opportunities unequal, in an effort to prevent the development of the kind of political environment that allowed the Nazis to rise to power.[16] The Weimar Republic, it was noted, was weakened by the birth of numerous fringe parties. German public funding laws were thus formulated to limit the growth of such parties. Today, with such court cases as that of the *Green Party vs. the German Bundestag*, in which there were questions raised about the fairness of certain tax deductions for corporate donations to political parties, equal opporunity remains a live issue in the politics of West German public funding.[17]

A second example of equal opportunity as an issue of public financing is reported in Pilar del Castillo's chapter on Spain in this volume. Castillo argues that the 1977 law which established public financing in Spain discriminates against both extra-parliamentary and minor-parliamentary parties, discriminating against the former by requiring that a party have its adherents elected to parliament before it can be eligible for public funding, and against the latter by basing public financing on a unique electoral formula which grants bonus seats to parties that receive the most votes.[18] By enacting schemes which do not allow equal chances for parties to emerge and grow, as Paltiel observed, policy makers run the risk of alienating citizens from the democratic process. In turn, he writes, such alienation "may stimulate recourse to extra-parliamentary opposition tactics of violent confrontation."[19] An opposite danger of public funding is that it might petrify the political system by embracing all parties, bringing them into the mainstream or within the parameters of the system. While this may channel conflict within the system, it also may lead to stalemate if a few major parties cannot lead. While all standards are arbitrary, some are more arbitrary than others.

Whatever the form of direct or indirect state aid, there always is the possibility that the power of government may be used unfairly, through employment practices, the granting of contracts, threats or changes in policies, or use of the airwaves or mails, to favor one party or candidate over another.

Public funding can add to the power of government if the party in power gains control over the funding of its opposition. The advantages of incumbency extend to the formulas used to define who gets public funding and under what conditions. As Paltiel wrote, the laws regulating public funding can lead to the institutionalization of existing party systems, generally favoring central party organizations over local ones, freezing relationships among major parties or dominant coalitions, or locking out new or emerging movements while maintaining current parties in existence perhaps after their support has diminished.[20]

These problems with public funding are not insurmountable. For example, one way to avoid the situation of a party in power gaining control over its opposition is if adequate provision is made for long-term funding supplied by an automatic mechanism that is not dependent on the vicissitudes of politics. Attention, however, should be drawn to the fact that what is at stake in public financing is the viability of free elections. Similar questions have been raised about the dominance of private money in elections. But the entry of government itself into the game exacerbates such concerns in considerable measure.

The role of government is extended when, as in the U.S., expenditure limits are imposed on monies permitted to be spent by candidates or parties. According to the U.S. Supreme Court, in the case of *Buckley v. Valeo*, expenditure limits can be applied only as a condition of acceptance of public funding by a candidate or party.[21] In all other circumstances the Court found spending limits to be unconstitutional, and this also applies to amounts candidates can spend of their personal funds in their own campaigns. Expenditure limits raise many questions: whether they can be effective, whether they trigger independent expenditures and other means of avoidance, whether they tend to rigidify the system. On this latter point, expenditure limits make it difficult for candidates who have spent close to the maximum allowed, to alter their campaign strategy towards the end of a campaign in order to fend off new challenges or to take new developments into account once spending commitments have been made. Moreover, expenditure limits cause candidates to centralize control of spending in their campaigns, in order to assure that they remain within the limits, thus reducing spontaneous or decentralized spending by campaign operatives.

Even given strong and effective enforcement, the implementation of overall limitations is most difficult. In pluralistic societies, there are many openings for disbursement to support a candidate or party: (1) through labor, business, professional, or miscellaneous committees or federations, if not through candidate or party committees; (2) through direct disbursements by the candidate, his family, or other individuals (not channeled through organized groups); (3) through issue organizations such as peace groups and gun lobbies. In the circumstances that money will likely carve new channels, limitations can readily become unenforceable and thus a mockery.

Contribution limits, disclosure, prohibitions of various sorts, and other restrictions within an electoral system, also serve to make government a key player affecting politics in a country.

CONCLUSION

In recent decades, public funding has emerged as an important force in democratic political systems. Such funding has come about as the result of concern with the dominance of private money in the political process, and the consequent abuses and private influences on national policies. Now that public funding is in place in so many of the mature democracies, new issues have emerged concerning the political consequences of the influx of public money into the political system. The task for public policy making in this context is to strike an appropriate balance between the competing forces of private and public monies. Either alone may not be adequate or desirable, and hence in most mature democracies, some combination is advisable. While there are common issues – and, perhaps, even imperatives – regarding both public and private sources of funds, the appropriate mixture is best left to be decided by individual countries with their own particular processes and cultures.

In this analysis, I have raised more questions than I have answered. Public funding has not been in existence long enough to evaluate conclusively its impact. Undoubtedly more countries will adopt public funding, with whatever mixture of public and private funds. Yet, as Hans Peter Schneider points out, it is important for government to take suitable measures to support the efforts of parties to raise private funds from members or the citizenry at large.[22] This follows the notions that parties should seek to remain independent of the state, and that citizens' rights to participate financially are assured.

This analysis of the various actions of government which affect the use of money in politics recognizes the possibility that government regulations and the infusion of public money may affect the outcome of elections. Government involvement is, of course, desirable if laws apply equally to all contestants, but the consequences of government policies do not always impact equally on different parties or candidates. Some accommodate better than others. The party or parties in power may regulate to their advantage, or may write laws that tend to squeeze out minor emerging parties.

In weighing governments as participants in the electoral process, and in building a conceptual framework relating to their roles, recognition is imperative that however well-intentioned their motives in enacting laws, intended as well as unintended consequences may result. In order to progress, a tradeoff may be necessary, in which the greater good outweighs the occasional hurts.

This essay has stressed the consequences of governments' activities, not to criticize their roles, but to admit their presence as significant actors in the electoral process. The ideas of votes counting for more than dollars, or of the use of dollars unduly influencing voting outcomes, require understanding of the additional dimension of government providing dollars and imposing regulations, and in turn affecting both aggregations of voters and concentrations of wealth. While previous theoretical formulations failed to take the roles of government into account, admittedly, further experience and refinement are necessary before authoritative conclusions and a fully integrated theory can be presented.

Notes

1 Herbert E. Alexander, "Political Finance Regulations in International Perspective," in Michael J. Malbin, ed., *Parties, Interested Groups, and Campaign Finance Laws* (Washington: American Enterprise Institute, 1980), pp. 333–5.
2 Herbert E. Alexander, *Financing Politics: Money, Elections and Political Reform* (Third Edition) (Washington: Congressional Quarterly, 1984), p. 3.
3 Herbert E. Alexander, "Campaign Resources," in *Dictionary of American History* (New York: Charles Scribner's Sons, 1976), pp. 413–14.
4 Robert Bierstadt, "An Analysis of Social Power," *American Sociological Review*, XV December, 1950, p. 737.
5 See Henry Bretton, *The Power of Money: A Political-Economic Analysis with Special Emphasis on the American Political System* (Albany: State University of New York Press, 1980), p. 331.
6 The compilation of countries is derived from: David W. Adamany and George E. Agree, *Political Money: A Strategy For Campaign Financing in America* (Baltimore: The Johns Hopkins University Press, 1975); Brazilian *Law* No. S.682, July 21, 1971; Commission on Election Contributions and Expenses, *A Comparative Survey of Election Finance Legislation, 1983* (Toronto: Commission on Election Contributions and Expenses, 1983); Costa Rican *Constitution of 1949*, Article 96, Chapter 2; for Venezuelan public funding, see letter from Henry Wells to Herbert E. Alexander, August 27, 1987; Harry Forsell, "Some Aspects of the Communal Party Subsidy in Sweden" (Los Angeles: Citizens' Research Foundation, 1973); Arnold J. Heidenheimer, ed., *Comparative Political Finance: The Financing of Party Organizations and Election Campaigns* (Lexington, MA: D. C. Heath and Company, 1970); The Rt. Hon. Lord Houghton of Sowerby, *Report of the Committee On Financial Aid to Political Parties* (London: Her Majesty's Stationery Office, 1976); Harry Kantor, "Public Finances Parties," *National Municipal Review*, March, 1958; Dick Leonard, "Contrasts in Selected Western Democracies: Germany, Sweden, Britain," in Herbert E. Alexander, ed., *Political Finance* (Beverly Hills: Sage, 1979), pp. 41–73; Mexican *Ley Federal De Organaciones Politicas Y Processos Electorales*, December 30, 1977; David Millar, "European Election Procedures," in Juliet Lodge, ed., *Direct Elections to the European Parliament* (New York: St. Martin's Press, 1986), pp. 44–6; see Khayyam Zev Paltiel, "Public Financing Abroad: Contrasts and Effects," in Michael J. Malbin, ed., *Parties,*

Interest Groups and Campaign Finance Laws (Washington: American Enterprise Institute, 1980), pp. 354–70; Khayyam Zev Paltiel, "Campaign Finance: Contrasting Practices and Reforms," in David Butler, Howard R. Penniman, and Austin Ranny, eds., *Democracy at the Polls: A Comparative Study of Competitive National Elections* (Washington: American Enterprise Institute, 1981), pp. 138–72; Khayyam Zev Paltiel, "The Impact of Election Expenses Legislation in Canada, Western Europe and Israel," in Herbert E. Alexander, ed., *Political Finance* (Beverly Hills: Sage, 1979), pp. 15–39.; Dick Leonard, *Paying For Party Politics: The Case For Public Subsidies* (London: Political and Economic Planning, 1975); Roy Pierce, "Presidential Selection in France: The Historical Background" in Howard R. Penniman, ed., *France at the Polls: the Presidential Election of 1974* (Washington: American Enterprise Institute, 1975), p. 21; Pertti Pesonen, "Impact of Public Financing of Political Parties: The Finnish Experience," (Los Angeles: Citizens' Research Foundation, 1973); Karlheinz Reif, ed., *Ten European Elections* (Brookfield, Vermont: Gower Publishing Company, 1985); Richard Rose and Arnold Heidenheimer, eds., "Comparative Political Finance: A Symposium," *The Journal of Politics*, Vol. 25, No. 3, August, 1963; Turkish *Law* Article 2820, April 22, 1983; Henry Wells, "Party Finance in Costa Rica," paper presented at the Eighth World Congress of the International Political Science Association, Munich, Germany, September 1, 1970.

7 See, for example, for German laender funding, letter from Karl-Heinz Nassmacher to Herbert E. Alexander, February 8, 1987, and letter from Hans-Peter Schneider to Herbert E. Alexander, October 22, 1987; Seattle Ordinance Number 112008, 1984; and "Initiative Update: Voters in Tucson Approve Public Financing," *Campaign Practices Reports*, November 18, 1985, p. 8; for party funding in the Austrian laender, see Herbert Dachs, "Oeffentliche Parteienfinanzierung in den oesterreichischen Bundeslaendern," *Oesterreichisches Jahrbuch fuer Politik*, 1985, pp. 439–54 and Wolfgang C. Mueller and Martin Hartmann, "Finanzen im Dunkeln: Aspekte der Parteienfinanzierung," in Peter Gerlich and Wolfgang C. Mueller, eds., *Zwischen Koalition und Konleurrenz: Oesterreichs Parteien Seit 1945* (Wien: Wilhelm Braumueller, 1983); assistance in interpreting the Austrian information was provided by Rainer Nick.

8 See Herbert E. Alexander and Mike Eberts, *Public Financing of State Elections: A Data Book on Tax-Assisted Funding of Political Parties And Candidates in Twenty States* (Los Angeles: Citizens' Research Foundation, 1986).

9 Party foundations are special organizations established by parties for continuing political research and education. They receive public subsidies in Austria, Israel, the Netherlands, the United States and West Germany. The West German party foundations also are involved in international activities, such as the Konrad Adenauer Foundation's work to establish cooperatives, community development projects and trade unions in Ceylon and Latin America, and the Frederic Ebert Foundation's assistance to fraternal parties in Italy and Spain.

10 See Nassmacher in this volume, pp. 250–1.

11 Otto Kirchheimer, "The Transformation of Western European Party Systems," in Joseph LaPalombara and Myron Weiner, eds., *Political Parties and Political Development* (Princeton: Princeton University Press, 1966), pp. 177–200.

12 Khayyam Zev Paltiel, "Public Financing Abroad, Contrasts and Effects," in Michael J. Malbin, ed., *Parties, Interest Groups and Campaign Finance Laws* (Washington, D.C.: American Enterprise Institute, 1980), p. 354.

13 See Schneider in this volume, pp. 224–6.

14 Michael Pinto-Duschinsky, *British Political Finance 1830–1980* (Washington, D.C.: American Enterprise Institute, 1981), p. 9.

15 Ibid., p. 292.

16 Ibid., p. 299n.

17 See Schneider in this volume, pp. 231–3.

18 See Castillo in this volume, pp. 176–9.

19 Khayyam Zev Paltiel, "Public Financing Abroad, Contrasts and Effects," in Michael J. Malbin, *Parties, Interest Groups and Campaign Finance Laws* (Washington, D.C.: American Enterprise Institute, 1980), p. 370.

20 Ibid., pp. 364–70.

21 *Buckley v. Valeo*, 424 U.S. 1 (1976).

22 See Schneider in this volume, pp. 220–1, 224–6.

2

Trends in British political funding, 1979–84

MICHAEL PINTO-DUSCHINSKY

Following the British general election of 1983, attention was again drawn to the problems of political funding by two pieces of legislation intended, according to opponents of the government, to increase the fund-raising advantages enjoyed by the Conservative Party over its adversaries. Under the terms of the Trade Union Act 1984, all the major unions which had political levy funds were obliged to poll their members by March 31, 1986 for their approval to continue raising money for political purposes (a practice of the Labor Party). The act also widened the definition of "political purposes" for which money could not be spent from a union's general funds. If a number of the largest unions voted against the political levy, this would not only deal a symbolic blow to Labor, it could severely affect the party's finances.

A second, less significant reform, was the proposal brought before the House of Commons in 1984 to raise the deposit required for parliamentary candidates from £150 to £1,000 and, at the same time, to lower the vote required to avoid its loss from 12.5 percent to 5 percent. After initially proposing the higher amount, the government agreed in 1985 to a compromise figure of £500. Since Conservative Party candidates are generally thought to be better financed than their opponents, this was attacked as another partisan measure.

Supporters of the government had several answers to the critics. The measures relating to political funds, they argued, were part of a larger package of reforms designed to make union leaders more accountable to their members. Trade union democracy, not the impoverishment of the Labor Party, was the central aim. Most unions had never consulted their members about making political payments since party funds were originally established in 1913. The new legislation merely required them to obtain majority consent once every ten years to raise political money. Once this

24

had been obtained, they could automatically levy payments on all members except those who signed forms "contracting out."

The raising of the deposit for parliamentary candidates enjoyed a measure of support from all parties. The £150 deposit was introduced in 1918 (when it was worth £2,500 at 1984 values). Because of inflation, it no longer acted as a deterrent to frivolous candidates who had stood in considerable numbers in recent elections (particularly by-elections) under such banners as the Monster Raving Loony Party.

In contrast to the government's reforms, Labor and the Alliance both favored a package that would include state subsidies to parties and restrictions on company payments to balance those imposed on unions. There was considerable support, particularly from the Alliance, for setting a limit on the expenditure of central party organizations and for compelling them to publish accounts. Labor and the Alliance differed widely in their views concerning the form subsidies should take. Many Alliance supporters would link the introduction of state aid with a ban on contributions by unions (and companies), whereas the Labor proposal was a supplement to the established system of union payments. They also disagreed about whether there should be block payments, which were favored by Labor, or grants matching the sums raised by the parties from small individual contributions.[1]

The continuing debate about how the funding of parties should be changed has tended to deflect attention from the actual state of political finance. The present chapter outlines the main trends in party funding in the parliamentary cycle 1979–83.[2] This review is significant, quite apart from its implications for arguments about the regulation of political money, for the light it throws on the condition of the rival parties during the first Thatcher administration. The overwhelming political superiority of the Conservative Party was not matched by its success in fund raising. The Labor Party, on the other hand, performed relatively well, considering its unpopularity and the shrinkage of union membership resulting from unemployment.

CONSERVATIVE PARTY FINANCES

At the time of the 1979 election, Conservative Central Office had still not recovered from the heavy financial loss sustained during the campaigns of February and October 1974.[3] The situation was aggravated by the further deficit during the 1979 campaign. During 1978–9 and 1979–80, spending exceeded income by £1,966,000 and Central Office exhausted all its reserves. Its cash and invested reserves at the end of 1977–8 – the last year for which this information was published – had totaled only £726,000. To make matters worse, 1980–1 saw another huge deficit of £2,315,000. From 1978 to 1981, central party expenditure was 35 percent above income and the deficit, totaling £4.3 million, was nearly double the amount spent by Central Office on the 1979 general election.

This state of affairs not only led to severe staff cuts at Central Office in 1980 and 1981, but also made it necessary to borrow large sums and to provide interest payments which, at the height of the crisis, amounted to over £300,000 a year. In 1982, the party treasurers completed a sale and leaseback arrangement for the party headquarters building at 21 Smith Square, Westminster. The sale reportedly netted about £1 million to pay off some of the debts, but it meant that Central Office would henceforward need to pay rent for the headquarters. Reluctance to reveal the extent of the deficit was probably the main reason for the long delay in issuing Central Office accounts for years following 1979–80. While no formal decision to stop publication seems to have been announced, previous arrangements for their widespread distribution were, at least temporarily, changed.

Despite the shaky state of the central party finances, the campaign strategists took the bold step of drawing up an election budget in 1983 of the same size, when adjusted for inflation, as that of 1979. Though the £3.8 million spent by Central Office on the election was modest by the standards of the 1959 and 1964 campaigns, it was higher in real terms than the amounts spent in 1966, 1970, February 1974 and October 1974. At the time of the 1983 campaign, there was no way of guaranteeing that money could be found to pay for the election on top of the £5 million or more for the routine maintenance of the headquarters. Estimates released by Central Office show that it raised and spent nearly £10 million in 1983–4, thereby avoiding an election year deficit similar to those incurred during the two previous general elections. The gradual recovery in financial support during the two years before the 1983 election meant that Conservative central income, in real terms, was marginally higher in the years between 1979–80 and 1982–3 than during the previous parliamentary cycle (1974–9). However, the level of income remained 10–20 percent lower than that of the 1950s and 1960s. In addition, Central Office was faced in the early 1980s with extra demands for redundancy or retirement payments and interest, which was the result of the erosion of the reserves in the 1970s and of the losses during the 1979 general election. By 1983, Central Office staff (excluding the area offices) numbered about 150, compared with some 200 in the late 1960s. In 1983, by contrast, Labor's Head Office employed about 130. A further deficit of more than £1 million in 1984–5 showed that the financial problems of the central Conservative organization have yet to be solved.

Table 1. *Conservative, central income and expenditure, 1973–4 to 1984–5 (£m)*

	Income					Expenditure		
	Donations	Constituency	Interest	State aid	Total	Routine	General election	Total
1973–4*	2.4m	0.4m	0.1m	–	2.8m	1.5m	0.6m	2.1m
1974–5*	1.2m	0.3m	0.1m	–	1.6m	2.0m	0.9m	2.9m
1975–6	1.1m	0.6m	–	0.2m	1.9m	1.9m	–	1.9m
1976–7	1.3m	0.6m	–	0.2m	2.1m	2.2m	–	2.2m
1977–8	1.9m	0.7m	–	0.2m	2.8m	2.8m	–	2.8m
1978–9*	2.4m	0.8m	–	0.2m	3.4m	3.7m	1.0m	4.8m
1979–80*	4.5m	0.9m	0.2m	–	5.6m	4.9m	1.3m	6.2m
1980–1	2.2m	0.9m	–	–	3.2m	5.5m	–	5.5m
1981–2	2.9m	1.0m	–	–	4.1m[a]	4.2m	–	4.2m
1982–3	3.7m	1.0m	–	–	4.8m	4.6m	0.1m[b]	4.7m
1983–4*	8.7m	1.1m	–	–	9.8m	6.1m	3.7m	9.8m
1984–5	3.4m	1.0m	–	–	4.4m	5.5m	–	5.5m

* General election years. The statistics have been drawn up on the same basis as those in *British Political Finance*, Table 28. Figures for 1983–5 are estimates. Interest received is net of tax and net of interest paid. Donations are net of fund-raising costs. Constituency income includes quota credits. State aid is grants to opposition parties in the Commons. Inconsistencies in total are due to rounding.

[a] Includes repayment of tax overpaid in previous years.

[b] Author's estimate.

Source: Conservative Central Office Annual Reports and supplementary information.

Although the total Central Office budget in the 1983 general election was about the same in real terms as in 1979, the pattern of spending was novel. Unlike previous campaigns with national advertising during the months – and even years – before the announcement of the election date, virtually all advertising expenditure in 1983 was concentrated into the weeks before the poll. This was, first of all, because the party strategists felt that advertising quickly lost its effectiveness. Secondly, a Conservative advertising campaign could signal to the opposition the likelihood of an early dissolution of Parliament. Thirdly, there was no longer a legal need to spend earlier. According to new interpretations of election law, national party organizations could spend money during election campaigns on newspaper and poster advertising without contravening the limits on spending by individual candidates, provided the advertisements did not mention their names and were not concentrated into target constituencies.[4]

Apart from £0.1 million spent on advertising for the local government election of May 1983 and some expenditures for the production of party political broadcasts during 1982–3, the entire election budget of Conservative Central Office was devoted to the four weeks between the announcement of the election date and the poll, when it spent £3,558,000. Advertising accounted for £2,568,000, including £843,000 for posters and £1,725,000 for press advertisements. The production costs of party political broadcasts came to £306,000; opinion research to £96,000; party publications (net of receipts) to £212,000; staff and administration costs to £262,000. Grants to constituency campaigns amounted to £62,000 and the net cost of the leader's tours to £52,000, a low figure achieved by payments from journalists for places on the campaign aeroplane, and, apparently, by the fact that the aeroplane had been loaned by a party supporter.

At the local level, Conservative membership and finances are still far healthier than those of other political parties. There has nevertheless been a serious drop in local activity. Firm statistics are not available, but party officials have indicated that membership before the 1983 election was probably between 1.1 and 1.2 million (compared with 1.5 million at the time of the Houghton Committee's survey in the early 1970s). The income of constituency associations totaled approximately £8 million in 1981–2, nearly £13,000 per constituency. If inflation is taken into account, constituency incomes at December 1984 prices averaged £23,000 in 1966–7, £20,000 in 1973, £15,000 in 1981–2. Financial shortages meant that quota payments by constituency associations to Central Office were, in real terms, 25 percent lower in 1983–4 than in 1979–80.

If all Conservative expenditures in the 1979–83 parliamentary cycle (central and local, routine and campaign) are taken into account, the

Table 2. *The pattern of Conservative political expenditure, 1874–83*

	Aristocratic era 1874–80	Plutocratic era 1906–10	Transitional era 1925–9	Post-war era 1966–70	Contemporary era 1979–83
Overall expenditure (£m)	1.9m	1.9m	3.7m	14.2m	52.5m
Overall expenditure at 1984 prices (£m)	65.9m	70.0m	79.3m	86.0m	66.7m
Total Conservative vote at subsequent election	0.9m	3.1m	8.7m	12.1m	13.0m
Overall cost per vote at December 1984 prices (£)	74.70	22.40	9.20	6.60	5.10
Percentage of overall expenditure devoted to					
Central routine	2.1	16.4	20.7	30.8	36.4
campaign	—	1.3	5.4	4.5	6.2
Local routine	20.6	47.7	59.6	60.6	54.0
campaign	77.3	34.5	14.4	4.1	3.4

Estimates of routine central and constituency expenditures have been adjusted to represent spending over a four-year period. Statistics for cycles until 1966–70 are taken from Michael Pinto-Duschinsky, *British Political Finance* (Washington, D.C.: American Enterprise Institute for Public Policy Research, 1981), Table 73.

general election of 1983 amounted to a tenth of the total. The largest category was routine spending by constituency associations (54 percent of the total) and the smallest was campaign spending by parliamentary candidates (£2.1 million, an average of £3,320).[5] Long-term developments in the pattern of party funding are shown in Table 2, which compares the structure of Conservative finances in 1979–83 with that of selected earlier parliamentary cycles.

Since campaign spending by parliamentary candidates is alone directly restricted by law, it would be possible for routine spending, national and local, and total national campaign spending, to escalate as a result. Nevertheless, there has been no explosion of expenditures in Britain as has been seen in other countries. Overall spending on Conservative politics since the Disraelian period has remained, in real terms, remarkably stable, despite the enlargement of the electorate. In the shorter term, there has been a significant fall, in real terms, between the late 1960s and the early 1980s. This has been due mainly to the decline in the routine income and expenditures of constituency associations – the result of falling membership – and partly from a fall in contributions to the Central organization. The total outlay of local parties still exceeds that of the national organization, but the long-term trend towards the centralization of political spending has continued. This has also been a result (at least since the 1960s) of the decline in constituency activity.

LABOR PARTY FINANCES

The income and expenditures of the National Executive Committee of the Labor Party are shown in Table 3. The totals include campaign as well as routine income and expenditure, though additional monies raised and spent at the regional level are not included.

Since the 1960s, Labor's central income has easily outstripped inflation. This is shown by a comparison of various non-election years. In 1967–9, National Executive Committee income (at December 1984 prices) averaged £2.1 million; £3.1 million in 1971–3; £3.4 million in 1975–7; and £4.0 million in 1980–2. These figures exclude Labor's share of the so-called "Short money," the state grant to opposition parties to aid their parliamentary activities, received since its defeat in 1979.

The main source of this improvement has been a rise in union affiliation fees to the party headquarters. Political levy funds have grown faster than inflation. Moreover, unions which previously made donations from their levies to constituency Labor parties as well as to the party nationally have

Table 3. *Labor central income and expenditure, 1973–84 (£m)*

	Income					Expenditure		
	Trade union Affiliation fees	Constituency Affiliation fees	State aid	Other	Total	Routine	General election	Total
1973	0.7m	0.1m	—	0.1m	0.8m	0.9m	—	0.9m
1974*	0.7m	0.1m	—	1.0m	1.8m	0.9m	0.9m	1.9m
1975	1.1m	0.1m	—	0.2m	1.4m	1.2m	—	1.2m
1976	1.2m	0.1m	—	0.1m	1.5m	1.3m	—	1.3m
1977	1.3m	0.1m	—	0.1m	1.5m	1.5m	—	1.5m
1978	1.5m	0.1m	—	0.6m	2.1m	2.0m	0.2m	2.0m
1979*	1.8m	0.2m	0.1m	1.0m	3.1m	2.1m	1.2m	3.4m
1980	2.0m	0.4m	0.2m	0.2m	2.8m	3.1m	—	3.1m
1981	2.5m	0.6m	0.3m	0.3m	3.7m	3.8m	—	3.8m
1982	2.8m	0.6m	0.3m	0.3m	3.9m	4.0m	—	4.0m
1983*	3.0m	0.6m	0.3m	2.4m[a]	6.2m	4.1m	2.1m	6.1m
1984	2.9m	0.7m	0.3m	1.0m[b]	5.0m	4.9m[c]	—	4.9m

* General election years. Totals include special funds as well as the general fund. Separately collected regional funds are not included. The table has been drawn up on the same basis as in Michael Pinto-Duschinsky, *British Political Finance*, Tables 16 and 38. State aid as in Table 1. Other income in general election years consists largely of trade union contributions to the National Executive Committee's general election fund.

[a] Includes repayment of tax overpaid in previous years.
[b] Includes grant of £734,000 from the Socialist Group in the European Parliament for the European parliamentary election.
[c] Includes expenditure of £859,000 on the European parliamentary election.
Source: Labor Party Annual Reports and supplementary information.

tended to direct a higher proportion of their payments to the National Executive Committee.

The rate for union affiliation to the National Executive Committee rose from 5 pence per member in 1969 to 28 pence in 1979 and 50 pence in 1983 (an increase of 86 percent in real terms). The unions have larger numbers: a record of 6.5 million affiliated members in 1979 compared with 5.5 million in 1969. While the rise in unemployment since 1979 has led to a sharp fall in union membership and in the numbers contributing to political levy funds, this had only limited effects on the numbers affiliated with the Labor Party from 1979 to 1984. The affiliations – and the number of votes individual unions possess at party conferences – are not an exact reflection of membership but depend on the size of political payments the unions are prepared to make. In other words, the unions purchased their proportionate influence in party votes. Some unions affiliate on the basis of a number exceeding their total levy-paying memberships and others on a far smaller number. In 1982, for example, the Engineering Section of AEUW had 655,894 levy-paying members but affiliated on the basis of 850,000; the Transport and General Workers' Union had 1,604,230 levy-paying members and paid an affiliation fee entitling it to 1,250,000 votes. In 1984, unions paid fees on behalf of 5.8 million members, a drop of only 10 percent from the record total of 1979.

Along with rising payments from the unions, there have been sharp increases in affiliation payments by constituency Labor parties, which are approaching the level of quota payments by Conservative constituency associations. They rose from £210,000 in 1979 to £710,000 in 1984, an increase of more than 100 percent in real terms. However, it is unclear how far this represents an increase in donations by local party members or money raised by local Labor parties from trade unions.

After the 1979 election, the Labor Party Head Office moved from the headquarters of the Transport and General Workers' Union in Smith Square, Westminster, to a renovated building in Walworth Road, Southwark. A loan towards its cost was obtained from a consortium of trade unions, which provided the money from their general funds. This led to legal action and a judgment in 1983 that the unions involved should pay for the loan from their political levy funds.[6] This did not directly affect the Labor Party, though it threatened to reduce union political levy reserves that might otherwise have been transferred to the party.

Despite growing income, Labor's Head Office operated at a loss each year between 1979 and 1982, though the deficits were much smaller than those of Conservative Central Office during the same period. This led to a wage freeze, budget cuts and economizing in other areas. Even so, the level of central income remained higher than it had in the 1970s.

Whereas the Conservatives were prepared to take financial risks in order to maximize spending on the 1983 election campaign, the Labor managers showed their traditional caution and gave priority to the routine needs of the party headquarters. The National Executive Committee's general election fund collected £2.3 million, 98 percent of which came from trade unions, while its expenditures on the campaign totaled only £2,057,000. The main items were £305,000 for grants to local campaigns; £878,000 for posters and advertisements (including those issued during the run-up to the campaign); £182,000 for producing television and radio election broadcasts; £145,000 for private opinion polls; £140,000 for party publications; £58,000 for the leader's tour; and £319,000 for headquarters salaries, administrative costs, and miscellaneous expenses.[7] In addition there was the money collected for the election by the regional organizations of the party, which were mostly payments by the unions for grants to parliamentary candidates. This brought Labor's central spending to about £2.3 million.

The absence of information makes it impossible to give current estimates of local Labor finances. However, there does appear to have been some improvement in activity in the constituencies. At least, the earlier sharp decline seems to have been arrested. Individual party membership dropped from nearly 1 million in the early 1950s to barely 300,000 by the late 1960s. According to official figures – which are more reliable than before because of changes in the rules relating to constituency affiliations to the national party – there were 324,000 members in 1984. In comparison, there were 348,000 members in 1980, 277,000 in 1981, 274,000 in 1982 and 295,000 in 1983. In view of the rise in membership subscription rates from £1.20 in 1978 to £6 in 1982, one might have expected a sharper fall than actually occurred. A rising level of party activity in the constituencies may be reflected in the increasing sums paid by local Labor organizations to the Head Office.

In the 1983 general election, Labor candidates spent an average of £2,927, and a total of nearly £1.9 million. While this was not far short of the total spent by Conservative candidates, the financial gap still remaining between the constituency organizations of the two parties is shown by the fact that aid received by Labor candidates from the National Executive Committee and from regional organizations probably exceeded £½ million, whereas the Conservative total was only £62,000. At the central level, too, the Conservatives retained a financial edge. The most notable point, however, was the extent to which the gap had narrowed. In the 1979–83 parliamentary cycle, Conservative central income (routine and campaign) was about 30 percent higher than Labor's; in 1952–5, it was three and a half times as great. The gap between the two parties' central revenues narrowed during each of the parliamentary cycles from 1966 onwards.[8]

LIBERAL AND SOCIAL DEMOCRATIC PARTY FINANCES

The year 1981 saw the formation, amid a blaze of publicity, of a new political party, the Social Democrats (SDP). The four Labor ex-ministers who were its leaders soon negotiated an electoral alliance with the Liberals. The two parties retained separate central and local organizations and their fund-raising efforts remained almost entirely independent; their styles were different.

The Liberal Party believed in governmental decentralization and community politics. Their strength lay in provincial roots. Since the 1930s, the extra-parliamentary headquarters, the Liberal Party Organization had been small, weak and poorly financed. In accordance with the philosophy of decentralization, the party's main financial backer, the Joseph Rowntree Social Service Trust Ltd., directed most of its grants to local Liberal purposes and not to the party headquarters.

By contrast, the SDP was led by a group of metropolitan insiders, including a former Chancellor of the Exchequer and former Foreign Secretary, and was supported by establishment figures including churchmen, professionals and businessmen. It was a party created from the center and soon built up an headquarters organization considerably larger than the Liberals. From the beginning, the SDP exploited modern technologies for recruiting members and for communicating with them by direct mail. It asked for a relatively high subscription (£9 in 1981), payable by credit card over the phone. In its first year of existence the SDP recruited 78,000 members and received £760,000 in subscriptions. After the initial bout of enthusiasm, subscriptions fell to £424,000 in 1983–4 and £393,000 in 1984–5. The SDP also worked actively for business support. Though few companies agreed to contribute, it was more successful with individual businessmen and reportedly received several hundred thousand pounds from David Sainsbury, a leading shareholder in a family chain of supermarkets.

Central Liberal income is shown in Tables 4 and 5. The decentralized structure of Liberal organizations means that different central and regional Liberal bodies maintain separate funds. The tables thus exclude some significant aspects of central activity and cannot be accurately

Table 4. *Liberal Party organization routine income and expenditure, 1973–84 (£)*

	Income	Expenditure
1973	125,000	97,000
1974	87,000	119,000
1975	101,000	106,000
1976	81,000	111,000
1977	130,000	105,000
1978	169,000	157,000
1979	299,000	252,000
1980	127,000	171,000
1981	191,000	208,000
1982	258,000	268,000
1983	383,000	385,000
1984	426,000	394,000

The totals exclude the by-election guarantee fund.
Source: Liberal Party Organization Annual Reports.

Table 5. *Liberal central association income and expenditure, 1973–84 (£)*

	Income			Expenditure
	State aid	Other	Total	
1973	—	9,000	9,000	13,000
1974	—	8,000	8,000	9,000
1975	33,000	2,000	35,000	40,000
1976	33,000	2,000	35,000	33,000
1977	33,000	1,000	34,000	34,000
1978	37,000	2,000	38,000	37,000
1979	n.a.	n.a.	n.a.	n.a.
1980	n.a.	n.a.	n.a.	n.a.
1981	52,000	6,000	58,000	57,000
1982	52,000	10,000	62,000	63,000
1983	57,000	8,000	45,000	69,000
1984	64,000	12,000	76,000	66,000

Source: Liberal Party Organization Annual Reports and supplementary information.

compared with the national accounts of the Conservative and Labor Parties. The main sources of the Liberal Party organization's routine income in 1984 were listed as £232,000 in donations and grants; £33,000 in bequests; constituency affiliation income, £92,000; and receipts from the appeal at the annual Liberal Asembly, £59,000. The Liberal Central Assocation has in recent years been little more than a repository of the Liberal share of the "Short money," the state grant introduced in 1975 to aid opposition parties in the House of Commons.

The central SDP accounts during the first four years of its existence are shown in Table 6. Thanks largely to the SDP, the routine central expenditure of the two Alliance Parties had reached £1.3 million by 1982–3, compared with only £0.2 million by the Liberals in 1980. This amounted to a four-fold growth, in real terms.

In the 1983 election the Liberals and SDP campaigns were only loosely coordinated and each raised a separate central fund. In addition, there was a third "Alliance" fund headed by David Owen and by John Griffiths, the Liberal president. Since most of this money was provided by David Sainsbury and some associates, the SDP members played the most important roles.

The SDP headquarters spent £467,000 on preparations for the general election, including about £250,000 on pre-campaign advertising. During the campaign, the central SDP spending amounted to £1,054,000, including money raised by the Alliance fund. The election thus cost the SDP Head Office £1,521,000. The largest item of campaign expenditure was £380,000 in grants to parliamentary candidates. Advertising costs during the campaign amounted to £181,000, including the SDP's share of the production costs of the Alliance Party election broadcasts. Other costs included £48,000 for private opinion polling, £39,000 for leaders' tours and £130,000 for party publications (net of receipts). Campaign spending by Liberal headquarters amounted to £120,000. In addition, the Joseph Rowntree Social Service Trust Ltd., donated £245,000, of which £140,000 was earmarked for Liberal candidates, £20,000 for the party leaders' tours and £57,000 for joint publicity with the SDP. In total, central election spending by the Alliance amounted to £1,934,000. By far the largest item was grants to parliamentary candidates, which amounted to over half a million pounds. The Alliance election budget in 1983 was, in real terms, six times greater than the £0.2 million spent centrally by Liberals in the 1979 election.

The largest contributor to the Liberal campaign was the Joseph Rowntree Trust whose contribution to the party in 1983 – centrally and locally – totaled £322,663. It gave an additional £10,000 to the SDP and

Table 6. *Social Democratic Party head office income and expenditure account, 1981–2 – 1984–5 (£)*

	Income			Expenditure		
	Members' subscriptions	Other	Total	Routine	General election	Total
1981–82	760,000	145,000	905,000	852,000	—	852,000
1982–83	584,000	928,000	1,512,000[a]	962,000	397,000	1,359,000
1983–84	424,000	1,215,000[b]	1,639,000	707,000	1,124,000	1,831,000
1984–85	393,000	513,000[b]	906,000	796,000	—	796,000

[a] Includes net receipts of by-election insurance fund.
[b] Includes state aid for SDP in the Commons.
Source: Social Democratic Party Annual Reports and supplementary information.

£3,388 to the Alliance fund. Earlier Rowntree grants to the Liberals – largely for local purposes – totaled £103,730 in 1979; £26,016 in 1980; £41,534 in 1981; and £80,360 in 1982. Additional grants to the SDP and Alliance funds in 1981 and 1982 amounted to £29,147. Another major Liberal contributor was BSM Holdings Ltd., which gave £40,000 to the party's general election fund in 1983 and an additional £98,000 for routine purposes in 1983–5.

Because of a lack of information, estimates cannot be made of the routine finances of local Liberal and SDP organizations. It is probable that Liberal constituency associations raise and spend more than the recently created local units of the SDP, which does not have constituency associations but is based on area organizations covering a group of parliamentary seats. According to official returns of election expenses in the 1983 election, the 311 SDP candidates spent an average of £2,777 each and the 211 Liberal candidates £2,282. Total spending by Alliance candidates amounted to £1.6 million. In real terms, this was 65 percent higher than that of Liberal candidates in 1979.

THE COST OF THE 1983 GENERAL ELECTION

Election costs consist of three elements: (1) central spending, (2) local spending, (3) the value of subsidies-in-kind, mainly free postage for candidates, free use of halls for election meetings, and free broadcasting time. In the 1983 campaign, the Conservative and Labor Parties each received five slots of ten minutes each on all television channels and the Alliance received four slots. One estimate assumed that a ten-minute broadcast had the same value as four minutes of commercial advertising and included broadcasts during the year before the announcement of the election date as well as those during the campaign.[9] Table 7 shows how subsidies in kind had the effect of equalizing the campaigning resources available to the three main contestants.

A noteworthy feature of the 1983 election was advertising by interest groups. In the 1960s, such "politically relevant" expenditures were mostly by business groups favoring the Conservatives; in 1983, the bulk was pro-Labor. After the 1964 election, Richard Rose calculated that the British Iron and Steel Federation, the employers' organizations Aims of Industry and the Economic League, and individual steel companies threatened by the Labor Party's nationalization plans, spent £1.9 million (£14 million at 1984 values) on pre-election advertising.[10] In 1983, Aims of Industry spent nearly a quarter million pounds on advertising in the national and provincial press and in leaflets, focusing attention on the issue of

Table 7. *Estimated total Conservative, Labor and Alliance campaign spending, 1983 (£m)*

	Conservatives	Labor	Alliance
Central campaign expenditures (excluding grants to parliamentary candidates)	3.8m	1.8m	1.0m
Local spending (including grants from central party organizations)	2.1m	1.9m	1.6m
Total (excluding subsidies-in-kind)	5.9m	3.7m	2.6m
Estimated value of subsidies-in-kind	4.8m	4.8m	4.0m
Total campaign costs (including subsidies-in-kind)	10.7m	8.5m	6.6m
Votes received (in millions)	13.0m	8.5m	7.8m
Expenditures per vote (excluding subsidies-in-kind)	45 pence	44 pence	33 pence
Total cost per vote (including subsidies-in-kind)	82 pence	100 pence	85 pence

Source: Labor, Liberal and Social Democratic Party Annual Reports, information supplied by Conservative Central Office, and Butler and Kavanagh, *The British General Election of 1983*, p. 266.

nationalization and highlighting some of the weaknesses of Alliance policies. Against the government, there was a range of publicity. Conservatives felt that the public relations efforts of some Labor-controlled local authorities, particularly the Greater London Council (GLC), constituted thinly veiled political advertising funded by local taxpayers. When the election date was announced, the GLC was in the midst of a poster campaign attacking government plans for cutting public expenditure and many of these posters remained in situ during the election. However, an issue of the GLC's free newspaper, "The Londoner," was withdrawn.

The election also coincided with a £1 million advertising campaign by the National Association of Local Government Officers opposing government job cuts. This union did not have a political levy fund and the advertising was paid for out of its general funds on the ground that NALGO was promoting the specific interests of its members, not engaging in general political propaganda. Other advertising came from the Animal Protection League, the International Fund for Animal Welfare and

Table 8. Average expenses of major party candidates in general elections, 1885–1983 (£)

	At current prices			At December 1984 prices		
	Conservative	Labor	Liberal	Conservative	Labor	Liberal
1885	890	—	891	35,000	—	35,100
1929	905	452	782	19,500	9,700	16,900
1945	780	595	532	10,900	8,300	7,400
1970	949	828	667	5,100	4,500	3,600
1974 (Feb.)	1,197	1,127	745	4,300	4,000	2,700
1974 (Oct.)	1,275	1,163	725	4,100	3,700	2,300
1979	2,190	1,897	1,013	3,700	3,200	1,700
			Alliance			Alliance
1983	3,320	2,927	2,525	3,500	3,000	2,600

Sources: Michael Pinto-Duschinsky, British Political Finance, Table 81 and David Butler and Dennis Kavanagh, The British General Election of 1983 (London: Macmillan, 1984), p. 266.

National Teachers in Further and Higher Education. According to Conservative calculations, press advertising by these groups immediately prior to and during the election cost £1.2 million. This was considerably larger than Labor Party advertising expenditure.

As far as long-term trends are concerned, the decline in the cost of constituency campaigning continued in 1983, as shown in Table 8. Most candidates still spent near the legal limit where they stood a prospect of winning, but there seems to have been a tendency for the two main parties to economize in constituencies considered unpromising. The spending limit has automatically been raised in line with inflation – as enacted in 1978 – to £2,700 plus 3.1 pence per elector in county constituencies and £2,700 plus 2.3 pence in boroughs. This worked out at £4,700 for an average county constituency and £4,200 for an average borough. Spending by Conservatives averaged 72 percent of the maximum, compared with 63 percent for Labor, 62 percent for SDP and 50 percent for Liberals.

The fall in local campaign spending has not been accompanied by a rise in election expenditure by the national party organizations. Until the First World War, the national campaign budgets of the Liberals and Conservatives were largely devoted to grants to constituencies. Even if these are excluded from the reckoning, national level spending by the Conservatives had reached its modern levels, in real terms, by 1929. The national campaigns in 1979 and 1983 have been more expensive for the two main parties than those between 1966 and 1974 but cheaper than those of 1959 and 1964 and, for the Conservatives, far cheaper than those of 1929 and 1935. Trends in central party spending in elections are shown in Table 9.

TRADE UNION VERSUS COMPANY DONATIONS

By 1979, union payments for Labor Party purposes had overtaken company donations to the Conservative Party. In the early 1980s, there were two developments that might have threatened this progress. First, unemployment was particularly severe in some of the manufacturing industries which serve as union strongholds. The total nominal membership of unions with political levy funds fell from 9.9 million in 1979 to 8.4 million in 1982. Secondly, election results showed that union members were becoming increasingly disaffected from the Labor Party. Opinion polls indicated that the proportion voting Labor fell from 55 percent in 1974 to 39 percent in 1983. Conservatives won 31 percent of union votes and the Alliance 29 percent. The relevance of such statistics has been disputed by K. D. Ewing and W. M. Rees, who argue that support for Labor was probably higher than average in unions which had political levy funds as

Table 9. *Central expenditure in general elections, 1929–83 (£m)*

	Conservative		Labor	
	At current prices	At February 1984 prices	At current prices	At December 1984 prices
1929	0.29m	6.3m	0.04m	0.9m
1935	0.45m	11.2m	0.03m	0.6m
1955	0.11m	1.3m	0.07m	0.6m
1959	0.61m	5.1m	0.24m	1.9m
1964	1.23m	8.8m	0.54m	3.7m
1970	0.63m	3.4m	0.53m	2.7m
1974 (Feb.)	0.68m	2.4m	0.44m	1.5m
1974 (Oct.)	0.95m	3.0m	0.52m	1.6m
1979	2.33m	3.9m	1.57m	2.5m
1983	3.83m	4.1m	2.3 m	2.5m

Totals include estimated spending by Labour regional councils except for 1979 and 1983, for which an estimate of such spending has been included. 1935 Conservative figures are approximate. Figures for 1983 are estimates.
Sources: For elections to 1979, Michael Pinto-Duschinsky, *British Political Finance*, Tables 31 and 41; for 1983, as for Table 7 above.

opposed to the middle-class unions of teachers, local government officers and civil servants, which did not.[11] Even so, the general trend is hardly likely to have left unaffected those which raised political levies.

Despite the potential challenges, however, the levy funds continued to advance during 1979–83. The political levy is collected automatically and almost painlessly. Because individual subscriptions are so small in relation to their overall union dues, it is easy to raise them and union leaders have protected the funds in this way. The growth of the political levy is shown in Table 10.

This shows that there was a 17 percent fall in membership of unions with levy funds between 1977 and 1983 and a 23 percent fall in the number contributing to them. However, average income per member grew by 221 percent (from 43 to 138 pence), an increase of 75 percent in real terms.

The fact that the number paying the levy fell more sharply than total union membership probably does not indicate any increase in the number "contracting out." The percentage of members contracting out is not shown in the statistics issued by the Certification Officer and is probably very small. The majority of those who fail to pay are excused from doing so.

Table 10. *Trade union political levy funds, 1977–84*

	Total membership of trade unions with political funds	Total contributing to political funds	Political funds total (£ millions)		
			Income	Expenditure	Reserves at end of the year
1977	9.72m	7.92m	3.39m	2.46m	4.11m
1978	9.89m	8.02m	4.05m	3.42m	4.53m
1979*	9.94m	8.10m	4.67m	5.04m	4.24m
1980	9.49m	7.73m	5.04m	4.05m	5.26m
1981	8.90m	7.17m	6.01m	4.84m	6.46m
1982	8.02m	6.49m	7.14m	5.92m	7.61m
1983*	8.06m	6.10m	8.41m	9.06m	6.60m
1984ᵃ	7.40m	5.70m	8.50m	6.00m	7.00m

* General election year.
ᵃ These figures are estimates and exclude the National Union of Mineworkers.
Source: Annual Reports of the Certification Officer for Trade Unions and Employers' Associations.

A recent study of the Durham Area of the National Union of Mineworkers showed that, although a mere 37.2 percent of the members paid the levy, only 99 members (less than 1 percent) contracted out. The rest were excused because they were retired members, members' widows, unemployed or permanently sick.[12] Since early retirement and unemployment have increased in recent years, this is the most likely explanation of the falling percentage of union members paying the levy. Despite Labor's political unpopularity, the result of inertia is that very few members actually contract out.

Almost all donations from unions are devoted to Labor Party purposes. The total cannot be accurately determined since unions contribute to local and regional units of the Labor Party and individual Members of Parliament as well as to the center. To make matters more complex, some unions distribute a share of levy income to their regions and branches and it is these which make contributions to the party. Analysis of levy fund accounts suggest that nearly 80 percent of total levy income is eventually paid to Labor Party organizations, about 9 percent is used to pay for the expenses of union delegates to party conferences and for political education, and the other 13 percent is devoted mainly to the costs of administering the funds.[13] Based on these calculations, unions gave an

Table 11. *Political payments by some major unions, 1983 (£)*

	Payments to Labor Head Office	Total union political levy expenditure
Transport Workers (TGWU)	1,320,752	1,449,163
General & Municipal Workers (GMBATU)	669,305	1,164,426
Engineering Workers (AUEW)	721,020	940,001
Public Employees (NUPE)	520,048	761,174
Mineworkers (NUM)	352,650	n.a.
Shopworkers (USDAW)	202,500	n.a.
Communication Workers (UCW)	183,163	n.a.

Payments to Head Office include affiliation fees and payments to the general election fund. Total levy expenditure includes payments to Labor Head Office, regional and local Labor parties, but excludes administrative expenditure.

Sources: Political fund accounts submitted to the Certification Officer and Labor Party Annual Report, 1983.

estimated £4.4 million to the Labor Party in 1982, of which £2.8 million was paid in affiliation fees to the National Executive Committee. Union contributions to the Labor Party, nationally and locally, in the election year of 1983 totaled about £7.1 million.

Normally unions build up their levy funds between general elections in order to make extra payments to the Labor Party in campaign years. A list of payments by large unions made in 1983 is given in Table 11.

As shown in Table 10, the growth in the levies has made it possible for unions to increase affiliations to the National Executive Committee and at the same time build up reserves. The 1983 election made little dent in these reserves. Increases in affiliation rates to some union levy funds which have been introduced since 1982 have led to further growth in the funds, whose income totaled £8.5 million in 1984 (excluding the National Union of Mineworkers, for which information is not yet available). Companies are required by the Companies Act of 1967 to report political payments in their annual reports. It is impossible to survey the reports of over half a million companies. The best sources of information in this area are surveys of major company reports carried out by the Labor Party's research department and an independent trade union organization called the Labor Research Department. According to the most recent Labor Party survey, corporate donations to the Conservative Party and its allied fundraising bodies (British United Industrialists and various regional industrialists' councils) totaled £2,566,000 in 1979–80; £1,620,000 in 1980–1; £1,788,000

Table 12. *Companies donating at least £50,000 to the Conservative Party and to allied organizations 1983–4 (£)*

British and Commonwealth Shipping	94,050
Allied-Lyons	80,000
Hanson Trust	80,000
Taylor Woodrow	79,035
Guardian Royal Exchange	76,000
Racing Electronics	75,000
European Ferries	60,000
London and Northern Group	54,000
Plessey	52,000
AGB Research	50,000
Consolidated Gold Fields	50,000
Distillers	50,000
Marks & Spencer	50,000
Trafalgar House	50,000

Source: Labor Party Research Department, "Company Donations to the Tory Party and other Political Organizations," *Information Paper No. 65*, September 1984.

in 1981–2; £2,042,000 in 1982–3; and £3,337,358 in the election year 1983–4. While these figures probably include all the contributions from major companies, they underestimate the combined total given. Assuming that the proportion of Conservative central and local income coming from companies remained the same from 1979 to 1983 as in the 1970s, total corporate donations to the Conservative Party nationally and locally amounted to an estimated £4.5 million in 1979–80, £2.6 million in 1980–1; £3.2 million 1981–2; £3.8 million in 1982–3; and £8–£8.5 million 1983–4. The largest company contributions revealed in the survey for the election year 1983–4 are listed in Table 12.

A recent theme of the Labor Research Department's publication, *Labor Research*, has been the "funding crisis" facing the Conservatives as a result of lessening business confidence in the government, reflected in falling company payments to the Conservative Party.[14] It is suggested that possibily because of the party's shortage of funds, the government has encouraged donations by giving peerages and knighthoods to large donors. While the direct exchange of honors for political payments has been illegal since the Honors (Prevention of Abuses) Act of 1925, *Labor Research* claims to have discovered "a remarkable correlation between some companies' generosity to Tory Party finances and the receipt of honors by directors,"[15] a charge that has been dismissed by the Conservatives.

A comparison of the estimated company donations during the three financial years preceding the 1983 election with the three years before the 1979 election indicates that company donations declined in real terms by some 5 percent. In itself, this does not appear significant. What makes it potentially serious is that company donations in the late 1970s were already considerably lower than normal.[16] Further, the continued stagnation of company payments contrasted with a rise of about one-fifth in the income of the union political levy funds during this period. In 1971–8, the amount received by the Conservative Party from companies was 27 percent less than that raised by the unions for Labor;[17] by 1979–82, company contributions were 33 percent below.

Labor's political unpopularity has led to some questioning of the organizational ties between unions and Labor. In the short run, however, there has been no loosening of these long-standing bonds. The changes in the party constitution which led in 1981 to a new procedure for electing the party leader gave the unions 40 percent of the voting strength in the new electoral college. At the financial level, the expansion of the levy funds has also served to strengthen the link between the unions and the party. By contrast, the connections between big business and the Conservatives has remained far weaker, as argued recently by Wyn Grant.[18]

It is hard to establish why political payments by companies have fallen behind those of the unions. A contributory factor may have been the enactment by the Labor government's Companies Act of 1967, which obliged companies to report political donations. Post-war Conservative governments, for their part, have long criticized the union levy system but have not taken any action against it until recently. "Contracting out," introduced in the Trade Union Act of 1913, was replaced with "contracting in" by a Conservative government in 1927. After Labor reintroduced "contracting out" in 1946, the Conservatives pledged in 1950 to reverse the law once again if elected to office. They narrowly lost that election and did not repeat the pledge in the 1951 election.

In January 1983, the Secretary of State for Employment, Norman Tebbit, published a Green Paper raising the question once again. It is believed that the business lobby, Aims of Industry, may have urged him to make this move. The newspaper *Democracy in Trade Unions* argued that some unions hindered their members from exercising their rights to contract-out of the political levy. Therefore, "it would be essential to require trade unions to do more to ensure that their members are aware of their ability to contract-out." Alternatively, the government proposed to substitute contracting-in for contracting-out.

Mr. Tebbit's document provoked a vigorous defence of the political levy system from Labor lawyers, some of whom were quick to argue that the laws relating to union political funds were more democratic than those governing company payments to the Conservative Party, since directors have no obligation to hold a ballot of shareholders before making political contributions and shareholders have no right to contract out. In reply to the Conservative argument that a shareholder is free to sell his shares (unlike a union member who is frequently obliged to join a particular union as a condition of employment), it was pointed out that individuals whose money was invested in shareholding pension funds were not able to do this.[19]

The Conservative election manifesto of 1983 included a commitment to introduce legislation requiring unions to hold periodic ballots to permit their members to decide whether to have a political fund. It also proposed "to invite the Trade Union Congress (TUC) to discuss the steps which the trade unions themselves could take to ensure that individual members were freely and effectively able to decide for themselves whether or not to pay the political levy." If the unions were unwilling to cooperate, the government would "be prepared to introduce measures to guarantee the free and effective right of choice."

Following the election, the government proceeded to introduce legislation. In accordance with the manifesto, it did not include contracting in as part of its Trade Union Bill but initiated negotiations with the TUC. In early 1984, it was agreed that the government would refrain from introducing legislation enforcing "contracting in" and that the union would undertake, in return, to make "contracting out" more accessible. In practice, this represented a victory for the unions. The Trade Union Act of 1984, contained two major provisions. First, unions will be required to hold ballots at least every ten years to decide whether to have a political levy fund; those which have not held such ballots in the last ten years will be required to do so within a year. Secondly, the definition of "political objects," for which payments must be made from political, not general, funds, will be widened. This is designed to prevent unions from making further loans to the Labor Party from their general funds (like the recent loan for the Head Office) and to block the use of general funds for political advertising such as that of NALGO during the 1983 election.

The act has predictably been interpreted as an attack by the Conservatives on Labor's main source of funds. If this was the aim, it has failed. In all twenty-nine unions which had held ballots by January 1986, a majority of members voted to continue raising a political levy fund. The average turnout was 51.7 percent. Of those who voted, 83 percent supported and 17 percent opposed political funds. These clear-cut results probably did not indicate solid support of members for union contributions to the Labor Party, however. Union leaders usually down-played the issue of payments to the Labor Party and campaigned on the argument that a vote against the political levy would prevent unions from campaigning for members' interests.

Even if some major unions had voted to discontinue their political levy funds, the financial damage to the Labor Party might still have been limited. The unions which continued to raise political levy could easily have increased the amounts collected from each member to compensate for the shortfall caused by the termination of other unions' levies. The ease with which the rate of a political levy can be increased was shown in April 1984 when the Transport and General Workers' Union increased it from 13 to 39 pence a quarter, a change that would raise an extra £1.5 million a year.

The real importance of the ballots required by the act and by other recent trade union legislation may prove to be their effect in concentrating attention on some fundamental questions about decision-making within trade unions. The democratization of at least some unions was possibly a more important Conservative objective than the desire to deny money to the Labor Party organization.

The complexities of party funding, lack of information, particularly about the budgets of local party organizations, and the uncertainties caused by the recent legislation about union levies, makes it unwise to draw simple conclusions about current trends. Two clear points can be made. First, 1979–83 saw the emergence of the Alliance, which proved far more successful in collecting both small and large individual contributions than any third party since the First World War. Secondly, the Conservative Party did not achieve in the late 1970s and early 1980s a response to its fund-raising efforts comparable to its political success. A period that saw a notable growth in its political lead over Labor saw its financial and organizational advantages eroding. This situation is surprising. In the U.S., the political Right has collected huge sums from small- and medium-sized contributors through the use of techniques of direct mail. Largely by this means, the Republican Party has established a large financial lead over its opponents. In 1982, it raised five times as much as the Democratic Party. In Britain, the only party which has made significant use of direct mail solicitations by the time of the 1983 general election was the SDP.

Notes

1 See Vernon Bogdanor, "Financing Political Parties in Britain," in Vernon Bogdanor, ed., *Parties and Democracy in Britain and America* (New York: Praeger, 1984); and Vernon Bogdanor, "Reflections on British Political Finance," *Parliamentary Affairs*, 1982.

2 For information on party finances before 1980, see Michael Pinto-Duschinsky, *British Political Finance 1830–1980* (Washington: American Enterprise Institute, 1981). The tables in this article have been drawn up on the same basis as the ones in that study. The present chapter also draws from my article, "Trends in Political Funding, 1979–1983," *Parliamentary Affairs*, Summer, 1985.

3 For an account of Central Office's financial problems in 1980 and 1981, see David Butler and Dennis Kavanagh, *The British General Election of 1983* (London: Macmillan, 1984), pp. 30–1.

4 See David Butler and Dennis Kavanagh, *The British General Election of February 1974* (London: Macmillan, 1974), pp. 240–2; and *British Political Finance*, p. 251.

5 Statistics on candidates' expenses are taken from Butler and Kavanagh, *The British General Election of 1983*, pp. 266–7.

6 See "Employment Appeal Tribunal: Association of Scientific, Technical and Management Staffs v. Parkin," *The Times*, October 7, 1983.

7 *Labour Party Annual Report 1984*, p. 87.

8 *British Political Finance*, p. 278.

9 For an estimate of subsidies-in-kind in 1979, see Michael Pinto-Duschinsky, "Financing the British General Election of 1979," in Howard R. Penniman ed., *Britain at the Polls, 1979: A Study of the General Election* (Washington: American Enterprise Institute, 1981), pp. 230–3.

10 Richard Rose, "Pre-election Public Relations and Advertising," in David Butler and Anthony King, eds., *The British General Election of 1964* (London: Macmillan, 1965), p. 378.

11 Keith D. Ewing and William M. Rees "Democracy in Trade Unions-I: The Political Levy," *New Law Journal* (133), 4 February, 1983, p. 100.

12 Ewing and Rees, "Democracy in Trade Unions."

13 *British Political Finance*, p. 224.

14 See, for instance, *Labour Research*, December 1983.

49

15 *Labour Research*, December 1983.
16 See *British Political Finance*, p. 232.
17 *British Political Finance*, p. 236.
18 Wyn Grant, "Business Interests and the British Conservative Party," *Government and Opposition* (15), 1980. He argues that relations between business and the Conservative Party are "more problematic and tenuous than is often assumed to be the case."
19 See Ewing and Rees, "Democracy in Trade Unions"; Ewing, *Trade Unions, The Labour Party and the Law* (Edinburgh: Edinburgh University Press, 1982), "The Conservatives, Trade Unions and Political Funding," *Fabian Tract No. 492* (London: Fabian Society, 1983) and "Company Donations and the Ultra Vires Rule," *Modern Law Review* (47), January 1984.

This chapter is adapted from an article published in *Parliamentary Affairs*, Vol. 83, No. 3, Summer 1985, and appears with pemission from Oxford University Press.

3

Canadian election expense legislation, 1963–85: a critical appraisal or was the effort worth it?

KHAYYAM ZEV PALTIEL

Since 1963, provincial, federal and municipal politicians have devoted considerable attention to problems associated with political finance and election expenses. Prompted by scandals – and the public reaction thereto – as well as by rising media costs and organizational expenses associated with sample surveys and the new techniques of political marketing, and shortfalls in party and candidate campaign funds, legislators at all levels have attempted to regulate the collection and spending of money by electoral competitors and the subsidization of political war-chests from the public purse. Consensus for change and the agreement of political rivals was obtained in almost all instances by way of royal commissions, advisory committees, party commissions and legislative committees whose hearings and recommendations served to build public support and formed the basis for much of the legislation which was subsequently enacted. The proposals made and the measures adopted have been legitimated as promoting the probity and honesty of the electoral process, the liberal values of equity, the equality of chances and opportunity, as well as facilitating the participation in – and the openness of – the election system, and the capping of escalating costs which benefit only the well-endowed to the detriment of those of lesser means.

Undoubtedly, the various regulatory schemes have constrained many of the gross abuses witnessed formerly, but few would argue that these have been completely eliminated. Recent prosecutions in Nova Scotia and allegations made following the latest provincial and federal elections indicate the contrary. Willful violations of these legislative reforms are serious problems, but more damaging to the proclaimed goals of their authors is the very structure of the control arrangements with their

51

deliberate as well as unintended consequences. Many factors have contributed to the crystallization of the existing party systems at the federal and provincial levels. History, the idiosyncracies of Canadian federalism, economic and ethnic regionalism, religion, and – to a lesser extent – class, as well as the "first-past-the-post" election system, have each played a part in this process. It is the purpose of this paper to explore the degree to which the reforms of political finance and the regulation of campaign spending have furthered the institutionalization of the traditional competitors on the Canadian electoral stage.

BACKGROUND

The problem of money in elections has been present in Canada from the earliest post-Confederation period.[1] The links between the traditional parties and the business community were made manifest in the series of transactions between John A. Macdonald and the promoters of the Pacific railway, known to history as the Pacific Scandal of 1873. This prompted the first attempt at reform by Alexander Mackenzie's Liberals who passed the Dominion Elections Act of 1874, which introduced the doctrine of agency to Canadian elections law and made candidates and their agents responsible for a statement of expenditures. But the law ignored the existence of parties and the sources of party funds, and provided no machinery for enforcement. Another series of railway scandals, involving Laurier's chief fund raiser, Israel Tarte, in the first decade of this century led to further ineffectual legislation in the form of amendments to the Dominion Elections Act in 1908 which purportedly sought to strengthen the doctrine of agency by making agents responsible for the receipt of all contributions to candidates and by prohibiting corporations from making campaign donations. Again parties were not defined and enforcement was neglected. A further amendment to the Dominion Elections Act enacted in 1920 had the effect of preventing contributions from trade unions to the fledgling labor parties which were springing up in that period. Eventually the efforts of the "ginger group," headed by J. S. Woodsworth and William Irvine, led to the repeal in 1930 of these abortive products of the Progressive Era. When the notorious Beauharnois Scandal broke over the heads of W. L. Mackenzie King and his Liberals in 1931, the emptiness and vacuity of the existing legislation was revealed, but strangely enough prompted no legislative response. It was not until three decades later, following the Great Depression, a second World War, a sea change in the style of politics and campaigning, and a communications revolution that Canadian legislators took up the problem of election finance in a serious fashion.

The provincial scene in the first century after Confederation did not differ substantially from that at the federal level. Some provinces had tinkered with the doctrine of agency, while others had attempted to limit contributions from certain sources, and a few had attempted to define and/or regulate parties in terms of sponsorship of candidates, votes cast or the expenditure and reporting of funds received. In none were the enforcement and sanctions worthy of the name. A complaisant public seemed to tolerate corruption in raising and spending provincial party campaign funds of a more blatant and pervasive kind than anything practiced by federal parties and their bag-men.

THE REFORM MOVEMENT

The ground for change was set by the collapse of two political organizations which had long determined the course of Canadian electoral politics. The defeat of the federal Liberals under Louis St. Laurent in 1957 and the death of Maurice Duplessis and subsequent defeat of his Union Nationale in 1960 presaged a new style of politics nationally and particularly in the province of Quebec. Trading on public revulsion for the excesses of the Duplessis regime and the deep-felt urge for modernization and "rattrapage" (catch-up), Jean Lesage and the Liberal "équipe du tonnere" (strike-force) promised fundamental reforms in the electoral morals of the province and most notably in the area of campaign finances. This involved the dismantling of the notorious system of "ristournes" (kick-backs) to the party in office, ending the "sale" of permits and licenses of various kinds and government party tolls on all goods and services purchased by the government as detailed in the Salvas Provincial Royal Commission inquiry.[2] Building on its election platform, the Quebec Liberal Federation commissioned a study by Professor Harold Angell of Concordia University which provided a basis for a series of party resolutions and convention debates, and in turn served to shape the election expense provisions of the Quebec Election Act passed in 1963 and which came into effect on January 1, 1964.[3] The act has since been amended several times, most notably by the Parti Québécois in March 1977 on the very morrow of its victory. The details and implications of the Quebec legislation are discussed in a later section, but its principal features must be outlined as they foreshadowed much of the legislation adopted in other Canadian jurisdictions.

The 1963 Quebec act imposed ceilings on the expenditures of parties and candidates; it provided for the reimbursement of a substantial portion of the permitted spending by candidates gaining one-fifth of the popular vote in their constituencies (but it particularly favored the candidates of the major parties whether or not they won 20 percent of the vote); the doctrine of agency was extended to apply to all candidates and parties and the agents were to be held legally responsible for all financial transactions incurred by their principals during the campaign; to participate in the campaigns all parties had to apply for recognition, and to gain such status had to present at least ten candidates in the previous or current campaign, although the incumbent government party and the party of the leader of the Official Opposition were automatically granted this status; reporting, disclosure, and publicity of campaign income and expenses were required subject to sanction as condition for payment of the reimbursements and for sitting and voting in the National Assembly; enforcement of these provisions was placed in the hands of the chief returning officer of the province who was given the status and tenure of a district judge. Subsequent amendments accorded public subsidies for a portion of the organizational expenses of recognized parties with seats in the legislature, the limitation of contributions by parties and candidates to gifts from registered voters in the province only, and a modest tax credit to stimulate such giving.

The 1957 and 1958 victories of the federal Progressive Conservatives temporarily brought a new complexion to Canadian politics, reflected in the populism of John Diefenbaker and the tilt towards a nationalist stance by the new Liberal team under Lester Pearson and his economic spokesman, Walter Gordon. Uncertain as to the direction of the major parties, the corporate, business and financial interests, which had supplied the wherewithal for their campaigns, now tended to withhold the support they had displayed in the past. Compounding this problem were the repeated calls for funds necessitated by the recurring general elections resulting from the uncertainties of minority government. Further, the emergence of television as the prime element in political campaigns exacerbated the monetary shortages. Revelations of the resort to questionable sources to make up the shortfalls provoked the Rivard Affair and precipitated action by the Pearson government to fulfil its campaign promises to reform party finances and to regulate election expenses by establishing the Barbeau Committee on Election Expenses in 1964.[4] It was headed by Alphonse Barbeau who had chaired the Quebec Liberal party commission which had recommended the reforms instituted in that province. The committee was composed of representatives of the Liberal, Progressive Conservative and New Democratic parties, and included Professor Norman Ward who had written extensively on Canadian elections, but no representatives of the Ralliement des Créditistes or Social Credit parties were named. After extensive hearings and research, the

Committee presented its report in October 1966 with the following recommendations:

Political parties ought to be legally recognized and registered and be made legally responsible through the doctrine of agency for their financial transactions;

financial equity among candidates and parties should be sought through the provision of certain services and subventions from the public purse, such as free mailings, the reimbursement of a portion of qualifying candidates' cost, and the provision of a maximum amount of radio and television time to be allocated proportionately without charge to the registered parties;

campaign costs should be reduced by shortening the election period and banning advertising except for the last four weeks before polling day;

to restore public confidence, parties and candidates should be required to report and disclose their incomes and expenditures;

broader public participation in the campaign process should be encouraged through a tax credit system for modest donations by individuals;

a supervisory mechanism buttressed by appropriate sanctions should be set up to enforce law and to verify and publish the required financial reports.

It was to be eight years before these proposals found their way into the statute books. The restoration of the Liberal ascendancy under Pierre-Elliott Trudeau had dampened enthusiasm for the project, despite the Prime Minister's youthful critique of his party's traditional practices. This was underlined by a doomed, tardy, and half-hearted move in the dying days of the Twenty-Eighth Parliament in May 1972. Scandal and rumour, however, continued to beset the fund-raising process at the federal and provincial levels. In Quebec there were revelations of contacts between prominent Liberal politicians, including a former minister, and supposed underworld characters. In Ontario, allegations of funds raised by Conservative collectors from property developers doing business with provincial agencies (the Fidinam Affair) prompted the Premier to move toward reform. Charges and counter-charges regarding the dependence of the two old parties on large multi-national corporations headquartered in the U.S. and the reliance of the New Democrats on U.S.-based international unions rekindled public interest. However, the timing and impetus for the 1974 act must be attributed to the 1972 campaign and election results in the U.S. and

Canada. The Watergate affair south of the border and the outcome of the 1972 Canadian federal election which left the Liberals in a minority government situation dependent on New Democratic Party (NDP) support set the scene for the final enactment of the long-sought reforms. Indeed, full disclosure and identification of all donors and their contributions, not originally contemplated by the Barbeau Committee, were part of the price elicited by the NDP in return for its support of the Liberal government.[5]

In the meantime, Nova Scotia enacted its scheme for the reimbursement of a portion of election costs in 1969. Shortly thereafter, following an extensive investigation, Ontario adapted the federal model by imposing limits on contributions and advertising expenses, and copying the tax credit scheme in 1975. Since that time all but two of the provinces – British Columbia and Prince Edward Island – have made extensive revisions to their election acts governing election expenses.[6]

Today, the federal parliament and eight of the ten provincial legislatures have statutes in place providing for some measure of definition and regulation, limitation, reporting and disclosure of campaign costs and revenue as well as financial assistance to qualifying parties and candidates in the form of subsidies or reimbursements of election costs incurred.[7] In addition, most Canadian jurisdictions grant tax credits or deductions for contributions to candidate and party funds. Since our concern in this paper is with the impact of this legislation on the structure and articulation of the Canadian party system, a detailed analysis of the individual statutes and control mechanisms will be eschewed except insofar as required to clarify the arguments advanced.

From the outset, this legislation took cognizance of the political realities by implicitly favoring the major parties and other parliamentary groups which designed the statutes. Thus the interests of the incumbent governing parties and the leading opposition groupings were usually protected. In Quebec, the 1963 reforms assured that candidates representing those parties which had come first or second in the previous general election in each constituency would be assured of reimbursements; this advantage to the two leading provincial parties continues to this day. In Ontario and Alberta, legislation permitted the existing parties, in effect the governing Conservatives in each case, to conceal monies collected prior to the proclamation of the new laws in trust funds, the size of which need not be disclosed. Where a party held office in the absence of a parliamentary majority, the election expense laws appear to have reflected some of the concerns of third parties and other minor groups represented in the legislature. Otherwise the interests of third or minor parties, and those of other political formations not represented in parliament were given short shrift. Indeed, many of the statutes constitute impediments to their foundation and activity as exemplified by the stringent registration provisions, the party broadcasting allocations and the qualifications for reimbursement of party costs embodied in the Canada Elections Act.[8]

REGISTRATION AND THE DOCTRINE OF AGENCY

It is generally accepted that legal recognition of the role of parties in the campaign process is a *sine qua non* for any attempt to accomplish the purported goals of the reform of election finance; together with the doctrine of agency applied to the parties and their candidates, such recognition is a cornerstone of the control machinery adopted in Canada and eight of its provinces. Formal registration is required of any party which wishes to raise or spend money for campaign and inter-electoral purposes, sponsor and promote candidates, or benefit from tax incentives, subvention and services made available at public cost. To gain this status, the parties must demonstrate that they have a leader, an agent, a bank account, a headquarters, proper records, an auditor, and field a minimum number of candidates.

However, in addition to establishing the *bona fides* of the parties, many of the statutes seek to eliminate allegedly frivolous groupings and to accomplish ends that result in advantages for – or lessen threats to – the positions of the incumbents and/or the traditional parliamentary parties. For example, automatic registration is granted to the parties of the Premier and Leader of the Opposition in Manitoba, Nova Scotia and Quebec. Other provinces require that a party present candidates in either five, ten or as many as half the ridings represented in the provincial legislature. The federal registration requirement of at least twelve sitting Members of Parliament or the sponsorship of fifty candidates clearly inhibits the establishment of regional groupings outside the two large Central Canadian provinces. Had the current provisions been in effect in the 1930s, they might well have prevented the emergence of the CCF and the Social Credit and extended the monopoly on policy and office of the two old parties with the consequent aggravation of sectional grievances. That such constraints on entry into the parliamentary and electoral arenas were tempting to the spokesmen of the established parliamentary groupings may be gathered from discussions of the Standing Committee on Privileges and Elections which endorsed the Chief Electoral Officer's proposals to tighten the federal registration procedures which were incorporated into the 1977 amendments to the Election Expenses Act. Whereas Ontario and Alberta provide for a method of registration during the inter-election period through a public petition signed by several thousand electors, federal law appears to opt for less rather than greater public participation, except through the established parties.

Federal law appears to sin against openness as well, due to the feature that requires candidates who wish the party name to appear after theirs on the ballot to present a letter of endorsement from the national leader to the constituency returning officer, together with their official nomination papers. This method was used by Robert Stanfield to deny the party label to Leonard Jones of Moncton, despite the fact that he had been nominated by the local association of the Progressive Conservative Party. Regardless of what one thinks of the merits of the issue (Jones's opposition to official bilingualism) which provoked this action by the Conservative leader, it is clear that the law as currently written has considerably centralized power in the registered parties by furthering the process which has reduced the influence of the rank-and-file and backbenchers in the parliamentary and party system.

Federal law also works against the interests of the independent Member of Parliament in the treatment of any surpluses which may be left over after the conclusion of an election campaign. Winning and losing candidates affiliated to registered parties are permitted to turn over to their local constituency associations or the national party organizations any surpluses left after the payment of all expenses and the receipt of reimbursements, presumably to be held in trust for future campaigns and for the carrying out of ongoing organizational work. Independent Members of Parliament and candidates may not set aside these funds for these purposes; instead, any of their surpluses must be turned over to the government's Consolidated Revenue fund which cannot be retrieved. Rebellion and nonconformity has its price in the Canadian electoral system.

Fixing legal responsibility and accountability for the financial aspect of election campaigns in Canada and its provinces has generally involved a prohibition on those other than parties, candidates and their agents from making election expenditures during the formal campaign period to promote or oppose one of the rivals for office. However, the 1974 federal act did permit expenditures during the campaign period made "in good faith" and "for the purpose of gaining support for views held by [a person] on an issue of public policy, or for the purpose of advancing the aims of any organization or association, other than a political party or an organization or association of a partisan political character . . ." Several attempts by the Chief Electoral Officer to prosecute alleged contravenors were frustrated by the "good faith" defence. Nevertheless, provoked by the confrontational tactics of advocacy and single-issue groups, exemplified by anti-abortion and prolife groups during the 1979 and 1980 campaigns, and the intentions of peace, nuclear disarmament and anti-cruise missile movements, as well as environmental, ecological and animal rights groups, the three parliamentary parties, acting through their directors on the ad hoc advisory committee, persuaded the Chief Electoral Officer to request the removal of the "good faith" defence. This amendment was enacted in a matter of days, without parliamentary review or debate, on November 17, 1983, as Bill C-169.[9] This bill also included major changes to the broadcasting provisions, financial limits, reimbursements and audit procedures, all of which were plainly to the advantage of the parliamentary parties and somewhat to the detriment of the non-represented parties.

The passage of Bill C-169 after the adoption of the *Canadian Charter of Rights and Freedoms* not only marks a failure by its authors to foresee the doubtful constitutionality of the amendment concerning "third party" activity during campaigns, but it also underlines the failure of the Chief Electoral Officer to display sufficient independence from the very groups he was charged to oversee and provides a classic case of the supposedly regulated writing the rules to suit themselves. In addition, lack of debate surrounding the passage of the act indicates the failure of the press and the media to take note of this rampant raid on the public treasury and the violation of constitutional norms; no editorial comment was made until the National Citizens' Coalition (NCC) launched its constitutional challenge! Furthermore, the fact that expense limits and reimbursements now rise automatically without public discussion also has gone unremarked. Parliament also failed in its obligations; tempted by what were clear advantages to themselves, the three parties each presented a single spokesman on first reading of the bill, which was not referred to the Standing Committee on Privileges and Elections as had been the custom in the past. Witnesses were not heard and there was no discussion at any of the later stages of the bill; the attempt by the Conservatives to distance themselves from the proceedings after the bill was passed and after the NCC launched its suit simply emphasizes the conspiracy of silence which prevailed.

THE CONSTITUTIONAL CHALLENGE

Given the far-reaching implications of the successful constitutional challenge by Colin Brown and the NCC, a detailed discussion is in order. On January 16, 1984, the National Citizens' Coalition and its leader Colin Brown launched a suit against the Attorney General for Canada in the

Court of Queen's Bench of Alberta, Calgary District, impugning the constitutional validity of Sections 70.1 (1) and 72 of the *Canada Elections Act*, as amended (in 1983).[10] They claimed that these sections prohibited them from using the print and broadcast media to promote or oppose a candidate or registered political party during an election without first obtaining the consent or authority of the registered party or candidate. Furthermore, they alleged that these clauses infringe upon or deny their rights to freedom of thought, belief, opinion and expression, including freedom of the press and other media of communication, guaranteed by the *Canadian Charter of Rights and Freedoms*. Since the right of a Canadian citizen to vote necessarily implies the right to an informed vote, these sections by limiting participation in the electoral debate jeopardize or deny the right to vote guaranteed by Section 3 of the *Canadian Charter of Rights and Freedoms*. An alternative claim was that these sections, collectively and separately, infringe upon or deny the right to freedom of speech and expression, and the right to participate freely in democratic elections, both of which rights are fundamental principles of parliamentary democracy guaranteed by the reference in the preamble to the *Constitution Act of 1867* to "a Constitution similar in Principle to that of the United Kingdom." Legislation which violates or denies rights which are principles of parliamentary democracy is *ultra vires* of the Parliament of Canada. The plaintiffs, therefore, requested a declaration that Sections 70.1 (1) and 72 infringed upon and denied rights guaranteed to them by the Charter and a statement that they were null and void, or a declaration that the sections in question were *ultra vires*.

The case was heard and tried in Calgary before Mr. Justice Donald Medhurst during the months of April, May and June 1984. At the outset, the attorneys for the Crown, as defendants, questioned whether the plaintiffs were entitled to seek a remedy for rights which had not as yet been infringed (no election having occurred since the passage of the amendments). However, the Court upheld the standing of the *NCC and Colin Brown* to challenge the validity of the law even though it was based on "impending breaches," because "the action is so reasonably foreseeable in the near future that concern is therefore present at this time." The defence then proceeded to claim that the law was designed to assure fairness and equality in the procedures governing the election of members of parliament, and of parliament itself, and as such was not a denial of rights and freedoms; furthermore, to the extent that these sections constitute limitations, which was denied, of rights and freedoms, these were "reasonable limits . . . demonstrably justified in a free and democratic society" as set out in Section 1 of the Charter.

In support of its position, the Crown produced briefs and presented evidence from a number of expert witnesses, including Professor John Courtney of the University of Saskatchewan and Dr. Leslie Seidle. The Chief Electoral Officer, M. Jean-Marc Hamel, reviewed the background to the amendments made in 1983, backed by examples provided by Joseph Gorman, the Commissioner of Elections. In the course of his testimony, the Chief Electoral Officer conceded that the reason for the 1983 amendment lay in the difficulty presented by the "good faith" defence which hampered successful prosecutions; he also admitted that the bulk of the suggestions for legislative change which he had presented to parliament originated with members of the *ad hoc* committee of paid party spokesmen for whom he was essentially acting as a conveyor belt. Professor Paul Bender, a noted American constitutional expert from the University of Pennsylvania, argued that the interpretation given by the U.S. Supreme Court in *Buckley vs. Valeo*, which treated campaign expenditures as the equivalent of free speech, which the plaintiffs were adducing in support of their claim, was "highly questionable." Clearly he would have preferred, had he known of it, the position taken by Mr. Justice Raymond Bernier in a parallel case involving the *Quebec Elections Act* and that province's Human Rights legislation. In that case, the Centrale de l'Enseignement du Québec had allegedly violated the provincial ban against "third party" advertising during campaigns. The court found that "la liberté d'expression n'est pas équivalente à la liberté de dépenses" and that the legislation limits "not the right of free speech but the right to spend money to express oneself" (Boucher c. C.E.Q., February 10, 1982, unreported, Quebec Provincial Court). Bender's key argument was that a concern "to equalize the relative ability of all citizens to affect the outcome of elections" justified limiting "the speech of the affluent"; in his view, this was constitutionally legitimated in Canada by Section 15(2) of the *Canadian Charter of Rights and Freedoms* which approved affirmative action programs to insure equal treatment. Professor Larry Berg of the University of Southern California, in a lengthy brief and testimony, pointed to the pernicious effect of political action committees (PACs) on the U.S. campaign process made possible by the *Buckley* decision which had endorsed so-called "independent" expenditures. Such expenditures by PACs and wealthy individuals "threaten to impose government by special interest" lacking "any accountability to the electorate and frequently little to their own members." The author, who had questioned the wisdom of the 1983 amendments, argued in a report prepared for the assistance of the Crown counsel that the integrity of the Canadian electoral process required that some limitation of "third party" spending was mandatory if the goals of expense controls were to be achieved and the patent inequities of the U.S. situations were to be avoided.

On June 26, 1984, Mr. Justice Medhurst ruled that "Section 70.1 (1) and Section 72 of the *Canada Elections Act* are inconsistent with Section 2(b) of the Charter and to this extent are of no force or effect." In his reasons for judgment, he stated that "the sections on their face do limit the actions of anyone other than registered parties or candidates from incurring election expenses during the prescribed time and in this sense there is a restriction on freedom of expression." To permit such a restriction, it would have to be shown that the limit was "reasonable," that it is "prescribed by law" and that it could be "demonstrably justified in a free and democratic society" as called for in Section 1 of the *Charter of Rights and Freedoms*. To determine whether the offending sections meet these tests, the Court reviewed the history of the legislation and the reasons which had prompted the Chief Electoral Officer in his 1983 report to Parliament to request the removal of the "good faith" defence. Tellingly, the judge observed that "There was very little actual evidence of the abuses of section 70.1 to support the recommendation that had been made by the Chief Electoral Officer." Further, in choosing to eliminate the *bona fide* defence, Parliament – on the recommendation of the CEO – had deliberately ignored an alternative course of action, namely "to rewrite subsection 4 [which contained the defence-KZP] to make it more specific in line with preserving the right of third parties to express themselves while maintaining the intent of the legislation." While there might be dangers and mischief from unrestricted "third party" spending during campaigns, the values of debate to the parliamentary system as proclaimed by Justices Cannon and Duff in their judgments in the *Alberta Press Act* case must be taken into account. The question before the Court was whether Parliament had chosen the appropriate means to check perceived and anticipated abuses and to maintain the values which the law sought to attain; it could not consider whether other means were available. "It is not for the court to rewrite legislation so that it might conform with freedoms protected by the Charter," the judge wrote. This would confuse the legislative and judicial functions.

Thus Justice Medhurst concluded:

Care must be taken to ensure that the freedom of expression, as guaranteed by section 2 of the Charter, is not arbitrarily or unjustifiably limited. *Fears or concerns of mischief that may occur are not adequate reasons for imposing a limitation. There should be actual demonstration of harm or real likelihood of harm to a society value before a limitation can be said to be justified.* In my view it has not been established to the degree required that the fundamental freedom of expression need be limited. The limitation has not been shown to be reasonable or demonstrably justified in a free and democratic society [author's emphasis].

Technically, the decision only governed elections in Alberta. However, it was given nation-wide application by the decisions of the then-Attorney General for Canada, Donald Johnston, in the light of the impending 1984 federal general election, not to appeal the judgment and subsequent decisions made by the Chief Electoral Officer which gave it effect across Canada. Unless constitutionally valid legislation is enacted to meet the problems created by this decision, single-issue organizations, interest groups and others will be allowed to spend money freely during federal election campaigns. Ironically, only registered parties and candidates will be subject to control. The Advisory Committee on Election Expenses and those who drafted the 1974 Act were fully aware of the problems presented by "third party" advertising during campaigns, yet they were sensitive to the constitutional niceties involved. The "good faith" defence was an imperfect instrument. It did, however, act as a check, requiring those who would have violated its provisions to prove that they had not wilfully sought to contravene the law. Its removal in the face of the Charter of Rights adopted in 1982 reveals that partisan interest blinded the authors to the consequences of their actions. New language will have to be found and a constitutionally acceptable formula devised to close the loophole opened by this decision. Otherwise, the way is now clear for unlimited "third party" spending which will make a mockery of the intent of the act, to the benefit of the affluent in particular. Advocacy groups, single-issue organizations and interest groups will be able to go beyond promoting the issues they favor to direct involvement in election campaigns – supporting or opposing, as the case may be, those parties and candidates who concur or disagree with their views on public policy. Failing parliamentary action, we may well see the emergence of the political action committee (PAC) phenomenon on Canadian soil.

A recent judgment in the trial division of the Supreme Court of Ontario in another Constitutional case involving the *Canadian Charter of Rights and Freedoms*, launched with the assistance of the National Citizens' Coalition, appears to strike at the heart of trade union support of political parties and may have drastic financial consequences for the New Democratic Party. On July 7, 1986, Mr. Justice John White handed down his decision in the case of *Merv Lavigne*, a community college teacher at the Haileybury School of Mines. The plaintiff claimed that the 1984 contract between the Ontario Public Service Employees Union and the college's Council of Regents violated his rights because about $2 of his $338 in compulsory annual dues is spent on causes such as the peace movement, abortion rights and the New Democratic Party, which he does not endorse.

In his judgment, Justice White found "that compulsory dues may only be used for the purpose which justifies their imposition. In other words, the use of compulsory dues for purposes other than collective bargaining and collective agreement administration cannot be justified in a free and democratic society where the *individual objects to such use* (author's emphasis)." The far-reaching implications of the judgment have prompted the union's president, James Clancy, to announce that the union plans to appeal the ruling "to the Supreme Court of Canada, if necessary."

BILL C-169 AND ITS LESSONS

If the constitutional mishap may be attributed to a lack of foresight on the part of its authors, the same cannot be said for other amendments embodied in Bill C-169. Certain changes in the spending limits had to be made to take account of inflation since 1974. Thus an automatic escalator in party and candidate limits was introduced, linking the latter to the rise in the Consumer Price Index since 1980; for the 1984 election, permitted spending per voter was thus 1.318 times the initial base. Furthermore, candidate reimbursements, which would have outstripped spending limits that were tied to the rise in the cost of first-class postage, had to be readjusted; they were set from half the actual – to a maximum of half the permitted – spending for qualifying candidates. The original scheme had linked candidate reimbursements to the cost of first-class mail; changes in postal administration have led to a sharp rise in the cost of first-class postage, far outstripping the rise in the consumer price index and inflation. These justifiable changes of the method of calculating expenditure ceilings and the reimbursements to qualifying candidates nevertheless substantially increased permitted spending; in addition, amendments were made to federal election broadcasting procedures, the reimbursement of a portion of registered party election costs, the limits on a candidate's "personal" spending, and the responsibility of party and candidate auditors. Throughout, one may detect a weakening in the verificatory mechanism, further relaxation of spending limits and a bias in favor of the three parliamentary parties.

The broadcasting amendments in Bill C-169 transferred responsibility for administering these provisions from the Canadian Radio-Television and Telecommunications Commission to a Broadcasting Arbitrator appointed by the Chief Electoral Officer on the unanimous recommendation of two representatives appointed by the leader of each registered party represented in the House of Commons. The formula that had previously been the practice in the allocation of the six-and-one-half hours of prime time among the registered parties was spelt out as follows: the percentage of seats won in the previous election, the percentage of votes received and the percentage of total registered party candidates endorsed by each registered party at the previous general election, with no party to receive more than half the total time, determine the broadcast allocation. While an additional potential total of 39 minutes of broadcast time was made available for allocation among "new" parties, the allocation system distinctly favors the three parliamentary parties. Thus in 1984, the Liberals, Progressive-Conservatives, and New Democrats were allocated 173, 129, and 69 minutes respectively, whereas apart from the Parti Rhinocéros, which was granted 8 minutes, no other party was accorded more than 5.5 minutes. Similar rules govern the division of "free" time. This advantage has been accentuated by the change in party reimbursements. Until 1983, a registered party was only entitled to a refund from the federal treasury of one-half the cost of broadcasting time purchased by it during the course of the campaign. This was done to remove apparent discrimination against the print and other media. The 1983 amendments converted the reimbursement of broadcasting costs into a general reimbursement of up to 22.5 percent of the maximum permitted expenditures for any registered political party *which had spent at least 10 percent of its permitted maximum*. Since only the three parliamentary parties spent these amounts, smaller formations, such as Social Credit, which in the past could have benefited from the broadcasting subsidy, were effectively eliminated as beneficiaries of public funds.

While some view the elimination of the requirement that a candidate's personal expenses exceeding $2,000 be included as an election expense as a minor matter, the weakening of the verificatory mechanism is more serious. The 1974 Act required that all party and candidate declarations be accompanied by an auditor's report verifying their authenticity: "The auditor . . . shall make a report . . . on the return respecting election expenses . . . and shall make such examinations as will enable him to state whether in his opinion the return presents fairly the financial transactions required . . . to be detailed in the . . . return." While this was a heavy responsibility, it was seen by its authors and the Barbeau Committee as an essential element in the verificatory process. Nevertheless, the professional accounting associations mounted a successful lobby against this provision which has been amended to read "to state in his report whether in his opinion the return presents fairly the financial transactions *contained in the books and records of the candidate*." Further, the auditors' reports which are appended to all party returns for the last general election contain the following or a parallel disclaimer: ". . . the Act does not require us to report, nor was it practicable for us to determine, that the accounting records include all transactions relating to the . . . Party of Canada for the general election held on September 4, 1984 . . . The Return . . . presents fairly the information contained in the accounting records . . ." These reports thus say nothing about the state or quality of these records.

The foregoing detailed review of Bill C-169 raises serious questions regarding the efficacy of the federal control mechanism which serves as a model for several provincial jurisdictions. Is it sufficient to rest this responsibility on the very groups which should be subject to regulation? The colonization of the regulators by the regulated, as exemplified by the "ad hoc committee," is a common enough phenomenon and its consequences are known and predictable. While convenient to those charged with the administration of the act, its results may well frustrate the intentions of its originators, reinforcing the position of those represented in the Parliament to the detriment of outsiders and challengers. Clearly, there is a need for a statutory body which will assure input from others than incumbents, and one whose transactions are made public and subject to public scrutiny. The recent complaints by the three parliamentary parties concerning the inordinate delays by the Commissioner of Elections in disposing of allegations of financial misconduct by federal candidates and their agents presage fundamental reform of the administration of the federal Election Expenses Act. Here the Ontario model of a formal Commission on Election Contributions and Expenses is preferable to the informal devices employed at the federal level and by several provinces.

CONTRIBUTION AND EXPENSE LIMITS

Canadian legislative opinion has been divided as to whether equity among political competitors can best be achieved through prohibitions on the sources of – and constraints on the size of – contributions on the one hand, or through monetary and other ceilings on overall costs and particular forms of spending on the other.

Federal law places no limit on the source or size of contributions provided that all donations over $100 are fully reported and disclosed as to amount, identity and class of giver; monies may be solicited from sources foreign and domestic, including individuals, trade unions, corporations and other organizations. Nova Scotia merely requires the reporting of the total amounts received by parties and candidates; the source, identity and size of each particular donation does not have to be disclosed; it should occasion little surprise that illegal payment scandals are rife in that province. Ontario and Alberta have opted for controlling the size of contributions to parties, candidates or local constituency associations. Annual maxima are doubled during election years for donations from individuals, businesses, trade unions and other groups; federal-provincial intra-party transfers are forbidden and donors must be domiciled in the province concerned. Nevertheless, the limits are so generous, particularly in Alberta, that the incumbent Conservatives have had no trouble raising funds from large contributors. Nor have foreign-controlled businesses been seriously hampered inasmuch as a provincial branch office or subsidiary grants them entree as contributors. Only Quebec has attempted to place effective controls on political contributions by placing an upper limit of $3,000 and allowing donations only from registered eligible voters in the province. This far-reaching reform was enacted early in 1977 at the outset of the Parti Québécois' term in office; legitimated as a major democratization of the financing process, it had the additional effect of limiting support from the business community to the then opposition provincial Liberals. However, Canadian experience regarding limitation on business contributions parallels the American; money contributes to and flows to power, and the monied have learned to live with disclosure.

Spending limits during the formal election campaign have been imposed in most Canadian jurisdictions. Federal law fixes a per-voter ceiling on registered party spending with a sliding scale for candidates at the local level. Spending on advertising is limited to the last twenty-eight days of the campaign and the purchase of time on the electronic media is constrained as to amount. Several provinces, including Quebec and Nova Scotia, follow a procedure similar to the federal except for the electronic media which are beyond their jurisdiction. Prior to legislative amendments made in the summer of 1986, Ontario had set a per-voter limit on advertising expenditures alone, but this was so generous for parties and candidates, and the working definition of advertising so narrow that the control was scarcely worthy of the name; in fact, the former Ontario limits permitted spending at roughly three times the federal average. The new Ontario legislation follows the pattern set by the recent amendments to federal law, although it has substantially increased the tax credit available for small contributions.

The major flaw in the attempt to limit campaign spending lies in the very narrow definition given to the concept of election expenses. These are usually defined in terms of amounts spent to promote or oppose directly the election of registered parties and candidates during the periods from the date of issuance of the writs of dissolution to polling day. Pre-writ spending made in anticipation of the campaign, particularly by incumbents in a position to determine the date of the election, generally escape control.

Moreover, nomination costs spent in an effort to gain the leadership of a party or its candidacy at the constituency level are ignored by the law. Further, expense declarations from the last federal general elections in 1984 revealed a lack of uniformity and a great disparity in the treatment of ongoing party expenses during the election campaign; thus, whereas the New Democratic Party attributed all of its national office spending during the summer of 1984 to election expenses, the Liberals treated two-thirds as such, while the Progressive-Conservatives allocated only slightly more than one-quarter of their national office expenditures during the campaign as election expenses.[11] Had the Liberals and Conservatives followed the practice of the NDP, both would have been in serious violation of the legal limits.

A serious loophole favoring the incumbent governing parties in Canada and most of the provinces lies in the failure to control government advertising during the period of the formal election campaign. A form of advocacy advertising, it is invariably designed to depict the governing party as the purveyor of all good things to the electorate by identifying government programs with the current incumbents. The promotional advertising slogan "Preserve It. Conserve It," sponsored by the Tory government of Ontario during the 1981 provincial election campaign, is one of the more notorious examples. Successive Liberal governments at the federal level, however, were not averse from using bill-boards, circulars and envelope stuffers fostering one or another government program as a means of blowing their own horn during election campaigns. Thus far only Saskatchewan and Manitoba have legislated against this abuse. Section 229(1) of the Saskatchewan Election Act prohibits any government publicity activity during the formal campaign period, except in public emergency; a subsequent section extends the ban to broadcasters, who must disclose violations. Manitoba has enacted a similar, if somewhat softer, prohibition. Since the federal government is the largest single advertiser in the country, and paid provincial publicity is not insignificant, the abuse of incumbency by election related government advertising has prompted the Chief Electoral Officer to ask Parliament to eliminate this unreported and uncontrolled campaign expense.

FISCAL BENEFITS – REIMBURSEMENTS, GRANTS AND TAX CREDITS

Probably the most important aspect of the campaign finance laws adopted in the various Canadian jurisdictions is the attempt to provide an alternative source of money for serious parties and candidates which would reduce their former dependence on the largesse of the monied interests. Three devices have been employed: subsidies from the federal and provincial treasuries in the form of reimbursement of a portion of election expenses incurred by qualifying candidates and parties, grants to the parliamentary and legislative caucuses of parties represented in the elected chambers, and tax credits or deductions to stimulate donations to party and candidate funds.

Candidate reimbursements were first introduced in Canada by Quebec in 1963, followed by Nova Scotia in 1969, the federal government in 1974, and Ontario in 1975. Today, some form of candidate reimbursement exists in almost all provinces. Based either on a sliding scale or a fixed amount per voter, or as a portion of actual costs incurred, these subventions are paid to candidates who have gained either 10, 15, or 20 percent of the total votes cast in their constituencies (in Quebec candidates of the two leading parties in the previous election are reimbursed automatically). These subventions have lessened the burden on the central party treasuries which formerly had to advance funds to many of their local standard bearers. The probability of such refunds has enabled many candidates to borrow funds, and has opened the door to less affluent candidates, even in the major parties. It is likely that the availability of these reimbursements has played a significant role in making it possible for an increased number of women to stand for office in all the parties.

As membership parties dependent on small collections at the grassroots, the New Democratic Party and the Parti Québécois have benefited from these subventions to their candidates both federally and provincially. But few others outside the magic circle of the two established major parties have. On the federal scene in 1980, 650 or 43 percent of the 1,497 candidates qualified for reimbursements; in 1984, the figures were 664 out of 1,449 or 46 percent of the total, 238 Liberals, 282 Progressive Conservatives, 140 New Democrats, 3 Confederation of Regions-Western Party, and 1 Independent. The new federal reimbursement of 22.5 percent of registered party costs described earlier has similarly benefited only the Liberals, the Progressive Conservatives and the New Democrats, since only they spent at least 10 percent of their permitted ceilings; the anomaly of the federal party subsidy lies in the fact that aid is linked not to spending but to the maximum permitted, and modesty suffers.

The federal treasury and most provinces make grants to parliamentary and legislative caucuses to help defray the research and administrative costs of the parties represented in the legislatures. These grants are linked to the number of seats held by each party and are meant to compensate for the advantage that the government party possesses in its access to the public service and its expertise. Only Quebec, thus far, makes annual grants to the parties to help maintain their extra-parliamentary organizations, based on the number of votes each received in the previous general election. Of great significance also is the assistance provided by the federal treasury, Ontario and several other provinces for the maintenance of constituency offices by Members of Parliament and the Legislative Assemblies. Ostensibly established for the purpose of maintaining contact between the Member and his constituents, these facilities also serve party political and electoral ends and constitute a marked advantage to incumbents from the established institutionalized groups.

Most provinces have imitated the federal system of tax credits for donations to registered political parties and candidates, Quebec's being the most modest, while some have added modest deduction for corporate donations, as in Ontario. These credits are available for donations to candidates at election time and to parties annually; where local constituency organizations are registered, they too may issue the required receipts on an annual basis. All parties and candidates have benefited from this stimulus to smaller donations. At the outset, the greatest beneficiary was the grass-roots organization of the New Democratic Party and its candidates who had customarily depended for support on numerous small gifts from members and sympathizers.[12] Examination of more recent reports submitted to federal election officials, however, reveals that the Progressive Conservative party has best exploited the opportunities opened up by the tax credit system.[13] Using structured mailing lists and personalized electronically produced letters from party leaders, the Conservatives have carved out and produced a new class of givers among the young, upwardly mobile free professionals and the techno-bureaucracy of the corporate and business world. Between 1980 and 1983, the number of individual contributors to the New Democrats rose by slightly more than 5 percent, Liberal contributors almost doubled, whereas the number of individual Conservative donors more than tripled. In monetary terms, Liberal contributions rose by less than one sixth in this period, New Democratic collections by 40 percent, but Progressive Conservative contributions almost doubled to more than $14,000,000, two-thirds of which came from individuals. Whereas business enterprises accounted for almost half of donations to the Liberal Party in 1983, this class provided only one-third of Conservative funds, and a large part of the latter came from small enterprises tapped by the same techniques used to contact individuals. The importance of this phenomenon lies in the fact that many of these contributors to the Progressive Conservatives, be they professionals or small businessmen, have been upgraded from simple donors to activists at the poll, constituency, regional and national levels.

The systematic efforts of the Progressive Conservative Party to establish a modern fund-raising system were confirmed in the financial reports submitted to the Chief Electoral Officer following the 1984 federal general election. Outstripping its principal rivals in all categories but one, the Tory Party and its candidates raised more than $32,000,000 from more than 174,000 contributions in 1984. By contrast, the Liberals and their local standard-bearers collected less than $19,000,000 from 75,000 donors, and the New Democrats slightly more than $10,000,000 from 101,000 contributors. Three times as many business corporations and enterprises made contributions to the Conservatives as to the Liberals, in amounts totaling approximately $16,500,000 and $7,650,000 respectively. In the individual category, the Tories raised almost $15,000,000 from slightly more than 135,000 donors, as compared with $7,500,000 from about 50,000 Liberal contributors, and less than $6,000,000 from about 99,000 N.D.P. supporters. Only in the trade union category were the Conservatives outshone, with the New Democrats and their candidates raising about $2,600,000 from 1,500 trade unions and their locals, and only some $12,500 of union funds going mainly to a few Liberal and Conservative candidates. The 1984 party and candidate returns emphasize the breakthrough made by the Conservatives, and help to explain the deficit of $3,500,000 accumulated by the Liberal Party which had for long neglected the potential incentive provided by the tax credit system.

In sum, it may be concluded that the system of tax credits and *ex post* reimbursements tends to favour incumbents and the registered parliamentary parties and their candidates. The thresholds for eligibility are so high as to make it difficult for candidates of new formations to cross the qualifying barrier. Furthermore, the fact that this subsidy is payable only after the election has taken place presumes that candidates will be able to obtain initial financing on their own, or from their sponsoring parties or be in a situation where they will be able to obtain credit against the future possibility of reimbursement; in the latter case as well, major party candidates are at a distinct advantage. The reimbursement to registered parties also favors the registered parties with large budgets since it is payable only to those parties which have spent at least 10 percent of the permitted limits. Thus, a party which presented candidates in all 282 constituencies in the last federal election would have had to spend at least $639,150 before it was eligible for a refund of a portion of costs from the federal treasury. A party which did so would be entitled to a refund of approximately $140,000, but ironically, if it conducted a modest campaign and spent less, it would receive no public support.

On the other hand, the tax credit systems for political donations adopted in most parts of Canada do appear to give substantial assistance to those parties and candidates prepared to organize efficacious fund-raising efforts at the grass roots. This appears perforce to favor those parties organized among mass lines or those in a position to exploit direct mail and other techniques reminiscent of United Appeals and subscription campaigns launched by so-called "quality" magazines. Thus far, the New Democrats and the Progressive Conservatives have been the most successful practitioners of these arts. After the 1984 federal general election, the Liberals launched a serious direct mail fund-raising effort under paid professional direction; progress has been reported, but the Grits still have a long way to go before they can match the results obtained by their Tory rivals.

Since the tax credit system is closely linked to the disclosure provisions and requires the issuance of official receipts, one *caveat* must be borne in mind regarding its impact on left-wing parties and other dissenting groups. Fears of persecution and discrimination against supporters may well deter potential contributors from lending financial assistance on the grounds that revelation of their actions to the authorities might make them subject to police surveillance and political harassment. It is interesting to note that the U.S. Supreme Court on December 8, 1982, in a decision written by Mr. Justice Thurgood Marshall, upheld a finding by the Federal Election Commission that the Socialist Workers Party be exempt from the disclosure provisions of state and federal election laws; the names of donors and the recipients of its campaign expenses need not be revealed because of the history of government harassment of its members, which made such revelations a violation of First Amendment rights to free association.

On the subject of grants to the legislative caucuses and extra-parliamentary organizations of political parties or the services provided to sitting members, it need only be said that the greatest beneficiaries are obviously the established, institutionalized parties.

CONCLUSIONS

This overview of the reform movement of the past two decades appears to demonstrate that the basic features of the traditional pattern of Canadian party finance remain intact. The grosser elements of campaign corruption have been eliminated, although recurrent scandals reveal the possibility of its return, despite disclosure and the provision of alternate sources of public funding. The corporate business community continues to be a major element in the financing of the two old parties. Tax credits have stimulated individual giving, particularly in the new middle class of the free professions and the techno-bureaucratic cadres of the private business bureaucracies which share much of the outlook of the corporate financial community. If business influence appears to be less apparent on the electoral level, the same cannot be said about the nomination process for the leadership of the two major parties at the federal and provincial levels; corporate involvement in the nomination contests has become common knowledge. The post-party and post-governmental careers of former major party leaders and elites in corporate law firms and company board rooms amply confirm the relationships.

Canadian law at all levels concentrates on the formal campaign period. The nomination process is ignored. Pre-writ spending goes largely unnoticed and uncontrolled, and the advantages of incumbency are barely compensated; essential elements of the electoral process are thus neglected. The absence of a substantial corpus of party law means that the Canadian electorate is faced with a request simply to ratify pre-selected choices made by the party elites. The commonly noted fact that policy and program receive short shrift in Canadian elections accentuates elite dominance of the political stage.[14] The centralizing tendency inherent in the campaign finance reforms buttresses this control.

Compulsory reporting and disclosure of campaign income and costs have had a sanitizing effect on Canadian elections. Spending ceilings have slowed the competitive escalation of election expenditures, but loose definitions of the items covered provide exploitable loopholes. In the absence of links to the major socio-economic groups of organized business and organized labor, new political formations find it difficult to launch and maintain successful electoral efforts. New entrants to the electoral arena have generally been limited to groups and movements which have successfully altered the prevailing political discourse, or, like the Parti Québécois, have risen on an ideological surge and the support of their devotees. The latter's contemporary financial difficulties, however, show that waning mass enthusiasm has its price.

The campaign finance reforms have introduced a measure of equity into the Canadian electoral process. Much information is now available by which the performance of parties and candidates may be judged. Money still counts in Canadian elections, however, as Isenberg's study reveals.[15] The established parliamentary and legislative parties have severally and collectively benefited from the legislation, but it has had little impact beyond this narrow circle.

Notes

1 Khayyam Z. Paltiel, *Political Party Financing in Canada* (Toronto: McGraw-Hill Ryerson, 1970).
2 The Report of the Provincial Royal Commission concerned the purchasing methods used in the Department of Colonization and the Government Purchasing Service from July 1, 1955 to June 30, 1960 (Quebec, 1963). It was known as the Salvas Commission from the name of its Chairman.
3 Harold M. Angell, "Political Finance in Quebec," unpublished paper presented to the Political Finance Panel, International Political Science Association, Rio de Janeiro, August 9–14, 1982.
4 *Report of the Committee on Election Expenses* (Ottawa: Queen's Printer, 1966), The Barbeau Commission Report.
5 F. Leslie Seidle, "The Election Expenses Act: The House of Commons and the Parties," in John C. Courtney, ed., *The Canadian House of Commons: Essays in Honour of Norman Ward* (Calgary: University of Calgary Press, 1985), pp. 113–34.
6 Khayyam Z. Paltiel, "Comparaison de lois régissant le financement des partis politiques au Canada," 23 pp., unpublished paper for a Colloque, "Le financement politique: Bilan de l'expérience québécoise," sponsored by the Quebec Director-General of political party financing, Montreal, March 26, 1982.
7 Khayyam Z. Paltiel, "The Control of Campaign Finance in Canada: An Overview," in Hugh G. Thorburn, ed., *Party Politics in Canada*, 5th edition (Scarborough: Prentice-Hall, 1984), pp. 115–27. *A Comparative Survey of Election Finance Legislation, 1983*, Commission on Election Contributions and Expenses, Ontario, Toronto, 1983.
8 *Canadian Election Reform: Dialogue on Issues and Effects, December 1982*, Commission on Election Contributions and Expenses, Ontario, Toronto, 1982.
9 *BILL C-169, An Act to Amend the Canada Elections Act (No. 3)*, received Royal Assent on November 17, 1983, First Session, Thirty-Second Parliament, 29–30–31–32 Elizabeth II, 1980–81–82–83.
10 *National Citizen's Coalition and Colin Brown vs. The Attorney General for Canada*, statements of claim, arguments, briefs and reasons for judgment, April, May, June 1984.

11 Khayyam Z. Paltiel, "The 1984 Federal General Election and Developments in Canadian Party Finance." Paper delivered to the Political Finance Panel of the Research Committee on Political Finance and Political Corruption, XIIIth World Congress, International Political Science Association, Paris, 1985. To be published in Howard R. Penniman, ed., *Canada at the Polls III: The Federal General Election of 1984* (American Enterprise Institute/Duke University Press, 1988).

12 F. Leslie Seidle and Khayyam Z. Paltiel, "Party Finance, the Election Expenses Act, and Campaign Spending in 1979 and 1980," in Howard R. Penniman, ed., *Canada at the Polls, 1979 and 1980: A Study of the General Elections* (Washington, D.C.: American Enterprise Institute, 1981), pp. 226–79.

13 Report of the Chief Electoral Officer, *Election Expenses, Thirty-third General Election, 1984* (Ottawa: Chief Electoral Officer of Canada, 1985). Office of the Chief Electoral Officer, press releases, party and candidate reports.

14 John Meisel, "The Decline of Party in Canada," in Hugh G. Thornburn, ed., *Party Politics in Canada*, 5th edition (Scarborough: Prentice-Hall, 1984), pp. 98–114.

15 S. Isenberg, "Can You Spend Your Way into the House of Commons?", *Optimum*, Vol. 11, no. 1 (1980), pp. 28–9. S. Isenberg, "Spend and win? Another look at federal election expenses," *Optimum*, Vol. 12, No. 4, pp. 5–15.

4

Public funding of elections in Australia

E. A. CHAPLES

The regulation of election finance has been an issue which has received considerable discussion in the past decade in Australia. For most of the period since independence, Australia has operated – at both the national and state levels – a system of free enterprise politics with campaigns organized around political parties. Parties in Australia are organized at the state level but have strong national coordinating units that control campaigning in federal elections.

The two major conservative parties, the Liberals and the Nationals (formerly the Country Party), have controlled the Federal Government in coalition for twenty-one of the past twenty-eight years, although they were in opposition in the national government and in four of the six states at the beginning of 1988. The conservative parties are each strongly organized at the state level, and their national organizations have only minimal control over the behavior of the state parties. The major left-oriented party, the Australian Labor Party (ALP), however, is more powerful at the national level. The national executive of the ALP can – and often does – intervene in the internal affairs of its state parties when it sees fit to do so.

Traditionally, both the conservative parties and the Labor Party have had the responsibility for organizing funds for election campaigns, as well as for regular party maintenance activities. The Labor Party has been heavily dependent on union affiliations and union donations for its election finance, and in recent decades has found itself hard-pressed to raise sufficient monies to remain electorally competitive. The conservative parties have appealed to wealthy individuals and corporations for their funding, and, except in rare instances, it is generally accepted that they have enjoyed a substantial advantage in fund raising. Evidence for this assumption, however, is spotty and often indirect as effective spending disclosure laws have never existed in Australia.

Four of the six states and the national government have in the past attempted to regulate campaign finance by legislation to place limits on campaign expenditures. But all five of these processes varied in the formulas the governments in question applied to limiting campaign spending, and all found that enforcement of these provisions had become nearly impossible in recent decades. At the 1977 national election, for example, the law theoretically limited Senate candidates, who are elected statewide, to an expenditure of $1,000 and candidates for the House of Representative to $500.[1] What actually occurred, as Colin Hughes described it, was that the "Commonwealth Act appeared to establish a system of tight controls over electoral expenses, with potentially severe penalties for violations. In practice, however, the act is widely disregarded . . . [s]ometimes it is openly breached, and often reports of supposed compliance strike the informed observer as somewhat unreal."[2]

In the state of Tasmania, for example, the law restricted parties to a limit of $1,500 per candidate. The Australian Democrats, a third party which specializes in electing candidates to upper houses and has controlled the balance of power in the Australian Senate since 1980, challenged the failure of the major parties to heed these limits during the 1980 Tasmanian state election. The Democrats won their court challenge and forced a rerun of that election in one of Tasmania's five electoral sub-divisions.[3] Tasmania failed to amend its act, and a State Supreme Court justice then forced the parties to cancel almost all of their television advertisements for the 1982 Tasmanian election in an attempt to force compliance.[4]

THE NEW SOUTH WALES LEGISLATION

For many years, the Australian Labor Party has been a strong advocate of public funding, but until 1979 no state Labor Party had ever legislated on the matter. However, the rapid escalation of campaign costs in the era of television campaigning, the increasing difficulty in raising funds to fight either a state or national campaign on virtually an annual basis[5] and the obvious superiority of the conservative parties in raising funds had made the issue much more salient for the Labor Party in the 1970s.

The first instance of a state Labor Party actually putting party policy on public funding into effect occurred in New South Wales (NSW) in 1981. The legislation passed, however, only after NSW Labor Party had withstood very considerable opposition from the conservative establishment in that state. This opposition included the bitter and sustained disapproval of both the major newspaper chains which publish in Sydney, the Fairfax and Murdoch organizations.[6]

Both the Liberals and the National Country Party bitterly opposed the legislation, in particular the requirement that the names of donors of more than $200 to a candidate or more than $1,000 to a party in any election be publicly disclosed. The campaigns of the opposition parties and the newspapers were based on the contention that public funding would have several undesirable consequences. These were summarized in a lead editorial of Sydney's major morning paper, the *Sydney Morning Herald*. The *Herald* maintained that public funding would:

> outrage voters who have strong moral objections to the philosophy and policies of a particular party;
>
> entrench existing parties to the detriment of new and small parties;
>
> weaken the links between politicians and the rank-and-file party members;
>
> not necessarily prevent the continued occurrence of illegal contributions;
>
> encourage more frequent elections (a pet objective of the *Herald* is a four-year term for state Parliaments);
>
> lead to onerous bureaucratic controls over parties;
>
> open up election finance to the future manipulation of successive governments.[7]

Premier Neville Wran defied the campaign of the conservatives and pressed ahead with plans to introduce Australia's first public funding legislation in time for the 1981 NSW election. This was only accomplished after a bipartisan joint parliamentary committee, under the chairmanship of Ernie Quinn, M.P., had spent a year studying the form such legislation might take. The committee held several days of hearings and organized an international tour to study the administration of public funding legislation in other western democracies.[8] Finally, the joint committee prepared a comprehensive report in November 1980 which, with only small changes, became the basis for the legislation that was passed in Parliament in June 1981.

The New South Wales scheme was first applied in the September 1981 state election and was subsequently applied in five by-elections between the 1981 and 1984 state elections and in eleven by-elections since the 1984 elections.[9] The major provisions of the act were as follows:

> A state election fund was created equalling 22c per enrolled voter. The fund was divided into two parts, a Central Fund and a Constituency Fund. The Central Fund was to be distributed among parties according to their share of the statewide vote for the Legislative Council. Money would be available to any party, election group or candidate for the Council which registered with the Public Funding

Authority and obtained enough votes to retain their deposit, while
the constituency Fund would be divided amongst registered candidates for Legislative Assembly seats who retained their deposit in the
election.[10]

Two thirds of the public monies would go into the Central Fund
($1,414,881 in 1981) and one third into the Constituency Fund
($707,440). Eligible parties and candidates would divide the fund
according to their share of the vote, but no party could receive more
than one half of the monies in the Central Fund ($707,440), however
large their majority. Also, no Assembly candidate could receive more
than one half of the funds available for any constituency ($3,609 for
1981). Registered candidates and parties could claim only receipted
election-related expenditure.[11]

The operations of the Act were placed under the direction of a Public
Funding Authority, chaired by the State Electoral Commissioner and
including one member and one alternate member each, to be
nominated by the Premier and the Leader of the Opposition.
Supervision of the act thus rests with a senior public servant and with
representatives of the two largest Parliamentary parties.

All legitimate expenditures incurred by every candidate, party and
election group seeking seats in either house of Parliament must be
reported to the Authority, regardless of whether such candidate or
party sought to obtain public funds. In addition, the names of all
private donors whose contributions exceeded $1,000 to parties and
$200 to Assembly candidates were to be reported.

The disclosure and expenditure provisions of the 1981 act were set to
begin on August 14, 1981. Since this date was just five weeks before
the election, much of the expenditure and many of the donations for
1981 were hidden. In subsequent elections, however, disclosure and
expenditure provisions commence from the date a candidate has been
pre-selected or has otherwise declared an intention to seek election to
Parliament. Contributions from donors are cumulative between
elections.

Following the 1981 election, the opposition parties in New South Wales
had a change of heart about receiving monies from public funding. Despite
the proclamation made in 1981 by their leader of the moment, John Mason,
that "The Parliamentary Liberal Party and the Parliamentary Country
Party have jointly determined that they will not register as political parties
under the terms of the proposed Act and that they will not accept one cent
of taxpayers' money," the opposition parties were to change their attitude
after being badly beaten in the 1981 election.[12]

Faced with a $2 million deficit and interest of $1,000 per day on their overdraft, David Patten, the State Liberal President, announced that the Liberals would not only apply for funding in future elections but would also attempt to qualify, retroactively, for funds for 1981. This ploy did not work – although the initial Funding Authority decision was favorable to the Liberals. In the process, however, the opposition's long-term campaign against public funding collapsed in New South Wales and substantially affected the coalition parties' opposition to public funding at the national level as well.

Like the Liberals, the National Party also reversed their position on whether to accept election funding. In the words of Ian Armstrong, now the deputy National Party leader in NSW, "The ALP accepted public funding, and the people of this state returned them with an overwhelming majority. It was not an election issue – it was a flop as far as we were concerned, and the electorate did not reward us for sticking to our principles."[13] The National Party, however, did not join the Liberals' eventually unsuccessful application for retroactive funding for 1981, but they did register for – and accept – funds for 1984 and subsequent by-elections.

PUBLIC FUNDING AND THE 1984 NSW ELECTION

Public funding of elections was well-established in NSW by the time the state election was held in March 1984. Public funding was obtained by both the Labor and Liberal parties at five metropolitan area by-elections between 1981 and 1984,[14] and both the Liberal and National parties registered for funding for 1984. Table 1 shows the expenditure and receipt of major party funds from the Central Fund in that election.

In addition, a total of $810,031 was paid out to individual candidates for the Assembly in 1984 from the Constituency Fund. This included $404,428 to candidates endorsed by the Australian Labor Party; $286,299 to Liberal Party candidates; $85,630 to National Party candidates and $33,674 to minor party and independent candidates.

Table 2 shows how statewide party expenditure was distributed in 1984. Table 2 shows that expenditure on commercial television advertising accounted for about 63 percent of Liberal Party campaign spending and 52 percent of Labor Party spending in 1984. The National Party figures in Table 2, however, underestimate their expenditure on television and radio. The Nationals chose to report much of this expenditure in the returns of individual candidates. As a result, this expenditure is not reflected in Table 2.

Table 1. *NSW election contributions and expenditure of the major parties and election groups, 1984**

Party	Claimed expenditure	Reported contributions	State public funding received[a]
Australian Labor Party	$1,263,067	$ 462,456	$887,856
Liberal Party	1,286,669	6,094,903	484,186
National Party	439,985	1,450,427	322,790
Call to Australia[b]	137,626	22,805	115,278
Australian Democrats[c]	122,566	122,566	59,680

* As reported to the Public Funding Authority of NSW, 1984.

[a] The Liberals and Nationals ran a joint Council ticket and agreed to divide their funds based on the votes for this ticket with 60 percent to the Liberals and 40 percent to the Nationals.

[b] The Call to Australia was officially registered as the Jim Cameron Legislative Council Group for the 1984 election.

[c] The Australian Democrats again combined their expenses for their statewide campaign and for their fifty-two individual Assembly candidates in a single return. This was allowed by the Authority in both 1981 and 1984 on the grounds that the Assembly campaigns were supplementary to the Democrats' efforts to elect their Council candidates.

THE FEDERAL GOVERNMENT LEGISLATION

Undoubtedly encouraged by the collapse of coalition opposition to public funding and private disclosure legislation in New South Wales, federal Labor was quick to move for a similar package following their major election victory in March 1983. While the legislative situation was slightly more complicated for the new national Labor government – they did not control the Senate – it was decided very early that public funding would be part of a major package of electoral reforms which would be introduced within their first year of government.

To design this package, the new government set up a joint parliamentary committee with instructions to report in less than four months on a whole range of electoral issues. Besides election funding, these included changes in the voting system, electoral distributions, changes in the definition of the franchise and the procedures for registration of voters, and proposals for increasing the size of the Parliament.

The Joint Committee issued its report in September 1983.[15] While taking testimony and submissions from several public witnesses and all of the

Table 2. *NSW party expenditures, 1984**

Party	Advertising expenditure Television	Radio	Newspapers	Others	Administrative expenditure	Total
Australian Labor Party	$653,063	$65,618	$212,869	$244,381	$87,136	$1,263,067
Liberal Party	779,585[a]	18,540	196,097	232,869[b]	59,578	1,286,669
National Party	259,112	125	9,659	61,917	109,172	439,985
Call to Australia	—	17,263	23,910	65,169	26,284	137,626
Australian Democrats[c]	1,223	16,552	18,356	57,628	28,807	122,566

* As detailed in reports to the Public Funding Authority, 1984.

[a] The Liberals report spending $306,487 before March 5 (when the election was announced) and $473,098 between March 5 and March 24.

[b] The Liberal Party return includes an additional $164,578 in advertising that is reported as being billed to individual electorate campaigns.

[c] Combined totals for Assembly and statewide campaigns.

political parties, the scheme for public funding which the Committee recommended very much reflected the thinking of the Labor majority members on the Committee, particularly Dr. R. E. Klugman, M.P., New South Wales, the Chairman, and Senator G. R. Richardson of New South Wales, the former Secretary of the New South Wales State branch until his election to the Senate in March 1983. Both are members of the dominant right wing Centre Unity machine which controls Labor politics in New South Wales.

The Committee's recommendations were quickly drafted into legislation by the government and passed through Parliament in the last parliamentary sitting week of 1983. Haste was required because the omnibus bill created a new Australian Electoral Commission to supervise federal elections and election funding and also provided for an extensive redistribution of lower house seats and for an increase in the size of both houses of Parliament. Since the Labor government wished to be in a position to call an election by late 1984 – at least a half-Senate election was required by Easter 1985 – the quick reporting of the Joint Committee and the legislative enactment of their recommendations was a high priority for the government.

Since the government held only thirty of the sixty-four seats in the Senate at the time, compromises were required with either the opposition parties and/or the Australian Democrats to obtain the thirty-three votes needed to pass new legislation through that chamber. Reaching agreement on the public funding and disclosure portions of the electoral legislation was relatively easy because the Australian Democrats also supported public funding and private contribution disclosure as party policy. The one area of compromise that required negotiation between the Labor government and the Australian Democrats involved setting a threshold for eligibility for funding. Both Labor and Liberals supported a relatively high eligibility threshold of 10 percent of the votes cast in their party submissions while the Democrats opposed all thresholds in their party's submission to the joint committee. The eventual compromise threshold figure of 4 percent is considerably more lenient than the threshold adopted by the Labor government in New South Wales for lower house candidates.

In brief, the provisions of the national election legislation were:

A formula for providing funds after an election to registered parties and candidates who achieve the 4 percent threshold. The formula provided 60 cents per voter for each House first preference vote and 30 cents per voter for each Senate first preference vote, except where half-Senate elections were held separate from House elections when 45 cents per Senate first preference vote was provided. As with the

NSW Act, the legislation also provided for indexation of payments to increases in the cost-price index for future elections.

Funds were only provided for receipted expenses incurred during the period after an election had actually been announced, up to the eligibility each party realized as determined above.

All election funding was to be paid to state party branches for all candidates for either the House or Senate who were endorsed by a registered party. Unlike New South Wales, no constituency fund was created to fund local candidates. Candidates who were not endorsed by a registered party could register as individual candidates and receive their payment directly if they qualified.

Unlike New South Wales, there was no maximum payment to any party or candidate, but a 4 percent threshold of votes was imposed for any candidate to accrue public subsidies.

The administration of all electoral matters, including election funding and disclosure of expenditure and private contributions, was placed under the new Australian Electoral Commission, chaired by a judge who was to be appointed for a seven year term. The other two Commission members were the Electoral Commissioner – a permanent civil servant – and a second, seven year part-time appointee who was to be the equivalent of a Permanent Head of Department in the Australian public service.

Complete disclosure of all campaign expenditure and private donations of all candidates/parties was required. In addition, the names of donors of $1,000 or more to parties or election groups and of $200 or more to individual candidates was required. Anonymous gifts were not allowed, and such contributions were to be returned to the Treasury. In addition, all television and radio broadcasters, all publishers and all printers were required to make independent disclosure concerning any election materials and advertising they produced for any given election. The disclosure provisions, however, did not require the submission of documentation for expenditure although such documentation was to be held by the parties and candidates and could be required if the Commission found it necessary.

Given the partisan debate and wrangling that surrounded the New South Wales legislation between 1979–81, it is amazing how little controversy surrounded the national funding legislation in 1983. The Liberal and National parties still opposed the legislation in Committee and in the Parliament, but they seemed resigned to its adoption. As a result, they prepared their submissions in a positive manner to try to influence the structure of the funding law and disclosure provisions rather than refusing to cooperate as was their strategy in New South Wales.

Since the funding and disclosure provisions were included with more controversial provisions in an omnibus bill, the media paid little attention to the election funding provisions in the proposed legislation. Nothing like the concerted opposition of the Fairfax and Murdoch press to the New South Wales legislation occurred for the national legislation.

Still, the Liberal and National parties placed themselves clearly on record as being opposed to several aspects of the government's legislation. The major areas of their dissent were:

1 That public funding itself is a bad principle which does not have community support and which impinges on individual freedom.

2 That disclosure of donors' identities does not work and is intimidating. Senator John Carrick (Liberal-New South Wales) maintained that disclosure is a "lawyers' and accountants' bonanza" and "is a strong deterrent against private or corporate donation. It provides a ready-made and published hit-list available for punitive action by a mean-minded and vengeful government."[16]

3 That, in the words of National Party Deputy Leader R. J. Hunt, "any decision to appropriate funds for election campaigns would be unwarranted in view of the many legitimate unmet demands on the public purse."[17]

4 That the provisions requiring registration of parties and limitations on parties concerning how they present themselves to the public are undesirable and are part of the "paraphernalia that will inevitably swell the bureaucracy when public funding is introduced."[18]

5 That the centralization of public funding in the Committee's scheme through party organizations was undesirable. Committee Vice-Chairman, Steele Hall, a former Liberal South Australian premier, saw the government's refusal to earmark any public funding for candidates as accentuating "the trend away from individual candidates to party machines."[19] This point was particularly biting since the New South Wales legislation provides one-third of its public funding for individual lower house candidates, and the national ALP submission to the Joint Committee recommended that one-fifth of the money to be set aside for house elections should be allocated for funding constituency campaigns.[20] But an influential Committee Member, Senator Graham Richardson, had opposed such a constituency fund in New South Wales when he had been General Secretary of the New South Wales Labor Party, and from the phrasing of his questions during Committee hearings, it was obvious

that he remained opposed to such a provision. In any case, Richardson won the day within the Committee, and his favored approach was adopted. Opposition attempts to alter the legislation in Parliament to earmark funds for constituency campaigns were defeated along party lines and were opposed by Labor government members and the Australian Democrats during the floor debate.

6 There was some disagreement over the eligibility threshold with the ALP and Liberal parties supporting 10 percent and the Democrats and Nationals opposing any threshold. However, the 4 percent compromise was accepted by the Democrats, even though Democrat Senator Macklin opposed it in his dissenting report in the Joint Committee.

FEDERAL PUBLIC FUNDING AT THE 1984 ELECTION

Since the new federal legislation combines all votes for both House and Senate candidates on a statewide basis to determine public funding levels, it is easier to determine the amount of public funding received under the federal legislation than under the NSW legislation. Only the occasional independent candidate or minor party candidate running in a House electorate receives enough votes to qualify for individual funding under the federal law, despite the low threshold of 4 percent required to qualify for those funds.

Table 3 shows the amount of public funding, reported expenditure and reported gifts to the major parties at the 1984 election, the first time that public funding legislation applied to a national election in Australia.

The bill for public funding at the 1984 election amounted to $7,806,778. While total expenditures for all parties and candidates was documented by the Electoral Commission to be over $13.8 million, five parties accounted for almost all of the public funding paid out by the government. They included three major parties – the Labor, Liberal, and National Parties – and two minor parties that were mainly involved in contesting Senate seats, the Australian Democrats and the Nuclear Disarmament Party. The Australian Democrats won one Senate seat each in five of the six states while the Nuclear Disarmament Party won a seat in the sixth state, Western Australia.[21] In addition, two other minor election groups qualified for funds based on their Senate vote in a single state or territory. They were the ACT Referendum Group in the Australian Capital Territory and the Harradine group in Tasmania. Ten independents and two minor parties also qualified for and received funds in individual House elections. The total funding paid to all of these minor candidates totaled only $34,403.

Table 3. *1984 National election expenditure, gifts and public funding received by major parties**

Party	Claimed expenditure[d]	Reported gifts	Public funding received[e]
Australian Labor Party[a]	$4,700,420	$1,156,210	$3,669,264
Liberal Party	4,798,619	1,483,793	2,597,283
National Party[b]	2,731,129	1,157,186	839,292
Australian Democrats	469,528	182,407	464,621
Nuclear Disarmament Party[c]	236,139	108,766	201,915

* Figures for expenditure and public funding received as documented in the Australian Electoral Commission, *Interim Report* (Canberra, 1985). Reported gifts compiled by the author from individual party returns available through November, 1985.

[a] The Labor Party divided each of its public funding entitlement checks so that 84 percent was paid to the state or territory organization and the remaining 16 percent to the national organization. Expenditure and gift totals include separate returns for 51 NSW House candidates which were not included in that state's Labor Party declaration.

[b] All figures include the declarations and funding for the Country-Liberal Party organization in the Northern Territory.

[c] The Nuclear Disarmament Party did not qualify for public funding in Tasmania or the Northern Territory.

[d] The Australian Electoral Commission also reported additional expenditure by minor parties and individual candidates of $560,611 plus $318,998 by other groups which did not run specific candidates for the 1984 election. Total expenditure for the 1984 election was $13,815,444. See Appendix I of the *Interim Report*, p. 100.

[e] The Electoral Commission also paid an additional $34,403 to ten independent House candidates and to four minor party groups which qualified for funds in individual states.

The degree to which public funding covered election expenses varied considerably among the parties with a realistic chance to win seats at this election. Overall, public funding covered about 58 percent of total party expenditures. For the two minor parties which mainly contested Senate seats, the Australian Democrats and the Nuclear Disarmament Party, public funding covered most declared expenditures. The Democrats received 99 percent of their expenditures back from public funding and the Nuclear Disarmament Party got 88 percent. Given their declared private fund raising, both ended up with a surplus of funds after the 1984 election.

The victorious Australian Labor Party, which retained control of government at this election with a fifteen seat majority in the House of Representatives, also did very well from public funding. The Labor Party had 79 percent of their expenditure covered by their public funding checks. Given their declared private contributions, the Labor Party ended up with a modest surplus of $154,000. For the two conservative parties, however, public funding providing a much smaller portion of their declared expenditures. Public funding covered 31 percent of the National Party expenditure and 54 percent of Liberal Party expenditure. This left the National Party with a deficit, after declared contributions, of about $720,000 and the Liberal Party with a deficit of about $739,000 for the 1984 election.

Table 4 shows how the major parties spent their money at this election. We can see that for the three major parties – the parties that contested seats in both houses with a hope of winning government – the electronic media accounted for almost one-half of their election spending. This is a somewhat smaller percentage of spending on television and radio than has been shown in NSW election (See Table 2).

All parties spent a similar proportion of their funds on newspaper advertising, except for the Nuclear Disarmament Party, which spent almost twice the portion of their budget on newspapers than did the other four parties. The Nuclear Disarmament Party and Australian Democrats also spent proportionally much greater amounts of their budgets on other printing, which would include pamphlets and how-to-vote cards. In contrast, these parties spent virtually nothing on commercial television advertising.

The one disclosure provision in the new federal legislation which does not appear to have worked any better in the national legislation than in NSW is the provision that parties disclose the names of donors of over $1,000 to any party or $200 to any candidate. The National Party, in particular, has continued to use a front organization, the National Free Enterprise Foundation, to launder large amounts of funds from private donors before channeling them into party campaigns.

In the case of the Queensland campaign, the national Free Enterprise Foundation filtered $300,000 back into the National Party campaign for House and Senate candidates in that state. When the Electoral Commission attempted to audit the spending returns of the National and Liberal Parties, both parties refused to cooperate. The legal right of the Commission to require such audits remains unresolved at this writing.[22]

The Labor Party also used loopholes in the law relating to the reporting of contributions to encourage the masking of names of otherwise

Table 4. *Sources of election spending by major parties, national election of 1984**

Party	Percent of Total Spent		
	Radio and television	Newspapers	Other printing[a]
Australian Labor Party	46%	18%	19%
Liberal Party	47	21	17
National Party	49	23	14
Australian Democrats	8	22	45
Nuclear Disarmament Party	19	37	39

* From state and territory (only), returns on expenditure as provided to the Australian Electoral Commission. Individual candidate returns are not included here.

[a] Includes all non-newspaper printing on items that require party authorization such as pamphlets, how-to-vote cards, etc. Does not include campaign novelties like t-shirts, badges, car stickers, etc., which do not require party authorization under the national election law.

reluctant contributors. Bob McMullan, the Labor Party's national secretary, for example, wrote to potential donors inviting them to contribute to the party's administrative fund, which does not require public disclosure of contributions. Given that it was a Labor government which sponsored the disclosure legislation, his fund raising request met with more than passing attention from the media.[23]

EVALUATING PUBLIC FUNDING IN AUSTRALIA TO DATE

Public funding and private donation disclosure laws are still in their infancy in Australia. The New South Wales law has only been tested in two general elections and several by-elections. The new Federal scheme operated for the first time at the December 1984 election. Still, a preliminary evaluation of progress to date seems in order.

While public funding and, in particular, disclosure of the names of private donors remains a partisan issue in Australia, the much more cooperative approach taken by the conservative parties in the 1983 parliamentary debate suggests that a consensus may evolve over the future direction which election finance legislation will take in Australia. This consensus still does not extend to disclosing the identity of specific private donors.

Both the New South Wales and the national legislatures have opted for a system which emphasizes putting a floor under significant participants in the political process to guarantee that those with a meaningful electoral following will have enough money to put a respectable election case to the voters.

The conservative parties still seem much more opposed to disclosing their sources of private finance than they are to seeing minimal public subsidies operate. In New South Wales, the conservative parties have made use of every loophole available to mask their large donors. The National Party, in particular, has continued its evasion under the federal legislation.

Some disagreement remains over who should control the monies accruing to parties from public subsidies for electioneering. At this point, New South Wales has opted to divert a substantial portion of its public subsidies – one-third – to local candidates while the national government has chosen to channel all monies through state party head offices. The debate over the proper administration of funding exists within all the major parties and is particularly significant within the Labor Party in which it is a factional issue.

Public funding may well expand into the states of South Australia, Victoria, and Western Australia in the foreseeable future. All had Labor governments which supported public funding as party policy in 1987, but all three had Labor governments which lacked outright control of their upper houses at that time. Finding a vehicle for overcoming the lack of a majority in the upper house will be necessary in each of these states before public funding is adopted.

The New South Wales disclosure legislation has been adhered to with great care by all parties and most local candidates on expenditure questions and on disclosure of overall fund raising. Only the question of disclosing the names of large donors remains particularly contentious. The results of the first two New South Wales elections have been a rich source of data for students of electoral politics.[24] Australians have never had access to such complete data on how campaigns are financed. The national legislation should expand our data base still further, although its reporting procedures are much less complete than those in the NSW legislation.

Significant questions remain about the costs of campaigns, such as whether and how they can be regulated and with what result. The Federal Joint Committee continues to study the question of whether the commercial electronic media should be required to devote free or low-cost air time to parties and candidates at election time (the nationally owned Australian Broadcasting Corporation is already required to do so) as part of their licensing requirements.

In summary, Australia has been slow to join the movement in Western democracies to require public funding for major election campaigns. But the 1980s have seen a very significant beginning in reforming Australian laws on funding, and the movement appears to be gaining in community acceptance. Every indication is that public funding of elections will be a significant part of the electoral rules of the game in Australia in the decades ahead.

Acknowledgements

I wish to thank Margaret McAllister for the assistance she gave me in researching the federal legislation and Peter McEvoy and Jenny Hocking for help in analyzing the material filed by parties and candidates after the 1981 and 1984 NSW elections. David Tierney of Senator Richardson's office provided me with access to much unpublished material on the work of the Federal Joint Committee. Joan Adams and George Glintasis of the NSW Public funding Authority gave generously of their time and understanding of the NSW funding material.

Notes

1 For a full discussion of spending limits over Australian history, see Colin A. Hughes, "Party Finance and Compulsory Voting: The Australian Experience," paper prepared for the International Political Science Association 11th World Congress, Moscow, 1979.

2 Colin A. Hughes, "Control of Electoral Expenses: Australia," *The Parliamentarian*, Vol. 50, No. 4, 1969, p. 288.

3 Tasmania elects all of its federal and state lower house parliamentarians in five election sub-divisions. In state elections, each of the five sub-divisions elects seven legislators by proportional representation.

4 See Peter Dwyer, "Judge Slaps Ban on Party Poll Spending," *The Australian*, April 28, 1982, p. 3.

5 In New South Wales, for example, state parties had to fight a federal election in 1972, 1974, 1975, 1977, 1980, 1983, and 1984. They had to fight a state election in 1973, 1976, 1978, 1981, and 1984. In addition, Labor contests local elections which are run every three years, and several state and federal by-election campaigns were fought in this period. It is no surprise, therefore, that the New South Wales Labor Party was constantly in debt and always preoccupied with trying to pay off their last campaign deficit. Other state Labor parties faced similar difficulties, especially in Queensland where Labor last won control of the state government in 1954, in Western Australia where until they won in 1983, Labor was almost always in opposition, and in Victoria where Labor was out of office from 1955 to 1982.

6 For a full discussion of this campaign, see E. A. Chaples, "Public Campaign Finance: New South Wales Bites the Bullet," *Australian Quarterly*, Vol. 53, No. 1, Autumn, 1981, pp. 4–14.

7 *Sydney Morning Herald*, November 10, 1979, p. 6.

8 The opposition boycotted the official committee trip but sent their own committee member, Lloyd Lange, MLC, on a privately financed study tour. Lange produced a detailed report on his studies which was virtually ignored by the opposition parties in dealing with the government's proposals.

9 The Drummoyne by-election of April, 1982 and four by-elections in Kogarah, Marrickville, Maroubra and Riverstone in October, 1983, two by-elections in Murray and Peats on February 2, 1985, three by-elections in Cabramatta,

Canterbury and Kiama on February 1, 1986, two by-elections in Pittwater and Vaucluse on May 31, 1986, two by-elections in Bass Hill and Rockdale on August 2, 1986 and two by-elections in Bankstown and Heathcote on January 31, 1987.

10 Candidates for the New South Wales parliament were required to pay a deposit upon filing their candidacy of $100 for the Assembly (lower house) and $200 for the Council (upper house). This was increased in 1987 to $500 for the Assembly and $700 for the Council. Candidates recover their deposit if they obtain one-fifth of the first preference votes of two winning candidates (Assembly) or if they or the ticket on which they run receives one-half of an election quota for the council (i.e. 3.125 percent of the statewide vote).

11 The NSW Act also provides for the automatic adjustment of the public funding monies to account for increases in the Cost-Price Index. For the 1984 state election, the amount per voter was raised, therefore, to 28.07 cents per voter. The total fund was increased to $2,804,687. The maximum available to any Assembly candidate was raised to $3,721. At the three by-elections of February 1, 1986, the amount per voter had been adjusted up to 30.39 cents per voter, based on the September, 1985 Consumer Price Index.

12 For a full discussion of the detailed conflict after the 1981 election, see the author's "Election Finance in NSW: The First Year of Public Funding" in *Australian Quarterly*, 55 (Autumn, 1983), pp. 66–79. The results for the Legislative Assembly election in 1981 were ALP 69, Liberals 14, National Country Party 14, Independents 2. In the Legislative Council (upper house) where one-third of the seats are contested at each election, the results were ALP 8, Liberal-National Country joint ticket 5, Australian Democrats 1, Call to Australia (Christian Fundamentalists) 1. The ALP held 24 of the 44 Council seats between the 1981 and 1984 elections.

13 Mike Steketee, "Letters show ALP Moves on Funds to Liberals," in the *Sydney Morning Herald*, July 2, 1982, p. 2.

14 For a further discussion of expenditure at these by-elections, see the author's "24 March, 1984: What Happened and Why" in Chaples, Nelson and Turner, eds., *The Wran Model* (Oxford: Oxford University Press, 1985), pp. 227–9. Tables 1 and 2 here are reprinted from that Chapter with minor amendment.

15 See *Joint Select Committee on Electoral Reform, First Report*, Australian Government Publishing. Service, September, 1983. Chapters 9–12 deal with matters relating to election finance.

16 Hon. Sir J. Carrick, "Dissenting Report," *Joint Select Committee on Electoral Reform, First Report*, pp. 237–8.

17 R. J. Hunt, M.P., "Dissenting Report," *Joint Select Committee on Electoral Reform, First Report*, p. 251.

18 R. S. Steele Hall, M.P., "Dissenting Report," *Joint Select Committee on Electoral Reform, First Report*, p. 247.

19 Ibid., p. 244.

20 R. F. McMullan, National Secretary, "Submission on Behalf of the Australian Labor Party," June 30, 1983, p. 1.

21 The Australian Democrats and Nuclear Disarmament Party exchanged preferences in the Senate voting in all states and both territories. While the

Nuclear Disarmament Party outpolled the Australian Democrats on first preference votes in NSW and Victoria, the Democrats won both seats on the preferences of the major parties.

22 See the *Sydney Morning Herald*, "Liberals and Nationals Shoot Their Boots," October 4, 1985, p. 7. The Parliamentary Joint Committee on Electoral Reform seems to have conceded the inability of Parliament to enforce existing disclosure provisions in its report of January 6, 1987. The Committee has recommended, upon advice from the Federal Director of Public Prosecutions, further amendments to the Electoral Act which would remove the requirement that contributions to unincorporated associations, which are used for election purposes, be reported with the name of each contributor included.

23 Anonymous donors to both administrative funds and to party foundations are both allowed, at present, under the national legislation. See editorial, "Public Money and Political Parties," *Sydney Morning Herald*, August 12, 1985, p. 12.

24 For a preliminary discussion of this material, see E. A. Chaples, "Public Campaign Finance: New South Wales Bites the Bullet," *Australian Quarterly*, Autumn, 1981, pp. 4–14 and E. A. Chaples, "Wran's Revolution," *Australian Society*, December 17, 1982, pp. 9–11.

5

American presidential elections since public funding, 1976–84

HERBERT E. ALEXANDER

In the 1970s, the laws regulating federal election campaign financing in the United States underwent dramatic change. The Federal Election Campaign Act of 1971 (FECA),[1] the Revenue Act of 1971,[2] and the FECA Amendments of 1974,[3] 1976[4] and 1979[5] thoroughly revised the rules of the game for political candidates, parties and contributors. In regard to presidential campaigns, the laws provided for public matching funds for qualified candidates in the pre-nomination period, public treasury grants to pay the costs of the two major parties' national nominating conventions, and public treasury grants for the major party general election candidates. They also established criteria whereby minor parties and new parties and their candidates could qualify for public funds to pay nominating convention and general election campaign costs.

The public funds were intended to help provide or to supply in entirety the money serious candidates need to present themselves and their ideas to the electorate. The public funds also were meant to diminish or to eliminate the need for money from wealthy donors and interest groups and thereby minimize opportunities for undue influence on officeholders by contributors. In the pre-nomination period, public funding was intended to make the nomination process more competitive and to encourage candidates to broaden their bases of support by seeking out large numbers of relatively small, matchable contributions.

The feasibility of public financing in presidential campaigns has depended on the taxpayers' willingness to earmark a small portion on their tax liabilities – $1 for individuals and $2 for married persons filing jointly – for the Presidential Election Campaign Fund by using the federal income tax checkoff. This procedure has provided more than enough money to cover the public funds certified to presidential pre-nomination and general election candidates and to the major parties for their national nominating conventions. In 1976 a total of $70.9 million was certified for candidates and conventions, and in 1980 the figure reached $100.6 million. In 1984 some $133 million were paid out. Although public acceptance of the program started slowly, it grew as taxpayers became more aware of the checkoff procedure. From 1974 through 1985 the percentage of individual tax returns checked off has ranged from 23.0 percent to 28.7 percent.

Contribution limits and expenditure limits also were enacted, although the Supreme Court subsequently ruled that spending limits are permissible only in publicly financed campaigns.[6] These laws were intended to control large donations with their potential for corruption, to minimize financial disparities among candidates, and to reduce opportunities for abuse. Finally, laws requiring full and timely disclosure of campaign receipts and expenditures were put in place to help the electorate make informed choices among candidates and to make it possible to monitor compliance with the campaign finance laws.

Three presidential elections have now been conducted under the FECA, its amendments and its companion laws, a sufficient experience from which to draw some conclusions about the impact of the laws and to determine whether they have had their intended effects.[7] The general conclusions are that the laws have accomplished some of their aims, but they also have had some unintended, and not always salutary, consequences. The degree to which the laws have failed to achieve their intended effects may testify at least as much to the inventiveness of political actors in circumventing the laws and to the intractability of election campaign finance as to the deficiencies of the laws themselves.

THE PRENOMINATION CAMPAIGNS

Under the FECA, candidates for the 1984 presidential nomination who accepted public matching funds were permitted to spend no more than $20.2 million plus 20 percent ($4.0 million) for fund raising. As Table 1 indicates, this represents a net increase of about $11.1 million compared with the 1976 limit, and an increase of about $6.5 million compared with the 1980 limit. In addition, the 1974 FECA Amendments limit candidate spending in each state to the greater of $200,000 or 16 cents per eligible voter, plus a cost-of-living increase. Candidates who do not accept public funding are not bound by the overall or individual state expenditure limits. Payments made by the candidates for legal and accounting services to comply with the campaign law are exempt from the law's spending limits, but candidates are required to report such payments.

All candidates are bound by the contribution limits stipulated in the

Table 1. *Major party presidential campaign expenditure limits and public funding (figures in millions)*

Year	Prenomination campaign			Nominating convention	General election campaign		
	National spending limit[a]	Exempt fund raising[b]	Overall spending limit[c]		Public treasury grant[d]	National party spending limit[e]	Overall spending limit[f]
1976	$10.9 +	$2.2 =	$13.1	$2.2[g]	$21.8 +	$3.2 =	$25.0
1980	14.7 +	2.9 =	17.7	4.4	29.4 +	4.6 =	34.0
1984	20.2 +	4.0 =	24.2	8.1	40.4 +	6.9 =	47.3

[a] Based on $10 million plus cost-of-living increases (COLA) using 1974 as the base year. Eligible candidates may receive no more than one-half the national spending limit in public matching funds. To become eligible candidates must raise $5,000 in private contributions of $250 or less in each of twenty states. The federal government matches each contribution to qualified candidates up to $250. Publicly funded candidates also must observe spending limits in the individual states equal to the greater of $200,000 + COLA (base year 1974), or $.16 × the voting-age population (VAP) of the state + COLA.

[b] Candidates may spend up to 20 percent of the national spending limit for fund raising.

[c] Legal and accounting expenses to insure compliance with the law are exempt for the spending limit.

[d] Based on $20 million + COLA (base year 1974).

[e] Based on $.02 × VAP of the United States + COLA.

[f] Compliance costs are exempt from the spending limit.

[g] Based on $2 million + COLA (base year 1974). Under the 1979 FECA Amendments, the basic grant was raised to $3 million. In 1984, Congress raised the basic grant to $4 million.

FECA. No candidate is permitted to accept more than $1,000 from an individual contributor or more than $5,000 from a multicandidate committee.[8] Candidates who accept public funding are allowed to contribute no more than $50,000 in personal or family funds to their own campaigns.

As in 1976 and in 1980, to qualify for public matching funds available under the FECA, in 1984 candidates were required to raise $5,000 in private contributions from individuals of $250 or less in each of twenty states. The federal government matched each individual contribution to eligible candidates up to $250, although the federal subsidy to any one candidate could not exceed $10.1 million, half of the $20.2 million pre-nomination campaign spending limit. The threshold requirements serve as a screening device whereby candidates who do not demonstrate widespread support are ineligible for public financial support.

The pre-nomination campaign contribution and expenditure limitations and matching fund requirements take effect once a candidate establishes a campaign committee. Actual payouts of public funds to candidates are made only in the election year, but candidates may seek eligibility, submit information about contributions for matching funds and be qualified by the Federal Election Commission (FEC) in the prior year.

THE IMPACT OF THE LAW

The federal campaign laws enacted in the 1970s have often led candidates seeking their parties' presidential nominations and those who support them to alter traditional campaign strategies and tactics. Many of these developments were not foreseen by the framers of the laws, and some of them appear hostile to the purposes the laws were intended to achieve.

The overall spending limit

The 1984 overall spending limit of $24.2 million ($20.2 million plus a 20 percent fund-raising overage) for candidates accepting matching funds required candidates to plan carefully when and where to spend the money they had available. The Mondale campaign invested large sums early in the pre-nomination contest. Encouraged by the former vice president's initial front-runner status and by a front-loaded delegate selection process designed to favor a well-known, well-funded candidate, the Mondale organization spent heavily in the early stages of the campaign, hoping to turn the race into a runaway. By the third week of March 1984, when only a third of the nominating convention delegates had been chosen, the campaign had already spent nearly 60 percent of the overall limit.[9] This strategy left Mondale's once seemingly invincible campaign vulnerable to the challenge of Senator Gary Hart, whose surprising success at the polls in New Hampshire, elsewhere in New England and in some southern states, resulted in sudden fund-raising successes that until that time had eluded the Hart campaign. In fact, in all of the major contests following the six primary and five caucus contests held on March 13, the Hart campaign was able to outspend the Mondale campaign by a margin of at least 2-to-1.[10] The Mondale campaign was forced by the overall spending limit and by a slowdown in campaign contributions to rely in good measure on other means of financing its efforts. Some of these means, notably use of labor union facilities, phone banks and volunteers and use of delegate committees funded in part by labor union PAC (Political Action Committee) money, contributed to Mondale's image as a candidate tied closely to so-called special interests. Mondale, whose campaign spent up to the $20.2 million limit, won the Democratic nomination by a narrow margin, but his image as a candidate beholden to special constituencies haunted him during his ill-fated general election campaign.

The overall spending limit posed no problems for incumbent President Ronald Reagan's campaign for renomination by the Republican Party, since the president faced no major opposition. In 1980, however, Reagan found himself in a position similar to Mondale's in 1984. His campaign spent heavily early in the 1980 contest. When a well-funded George Bush emerged as a legitimate challenger, the Reagan campaign was not able to spend as much as it would have liked to fend off the challenge. Nevertheless, the recognition and support Reagan had solidified early in the pre-nomination campaign were sufficient to bring him the nomination.

Since 1976, some candidates whose campaigns have had a realistic chance to remain in the race through the convention have complained that the overall spending limit is set too low. Although the limit is adjusted to account for inflation, the costs of many of the items and services campaigns must purchase increase at a rate far exceeding that of inflation. For example, between 1980 and 1984, network television advertising costs for commercial advertisers increased in general approximately 56 percent. The increase in costs to political advertisers was even greater.[11] During the same period, however, the Consumer Price Index rose 37.4 percent. Candidates who feel they must rely on television to reach the large numbers of potential voters who may take part in the primary elections must use a substantial portion of the funds they may spend to pay for television advertising. The Hart campaign, for example, spent more than $5.6 million on television time and production costs. Or candidates must depend on their ability to draw media attention so their messages can be transmitted to the public at no direct cost to their campaigns. Jesse Jackson, whose campaign raised less than one-fourth the amount raised by the Mondale campaign, was particularly successful in attracting coverage by television and radio networks and stations. Said Jackson: "If you make the news at 6, you don't have to buy commercials at 7:01."[12]

State limits

Like the overall spending limit, the ceiling established by the FECA for spending in individual states called for strategic pre-nomination campaign decisions, particularly in the early primary and caucus contests. These limits, too, were the subject of criticism by candidates and campaign officials. There is a substantial disparity between the overall spending limit imposed on publicly funded candidates and the sum of all the individual state limits, which is far greater. If individual candidates had succeeded in raising sufficient funds to spend up to the limit in all fifty states – a total of almost $60.2 million – they would have exceeded the national spending limit several times over. The two sets of limits are inconsistent, and they forced candidates to pick and choose which states would receive the greatest attention from their campaigns.

Candidates, of course, felt the need to do well in the early pre-nomination contests, which customarily are assigned more importance by the news media than the number of delegates at stake would otherwise warrant. The low spending ceilings in early contests in less populous states such as New Hampshire ($404,000) forced campaigns to budget tightly and forced national campaign organizations to maintain control of expenditures in each state.

Campaigns also resorted to a variety of subterfuges in an attempt to get around low state spending limits. For example, in states with early pre-nomination contests, candidates went to great lengths to make sure they spent fewer than 4.5 consecutive days in those states. In this case, according to a Federal Election Commission ruling, they could bill their costs to their national campaign organizations rather than apply them to the state limits.[13] Or candidates went to a nearby state to lease cars to be used in a state with a primary or caucus contest so the cost could be applied to the nearby state's limit.[14] Or they bought television advertising time on Boston stations, which reach most New Hampshire voters, so the costs could be applied proportionally to the more generous Massachusetts state spending limit.[15]

The campaigns of Alan Cranston and John Glenn reported having exceeded the spending limit in Iowa, where the nation's first delegate selection events were held. The Glenn campaign also reported having exceeded the limit in New Hampshire. In both states the Mondale campaign reported expenditures close to the stipulated limits. But in both states the candidate also was able to count on expenditures on his behalf not subject to the limits. In Iowa he benefited from money spent by labor organizations on communications advocating his nomination. He also received the benefit of existing labor union telephones, buildings and other facilities, thereby saving funds that otherwise would have to have been spent on having phone lines installed or on finding comparable space and facilities.[16] In New Hampshire, Mondale benefited from more than $100,000 in spending by two delegate committees which the campaign maintained were independent of the campaign;[17] elsewhere delegate committees also helped.

Contribution limits

The contribution limits also helped shape pre-nomination campaign strategy and occasioned the criticism of campaigners and observers. Even though the expenditure limits were adjusted upward to account for inflation (See Table 1) the individual contribution limit remained the same: $1,000 per candidate. When the Consumer Price Index is used as a measure, a $1,000 contribution to a candidate in 1984 was worth less than half that amount when compared with the buying power of $1,000 when the limit went into effect a decade before.

In 1984, as in 1980 and 1976, the limit achieved its intended effect of eliminating large contributions by wealthy donors directly to presidential candidates. But, by prohibiting candidates from gathering seed money for their campaigns through large contributions, the contribution limit gave an advantage to well-known candidates who had already achieved significant name recognition and forced less well-known candidates to begin fund raising for the campaigns as much as a year and a half before the nominating convention.

The limit also altered fund-raising patterns in significant ways. The role once filled by large contributors is now filled by well-connected volunteer fund raisers who can persuade a large number of persons to contribute up to the maximum $1,000 amount. Each of the leading Democratic candidates relied on the efforts of a number of such "elite solicitors."[18] Candidates also are forced to run to costly direct mail solicitations – in many instances the most effective way of reaching large numbers of small contributors – and to the direct mail specialists who have emerged as important forces in political campaigns since the enactment of the 1974 FECA Amendments. In 1984 Democratic candidates generally did not have great success with direct mail. The Mondale campaign, however, netted about $4.1 million from mail solicitations, some of it raised in the post-convention period to help retire the campaign's debt of $3.5 million. In all, the Mondale campaign raised about $17.4 million and received an additional $8.9 million in matching funds. The Reagan campaign brought in approximately $12 million through the mail by late April, about three-fourths of the $16 million it had raised by that time.[19] The campaign ceased its fund-raising activity in May, but contributions continued to arrive at campaign headquarters. By the time the campaign for nomination had concluded, without contest by a major challenger, the Reagan campaign had spent almost the entire $20.2 million it was permitted to spend plus additional millions on fund raising and compliance.[20]

Some candidates also rely on entertainers to hold benefit concerts for their campaigns. The volunteer services of such individuals are not subject to the $1,000 limitation. Entertainers, however, appeared to play a role of lesser importance in the 1984 campaigns than they did in some 1980 campaigns.

Multicandidate committees, popularly known as political action committees (PACs), are allowed to contribute up to $5,000 per candidate per election. They play a minimal role in the direct financing of presidential campaigns, however, in part because PAC contributions are not matchable under federal election law. In 1984, PAC contributions to the fourteen presidential candidates whose financial activity exceeded $100,000 came to $1.3 million, slightly more than 1 percent of the candidates' total receipts. Committees formed to further the selection of national nominating convention delegates supporting Walter Mondale, however, received additional contributions from labor union PACs; and independent expenditures by some PACs were substantial.

Circumventing the limits

The expenditure and contribution limits also were responsible in large part for the continuing use of such methods of avoiding the limits as independent expenditures and presidential political action committees, and the development of another method: delegate committees. In its 1976 *Buckley* decision, the Supreme Court ruled that individuals and groups could spend unlimited amounts on communications advocating the election or defeat of clearly identified candidates provided the expenditures were made without consultation or collaboration with the candidates or their campaigns.[21] By 1980 those inclined to make such expenditures had developed sufficient familiarity with the election law to spend a total of $2.7 million independently in nomination campaigns, about $1.6 million of that on Ronald Reagan's behalf. In 1984 Reagan was again the major beneficiary of independent expenditures. Political committees reported spending approximately $8.6 million on his behalf, even though he ran without major opposition. For example, the Fund for a Conservative Majority contributed to a campaign to write in Reagan's name on the Democratic ballot in New Hampshire. In all about $8.9 million was reported in independent expenditures for or against candidates seeking presidential nomination. Almost all of it was spent by political committees rather than individuals.

Long before the 1980 presidential campaigns officially commenced, four Republican hopefuls – Ronald Reagan, George Bush, John Connally and Robert Dole – formed political action committees, ostensibly to raise and spend money on behalf of favored candidates and party committees. These PACs were undoubtedly helpful to the candidates who received support from them, but they also were instrumental in furthering the ambitions of the prospective presidential candidates who sponsored them. The PACs allowed their sponsors to gain the favor and support of federal, state and local candidates and of state and local party organizations through the direct and in-kind contributions that the PACs made. They also allowed the prospective presidential candidates to travel extensively throughout the country, thus attracting media attention and increasing their name recognition among party activists and the electorate in general, without having the money raised and spent counted against the spending limits that would apply once the presidential hopefuls declared their candidacies and accepted federal matching funds.

In 1981 former Vice President Mondale and Senator Edward Kennedy, then thought to be the front-runners for the 1984 Democratic presidential nomination, established PACs of their own to fund their pre-announcement activities. During the 1981–2 election cycle, Mondale's PAC, the Committee for the Future of America (CFA), raised almost $2.2 million and spent a like amount. The CFA raised an additional $300,000 in 1983 before being disbanded. Kennedy's PAC, the Fund for a Democratic Majority, raised $2.3 million and spent about $2.2 million during the cycle. Following a successful Senate reelection campaign in 1982, Kennedy withdrew from consideration as a presidential candidate. His PAC, however, continued to function during the 1983–4 election cycle, during which it raised $3.6 million and spent about $3 million.

Mondale added a new dimension to presidential PAC fund raising. In addition to the Committee for the Future of America, which was registered with the FEC, four state-level PACs were formed to raise and spend money in ways that would be helpful to the prospective presidential candidate. These PACs were able to collect contributions under the laws in the individual states in which the PACs were registered. Often these laws gave freer rein to individual contributors than the federal law did and permitted contributions in amounts or from sources that would be prohibited under federal law. In all almost $400,000 was collected by these state-level PACs, including about $150,000 from corporations and $160,000 from labor unions.[22] Some $100,000 of the money collected was contributed to candidates for state and local office. Other money apparently was used to pay for the operating expenses of the PACs. The work of the state PACs was coordinated with the operations of the federal-level Committee for the Future of America. The existence of the state-level PACs, which were subject to state rather than federal disclosure laws, was only made public in a July 1984 issue of a Washington, D.C. business magazine – long after the CFA and its state "subsidiaries" had ceased to function and shortly before the Democratic National Convention.[23]

The Mondale campaign also sought to benefit from an additional means of avoiding the federal campaign contribution and spending limits by encouraging the establishment of committees supporting candidates for nominating convention delegates who advocated Mondale's nomination. According to rules promulgated by the FEC, if several persons, acting as a group, support the selection of one or more delegates by receiving contributions or making expenditures in excess of $1,000 a year, the group becomes a political committee.[24] These delegate committees may accept no more than $5,000 from any individual or other political committee and must report all contributions they receive. They also must report all of their expenditures. Any expenditures they make for political advertising which advocates the selection of a delegate and also refers to a candidate for presidential nomination is considered either an allocable in-kind contribution to the presidential candidate or an allocable independent expenditure on that candidate's behalf.

Early in 1984 Mondale's campaign headquarters issued a memorandum to candidates for delegate positions encouraging them to set up delegate committees. The memo pointed out that, although the presidential candidate himself had pledged not to allow his principal campaign committee to accept PAC contributions, delegate committees were free to make their own decisions about the propriety of accepting PAC money to further their goals.

Eventually more than 100 delegate committees were set up to aid Mondale, and they spent $740,000. Many of them accepted funds from a number of labor union PACs and from individuals who already had contributed the maximum amount directly to the Mondale campaign.

Some PACs and individuals contributed to a number of Mondale delegate committees. When the existence of the delegate committees became a matter of public knowledge and journalistic reports suggested a pattern of cooperation and coordination between the committees and the Mondale campaign, the candidate insisted the delegate committees were independent of his campaign and that the campaign organization had no control over them. Early in April 1984, Senator Gary Hart's campaign filed a complaint with the FEC charging that the delegate committees represented an illegal circumvention of the campaign spending laws. Mondale continued to insist that the committees were independent of his campaign. But late in April the force of criticism by his opponents and the negative publicity it engendered led the former vice president to order that the committees be disbanded. The candidate declared he would count the committees' spending against his own campaign's spending limit and would pay back from his campaign treasury all PAC funds contributed to the delegate committees, as well as individual contributions to the committees from persons who also had contributed the $1,000 legal maximum to his campaign. He made the decisions, he said, not because he believed his position was not legally defensible but in order to remove "any lingering doubt and put this issue behind us."[25]

In mid-May Mondale took out a bank loan to establish a $400,000 escrow account to repay the disputed contributions. The money was never repaid to the donors, however. Rather, on November 27, 1984, after the general election, the FEC resolved the Hart complaint of April 1984 and a similar complaint filed by the National Right to Work Committee by voting 4-to-2 to accept a conciliation agreement submitted on behalf of the Mondale pre-nomination campaign committee. Under the agreement the committee consented to pay $350,000 to the U.S. Treasury, an amount which represented contributions to the delegate committees which would not have been permissible had they been made directly to the campaign organization. The committee also agreed to pay an additional $29,640 to the Treasury, the federal matching fund share of the amount the Mondale committee and the delegate committees together spent in excess of the campaign organization's New Hampshire spending limit. Finally, the Mondale committee agreed to pay a $18,500 civil penalty. Nevertheless, the committee admitted no illegal behavior and agreed to the settlement, according to its treasurer, "to avoid protracted litigation over this matter."[26] In effect, the borrowed money that was intended to be used to repay delegate committee donors was turned over to the Treasury as part of settlement; the proposed repayments to donors were cancelled.

Matching funds

Since the federal matching fund system was first employed in the 1976 presidential pre-nomination campaigns, matching funds have provided potential candidates who lacked name recognition or access to large amounts of private campaign funds the opportunity to compete effectively for presidential nomination. If it was not for the combination of contribution limits and public funding, Jimmy Carter, who lacked access to traditional sources of large Democratic contributions, probably would have lost out early in the 1976 primary season to those candidates, such as Senator Henry M. Jackson, who enjoyed such access. In 1980 public funds helped George Bush establish himself as front-runner. Ronald Reagan's major competitor and stay the course of the primaries and caucuses. Public funds also helped John Anderson to become an influential force in some early Republican primaries and, more significantly, to start building the name recognition and national organization he needed to mount his independent candidacy for the presidency.

In 1984 matching funds helped Senator Gary Hart refill his depleted campaign treasury following his unexpected New Hampshire primary victory and the subsequent upsurge in contributions his campaign experienced. Matching funds also helped keep Jesse Jackson's under-funded but nevertheless well-publicized campaign afloat. In all these cases the matching fund provisions of the FECA opened up the electoral process to some candidates whose campaigns otherwise might not have been able to survive.

In 1984 Ronald Reagan became the first candidate since the matching fund system was inaugurated to qualify for the maximum amount of matching funds available to a candidate. His campaign received the full $10.1 million in public funds to match an equal amount which it raised in individual contributions of $250 or less. Since the campaign committee concluded its operation with a $1.5 million surplus, however, it refunded one-third of it – the portion it calculated had come from taxpayer funds – to the U.S. Treasury.[27]

Compliance

As in 1976 and in 1980, candidates who accepted matching funds in 1984 were required to supply the FEC with substantial documentation to demonstrate that their campaigns had remained within the spending limits specified by the FECA. All candidates were required to file regular reports with the FEC to demonstrate that their campaigns had complied with the law's contribution limits and to fulfill the law's disclosure requirements.

Lawyers and accountants who could lead candidates through the complexities of election campaign finance law and devise systems to keep track of receipts and expenditures were as prominent in some campaigns as political operatives. Efforts to comply with the law, of course, imposed additional expenses on campaigns. Even though these expenditures were exempt from the overall spending limit, they diverted funds and fund-raising energies from the campaigns themselves. Three 1984 candidates – Mondale, Glenn and Reagan – reported spending more than $1 million each on compliance-related costs.

THE NOMINATING CONVENTIONS

In addition to funding individual presidential nomination campaigns, the FECA also provides for federal grants to help finance the national conventions of the major political parties. Under the 1974 Amendments, the major parties were each eligible to receive a grant of $2 million plus a cost-of-living increase from the presidential checkoff fund. The 1979 FECA Amendments raised the basic grant to $3 million. In mid 1984, shortly before the nominating conventions were held, Congress increased the base amount to $4 million. Proponents of the measure cited increased security costs as the reason for the increase. Inflation brought the 1984 convention grant to approximately $8.1 million for each major party.

Under the FECA a minor political party also is eligible to receive a federal subsidy for its convention if its candidate received more than 5 percent of the vote in the previous presidential election. No minor party qualified for federal funding of its convention based on its showing in 1976. Had John Anderson entered the 1984 election contest as a third-party candidate, however, his showing in the 1980 contest, in which he won 6.6 percent of the popular vote, would have entitled his party to a federal grant for its 1984 convention.

The federal grants, which are used to pay for convention-related expenses such as convention security services, printing, telephone, travel and convention staff, food and lodging, were intended to replace the previous methods of convention financing whereby host cities and local businesses furnished cash and services to party conventions, and national corporations bought advertising space in national convention program books. FEC advisory opinions, however, have permitted certain types of outside contributions to convention arrangements committees and expenditures on their behalf in addition to the federal subsidy. State and local governments which host the conventions are permitted to provide certain services and facilities, such as convention halls, transportation and security services, the costs of which are not counted against the parties' expenditure limits. Parties may accept such items as free hotel rooms and conference facilities so long as other groups holding conventions of similar size and duration are offered similar benefits. Local businesses and national corporations with local outlets may contribute funds to host committees or civic associations seeking to attract or assist the political conventions, so long as they can reasonably expect "a commensurate commercial return during the life of the convention."[28]

The Republican party chose to hold its 1984 convention in Dallas, Texas. State law and long-standing tradition prevented tax revenues and other government monies from being used to finance convention-related costs. Accordingly the city sought and received a ruling from the FEC that it could establish and administer a non-profit, non-partisan convention fund to finance facilities and services for the convention provided the fund pay for such items and services at their fair market value.[29] The ruling stated that payments made by the city-administered fund for convention facilities and services and donations made to the fund would not constitute contributions to the Republican National Committee and would not count against the committee's spending ceiling of $8.1 million. Consequently the convention fund was able to collect donations of unlimited amounts from individuals, associations, businesses and corporations. In addition, the Dallas Convention Fund received a ruling from the Internal Revenue Service that all contributions to the fund would be 100 percent tax deductible. Spending by all sources totaled $13.7 for the Republican Convention. In 1983 the city of San Francisco, site of the 1984 Democratic National Convention, received a similar ruling from the FEC for its Convention Promotion and Services Fund.[30] Total spending amounted to $18 million for the Democratic Convention.

In addition both parties were able to arrange reduced-cost services, such as airfare for delegates and telephone and data processing services, by agreeing to designate the providers as "official suppliers" for their conventions.

To date the mix of public and private financing of party nominating conventions appears to be working satisfactorily. It remains to be seen, however, whether the development of new means of reintroducing private money into the convention financing process in 1984 will lead to further alteration of the process.

THE GENERAL ELECTION CAMPAIGNS

Under the Revenue Act of 1971 and the FECA Amendments of 1974, major party candidates who accept public funding in the general election period may not accept private contributions to further their campaigns and may spend no more than the amount of public and party funds to which they are entitled to finance their election campaign efforts. The laws provide that candidates of minor parties whose candidates received 5 percent or more but less than 25 percent of the previous presidential election vote are eligible for pre-election payments of public funds according to a complex formula based on the relationship of the number of votes cast for the minor party candidate to the average number of votes cast for the major party candidates. The laws also provide that minor party candidates are entitled to post-election federal grants if they receive 5 percent or more of the total number of popular votes cast for the office of president in the current election.

According to a formula set forth in the 1974 FECA Amendments, by 1984 each major party candidate was entitled to a grant of $40.4 million. This public funding may be supplemented by funds raised privately by each of the major national parties for spending on behalf of its presidential ticket. Under the 1974 FECA Amendments, the national party spending limit, which is based on the voting-age population of the nation, was $6.9 million for 1984. The combined total of $47.3 million that could be spent under the direction of each major party nominee's campaign organization was $22.3 million more than allowed in 1976 and about $13.3 million more than in 1980 (see Table 1). Finally, the campaign laws exempt from the ban on private contributions to publicly funded candidates those contributions given to help candidates defray compliance costs. Such contributions may not exceed $1,000 per donor.

Impact of the law

Although both major party candidates in 1984 accepted the federal grants provided under the campaign law and thus were not permitted to accept any private contributions to support their campaigns, from the point of view of money raised and spent to influence the outcome of the general election, three different but parallel campaigns were conducted, either by the candidates or on their behalf. Consequently, instead of some $47.3 million being spent on each candidate's campaign, as anticipated by the law, each candidate actually benefited from a patchwork of funds amounting to much more, with the financial advantage belonging to the Reagan campaign (see Table 2).

Publicly funded campaigns

The first campaign, in which spending was legally limited and mostly subsidized by the U.S. Treasury, was within the control of the major party nominees and their campaign organizations. The campaign was financed

Table 2. *Sources of funds, major party presidential candidates, 1984 general election (in millions)*

	- Sources of funds	Reagan	Mondale
Limited campaign	Federal grant	$40.4	$40.4
Candidate-controlled	National party	6.9	2.7
Unlimited campaigns	State and local party	15.6[a]	6.0[b]
	Labor[c]	2.0	20.0
Candidate may coordinate	Corporate/Association[c]	1.5	0.1
	Compliance	2.4	1.2
Independent of candidate	Independent expenditures[d]	8.5	0.7
Total		$77.3	$71.1

[a] Includes both money raised by the national party committee and channeled to state and local party committees and money raised by state and local party committees from their own sources.

[b] Includes only money raised by the national party committee and channeled to state and local party committees; an estimate of money raised for presidential campaign purposes by state and local party committees from their own sources is not available.

[c] Includes internal communication costs (both those in excess of $2,000, which are reported, as required by law, and those less than $2,000, which are not required to be reported), registration and voter turnout expenditures, overhead and other related costs.

[d] Does not include amounts spent to oppose the candidates.

Source: Citizens' Research Foundation.

primarily by public funds, which were supplemented by funds raised privately by each of the major party national committees for spending on behalf of the presidential ticket.

Since major party nominees Reagan and Mondale each received $40.4 million in public funds, spending in this first campaign was largely equalized. However, there was an imbalance in favor of Reagan. The Republican National Committee (RNC) easily raised the $6.9 million it was permitted to spend on behalf of the Republican presidential ticket to supplement the Reagan-Bush campaign's own expenditures. The Democratic National Committee (DNC) fell short, raising and spending only $2.7 million of the maximum amount allowed.

Coordinated campaigns

The second campaign, in which spending was provided for but not limited under the law, was in part under the direct control of the candidates and their organizations and in part outside their control. The funds spent in this campaign that were outside candidate control, however, could be coordinated with spending by candidates, although that did not always happen.

Three types of funding financed the activities which constituted this second campaign:

> Funds raised under the FECA by each candidate's campaign organization from private contributions to pay legal and accounting costs incurred in complying with the stipulations of the law.
>
> Funds raised by or on behalf of state and local party committees, which were allowed under the 1979 FECA Amendments to spend unlimited amounts on volunteer-oriented activity on behalf of the parties' presidential tickets.
>
> Funds spent on behalf of candidates by labor unions, corporations, trade associations and membership groups on partisan communications with their own constituencies and on nominally non-partisan activities directed at the general public.

The Reagan organization enjoyed an advantage in the second campaign both because more money was spent on its behalf and because the money that was spent was more effectively coordinated with the organization's own spending than money spent on behalf of the Mondale organization.

Reagan spent $2.4 million, and Mondale half as much, for compliance costs. These costs included not only those incurred in tracking receipts and expenditures during the campaigns and in filing required reports but also wind-down costs after the campaigns during FECA-mandated audits conducted by the FEC.

In the 1980 campaign, the Reagan-Bush Committee and the RNC were much more successful than their Democratic counterparts in assuring that state and local party committees were able to take full advantage of the provisions of the 1979 FECA Amendments that were enacted to encourage the local activity that was missing from the 1976 general election campaigns. Under the 1979 Amendments, state and local party committees may make unlimited expenditures on behalf of the presidential ticket for specified volunteer campaign activities, including volunteer-oriented telephone banks and voter registration and turnout drives on behalf of the party's presidential nominee. In 1980, candidates Reagan and Bush took part in fund-raising events designed to help fill Republican state and local party committee treasuries. More important, RNC operatives raised some $9 million from individuals – some of whom had already reached their $25,000 annual federal-election related contribution limits – and from corporations – which are prohibited from contributing to federal election campaigns – and channeled it into those states where such contributions to party committees were permitted and where spending for activities such as voter identification and turnout drives would have the greatest benefit.[31] State party committees raised at least $6 million more, for a total of $15 million. A large portion of those contributions, frequently called "soft money" because they are outside federal restraints, could be raised, spent and disclosed according to campaign finance laws in the individual states rather than according to federal law. A significant number of states permit corporate and/or labor union political contributions and give freer rein to individual and PAC contributions than the federal law does.

In 1980 the Democratic Party started its soft money drive late in the campaign. Only about $1.3 million was raised at the national level, from unions and individuals, and was funneled to state and local party committees in states that permitted such contributions, although local party committees added another $2.7 million. In 1984 Mondale-Ferraro campaign fund raisers announced a drive to raise as much as $25 million in soft money from individuals, corporations and other groups to be channeled to state parties.[32] Published estimates of how much actually was raised through the soft money drive vary. A Democratic Party spokesman maintained the party raised a total of $9.4 million in soft money channeled to four state accounts in 1983 and 1984.[33] Another estimate, however, placed the Democratic Party soft money total at $30 million.[34] A Mondale-Ferraro operative privately stated that only $6 million in soft money had been raised in efforts coordinated by the campaign itself. Some of the Democratic Party's soft money activities came to light when the existence of three Democratic National Committee "non-federal" accounts operating in three different states was disclosed when the DNC filed statements or reports to comply with the states' campaign laws. These disclosures revealed contributions of as much as $100,000 each from several wealthy individuals and a large number of lesser contributions from a great variety of corporations and trade organizations.[35] In any case, at least $6 million were spent in this category.

Despite the Republican Party's success with soft money in 1980, it downplayed soft money drives in 1984. Many state party committees were able to raise substantial amounts either on their own, or with the aid of the RNC, which between 1980 and 1984 paid the salaries of some state party finance directors who worked to build state fund-raising capabilities, or with the help of a private company – Leadership '84 – set up by a former Reagan-Bush pre-nomination campaign finance committee chairman and employed by the Republican National Committee, among others.[36] This money was raised and reported under federal campaign laws. In addition the Republican national party committees often were able to supplement state party funds by transferring "hard money" – money raised under the FECA limits – to the state parties from the ample treasuries of the national committees. Although the money transferred could not legally be used to fund state and local volunteer party activity on behalf of Reagan-Bush, it freed funds raised by the state committees to pay for such activities.[37] Moreover the use of soft money in 1980 became the object of criticism. In August 1984 the Center for Responsive Politics filed a complaint with the FEC alleging that both past and proposed uses of soft money by the two major parties' national-level committees represented the illegal use of non-federal funds to influence federal elections.

Nevertheless soft money did play a significant role in funding this parallel Republican campaign. A Republican Party spokesperson acknowledged privately that some $5.6 million in soft money had been raised under RNC auspices in the period between the Republican National Convention and the general election. This money was used primarily to finance voter registration and turnout activities in the states. Moreover, state committees, said the party spokesperson, may have raised an additional $10 million in soft money, a total of $15.6 million.

Although the RNC de-emphasized soft money, Leadership '84, working for the Republican Party, focused energies on channeling money from willing individuals, associations and corporations to a number of non-partisan, non-profit and tax-exempt conservative groups engaged in voter registration and turnout campaigns. Among groups to which these funds were channeled were a fundamentalist Christian organization that conducted a voter registration drive aimed at church members and a group organized to conduct voter registration drives among military personnel and opponents of gun control and abortion. The Democratic Party also attempted to funnel money from groups and individuals to a number of new and established non-partisan, tax-exempt organizations conducting voter drives. Often these drives were conducted among constituencies that have tended to vote Democratic, for example, blacks, Hispanics and low-income persons.

Both parties apparently experienced some success in these efforts to encourage tax-deductible contributions to organizations conducting voter drives. For example, Americans for Responsible Government, a tax-exempt foundation that espouses conservative causes, used the services of Leadership '84 to raise more than $2 million which it funneled to other conservative groups for voter registration and related activities. Moreover, a greater number of foundations made grants to groups conducting voter drives than ever before. According to one account, foundation money for such drives increased by an estimated 500 percent, from about $1.2 million in earlier years to about $6 million in 1984.[38] This is a low estimate, but, because contributions to such groups and expenditures by them are not subject to federal campaigns disclosure laws, the precise amounts spent on such activities may never be known.

Finally, substantial amounts were spent by labor organizations and lesser amounts by associations, corporations and membership groups to pay for communications costs and other activities intended to benefit one of the presidential tickets. Here Mondale-Ferraro enjoyed the advantage, with $20 million spent on behalf of the ticket. The vast majority of labor unions supported the Democratic ticket as they had supported Mondale in his quest for the Democratic nomination. Only a small portion of the expenditures they made on Mondale-Ferraro's behalf were subject to disclosure requirements. Labor unions, membership groups, trade associations and corporations are required to report to the FEC the cost of partisan communications to their respective members and their families, or stockholders, executive and administrative personnel and their families only when those costs exceed $2,000 per election. However, significant amounts of labor's expenditures for Mondale-Ferraro paid for partisan communications by unions that probably did not reach the $2,000 threshold. Moreover, some pro-Mondale appeals were part of communications that were deemed non-political. And nominally non-partisan voter registration and turnout drives may have been designed to favor Democratic candidates. Some corporations, associations and membership groups supported Reagan-Bush with about $1.5 million in expenditures for internal communications; and a few labor unions, such as the Teamsters, helped with about $2 million in expenditures.

Independent expenditure campaigns

The third parallel campaign conducted during the general election period was funded entirely by money raised and spent independently. As in 1980, the Reagan campaign attracted a substantial amount of independent expenditures on its behalf, most of it by ideologically conservative committees, such as the National Conservative Political Action Committee (NCPAC), the Fund for a Conservative Majority (FCM) and the Christian Voice Moral Government Fund. NCPAC claimed it spent $12 million and FCM claimed $2 million in independent expenditures to help reelect Ronald Reagan in 1984.[39] However, official reports indicate that $8.5 million were spent on behalf of Reagan-Bush in the general election period. The Mondale campaign had far less spent independently on its behalf, about $700,000. Environmental groups opposed to the Reagan administration's environmental policies were among those who provided Mondale-Ferraro with independent support.

Since the 1980 campaign, independent expenditures had been the subject of considerable litigation. In a suit arising from that campaign, a three-judge court in the District of Columbia circuit had ruled that a provision of the Presidential Election Campaign Fund Act prohibiting independent expenditures of more than $1,000 by organized political committees on behalf of publicly funded presidential candidates was unconstitutional. That provision had not been considered in the court's 1976 *Buckley* decision and was subsequently left untouched by Congress in the 1976 FECA Amendments. The lower court's verdict was upheld in a tie vote of the Supreme Court when the case was heard on appeal.[40] But since the vote was equally divided, the court's decision had no precedential value and applied only in the District of Columbia circuit.

In 1983 the FEC and the Democratic National Committee brought suit in the U.S. District Court for the Eastern District of Pennsylvania against NCPAC and FCM, two groups that made public their plans to make large independent expenditures in the 1984 presidential campaign. The Pennsylvania district court refused to allow the FEC to implement the provision, and the commission filed an appeal with the Supreme Court. The high court declined to expedite the appeal so the matter could be resolved before the general election.[41] In March 1985, the court, in a 7-to-2 decision, held that the law limiting to $1,000 independent spending by organized political committees on behalf of publicly funded presidential candidates was unconstitutional.

The Anderson factor

Throughout 1983 speculation that John Anderson, who ran as an independent candidate in 1980, might run as the presidential candidate of a new party in 1984 provided material for a variety of press reports. For Anderson, one of the attractions of running again was the prospect of receiving some $6 million in federal funds based on his 1980 showing. That he decided not to run indicates that the public money alone was not sufficient. He would have been required to qualify for the ballot in at least 10 states in order to receive the money. Anderson knew from his 1980 experience and from initial efforts in 1984 that ballot access costs for a minor party would have been great and the process of qualifying as a candidate for a minor party more tenuous and more arduous than as an independent candidate. Instead he chose to endorse the Mondale-Ferraro ticket and to campaign on its behalf.

CONCLUSIONS

The experience of three presidential campaigns indicates that the FECA has achieved mixed results. In the pre-nomination period, the campaign law's public funding provisions have improved access to the contest by supplementing the treasuries of candidates who attain a modest degree of private funding. When combined with the relatively low individual contribution limit, the public funding has increased the possibility that candidates without ready access to wealthy contributors may compete effectively with candidates who enjoy such access. Evidence may be found in the victorious campaign of initially little-known Jimmy Carter in 1976, in the ability of George Bush and John Anderson to wage effective campaigns in 1980 and of Gary Hart and Jesse Jackson to make their marks in 1984.

The public matching fund provision has increased the importance of contributors of small amounts in financing pre-nomination campaigns. Some observers maintain that the fact that only contributions from individuals may be matched reduces the likelihood that organized groups will play a significant role in pre-nomination campaign financing. Perhaps so, but it must be said that many organized groups traditionally avoid becoming deeply involved in intra-party contests to determine a party's nominee for president. Moreover, in 1984 labor organizations and their PACs demonstrated, through substantial expenditures for pro-Mondale internal communications and PAC contributions to pro-Mondale delegate committees, that making PAC contributions non-matchable does not necessarily impede the expenditure of interest group money seeking to influence the pre-nomination campaign result. And, of course, some PACs make independent expenditures.

The law's contribution limits have reduced the possibilities wealthy contributors may have to exert political influence. Its disclosure provisions have resulted in more campaign finance information than ever before being available to the public, and its compliance requirements have caused campaigns to place greater emphasis on money management and account-ability. These effects suggest that in some ways the laws have succeeded in altering the behavior of candidates, committees and contributors to achieve some of the goals of campaign reform.

Other results of the law, however, are less favorable. The low individual contribution limit has caused wealthy contributors to be replaced by a variety of fund raisers upon whom candidates may become equally dependent for campaign funds. These include direct mail consultants with access to mailing lists of proven donors to campaigns; entertainment industry promoters who can persuade their clients to hold benefit concerts for favored candidates; and "elite solicitors" who can tap into networks of individuals capable of contributing up to the maximum amount allowed.

Even with public matching funds, the low contribution limit may make it difficult for candidates to raise sufficient money to conduct their campaigns. Every eligible Democratic candidate concluded his pre-nomination campaign with a substantial debt, and the total indebtedness for all those candidates combined reached as much as $15 million. Pre-nomination debt reduction activities continued through the general election period, distracting attention and draining resources from the Democratic election campaign.

The low individual contribution limit and the expenditure limits have reduced campaign flexibility and rigidified the election campaign process. The contribution limit prevents potential candidates from mounting a campaign late in the pre-nomination season because it makes it extremely difficult to raise sufficient funds in a short time. The expenditure limit makes it difficult for candidates who have spent close to the maximum allowed to alter campaign strategy and tactics to fend off new challenges or to take new developments into account.

Instead the contribution limit works to the advantage of well-known candidates capable of raising money quickly, perhaps forestalling others from entering the contest. It forces less-known candidates to begin their fund raising earlier than ever before, thereby lengthening the campaign season. Also contributing to the lengthening of the campaign season in 1984 was the decision of the Democratic Party to compress the primary and caucus period. A number of states then moved their election contests to the early portion of the period to increase their importance to the candidates and the media, consequently putting pressure on the candidates to establish their credibility and to fill their campaign treasuries earlier than usual. Thus many candidates participated in expensive straw polls and competed for group endorsements through much of 1983, seeking the momentum they hoped would carry them through the front-loaded primary and caucus season in 1984.

The relatively low expenditure limits have encouraged candidates to favor mass media advertising, which is more cost-effective and less time-consuming than grass-roots campaigning but may not be as informative. It has caused candidates to centralize control of their campaign efforts in order to assure that they remain within the expenditure limits, but this centralization comes at the expense of local authority and direction. The low expenditure limits also have led candidates to resort to a variety of subterfuges to circumvent the limits. In the 1980 campaign they led Republican candidate John Connally to reject public matching funds in order to avoid the limits and gain greater campaign flexibility in an effort to overtake frontrunner Ronald Reagan.

The low contribution and expenditure limits have encouraged the development of a variety of ways to frustrate the intent of the limits, including the presidential PACs, delegate committees and independent expenditures used in the most recent campaign. Such developments demonstrate the difficulties in attempting to regulate money strictly in the U.S. political arena. In a pluralistic society, such as that of the U.S., in which freedom of speech is guaranteed, restricting money at any given point in the campaign process often results in new channels being carved through which monied individuals and groups can seek to bring their influence to bear on campaigns and officeholders.

Despite the increase in campaign finance information available to the public because of the FECA's disclosure provisions, there has been some significant erosion in the ability of these provisions to bring important data to light. For example, in December 1983, the FEC voted 4-to-2 to allow these candidates who contract with outside parties to conduct campaign-related activities on their behalf to meet their disclosure obligations merely by reporting payments made to those parties.[42] The decision allowed the Mondale for President Committee to avoid public disclosure of its itemized media costs, permitting the committee instead merely to report the lump sums it paid to its media firm. The commission failed to heed a warning from its own legal staff that under such a ruling campaigns could defeat the purpose of public disclosure of all campaign expenditures simply by contracting with a professional consulting firm to conduct campaign activities on their behalf and then reporting only the sums paid directly to the firm.

Further, the information of a large number of delegate committees supporting candidates for delegate who backed Walter Mondale spread the disclosure of campaign contributions and expenditures intended to assist the presidential candidate over many widely dispersed committees whose activities sometimes became known only after the primary elections they were meant to influence had already taken place. Moreover, the establishment of state-level PACs as "subsidiaries" of Mondale's federal-level presidential PAC, the Committee for the Future of America, allowed those PACs to collect and disburse funds to help Mondale's cause without having to disclose their receipts and expenditures to the FEC. In addition, the FEC decision to consider contributions to convention city promotion and services funds exempt from FECA limits and therefore non-reportable means that contributions to provide certain kinds of support for the political parties' quadrennial conventions may be collected from any source whatever, and that the contributors may never be known to the public.

Finally, the complexities of the law's compliance requirements have contributed to the professionalization of campaigns, possibly chilling enthusiasm for volunteer citizen participation in politics.

In the general election, public funding combined with a ban on private contributions to the major party nominees – except to defray compliance costs – was intended to equalize spending between major party candidates, to control or limit campaign spending and to eliminate the possibility of large individual or interest group contributions influencing presidential election results. In 1976, with a few exceptions, those purposes appeared to have been achieved. But in 1980, and again in 1984, due in large part to increased familiarity with the law's provisions as well as some changes in the law, political partisans discovered a variety of ways to upset the balance and reintroduce substantial amounts of private money into the campaigns: contributions to state and local party committees to pay for activities beneficial to the presidential candidates; contributions to tax-exempt organizations conducting nominally non-partisan voter drives which actually were intended to benefit the candidates of one or the other of the political parties; independent expenditures; spending by labor unions and other organizations on internal communications and other activities to help candidates.

The 1984 general election experience strongly suggests that in a political system such as that of the U.S., animated by a variety of competing interests each guaranteed freedom of expression, a tightly drawn system of expenditure limits does not work well. Such limits have served only to constrain the presidential campaign leadership because they have restricted the amount the central campaign organizations are able to spend directly but have placed outside the campaign's control potentially unlimited sums disbursed, quite legally, to influence the election result.

As in the pre-nomination period, the law's disclosure provisions have led to far more information for the public regarding political campaign money. But here, too, there are gaps. Some political money does not have to be reported. In this category, for example, is the substantial labor spending on non-reportable communications and other activities that have helped Democratic candidates in all three publicly funded election campaigns. So, too, are the contributions made to and expenditures made by tax-exempt, nominally non-partisan organizations that conducted voter drives in the 1984 campaigns. Other spending to influence the presidential election result is difficult to trace, such as the money raised under national political party committee auspices in 1980 and 1984 and channeled directly to state party organizations to finance state and local volunteer-oriented activities on behalf of the presidential tickets. Much of the spending was exempt from federal reporting requirements; specific information about it is available only from appropriate state officers in the individual states where the contributions or expenditures were made.

Among the potentially most consequential legislative proposals that would have affected presidential campaigns and elections were provisions of various tax-simplification measures offered by the Reagan administration and by the House Ways and Means Committee. Late in May 1985, the administration's Treasury department unveiled a massive tax-simplification plan that, among other things, would have eliminated both the income tax checkoff procedure by which public funding is provided for presidential campaigns and the 50 percent tax credit for modest contributions to federal, state, and local candidates, PACs and political party committees. Treasury department officials argued that the checkoff complicates the tax form and confuses taxpayers. The tax credit, claimed on slightly more than five million returns in 1984, cost the Treasury about $300 million in revenue lost. The tax checkoff costs about $40 million each tax year.

Opponents of elimination of the tax checkoff argued that the move might have several negative consequences for presidential campaign financing: it might increase the importance of interest group sponsored PACs, which have not contributed large amounts in publicly funded campaigns; it could lead candidates to narrow their geographical bases of fund raising, since they would no longer need to raise a threshold level of matchable contributions in each of twenty states before qualifying for public funds; it might also require candidates to spend more time than ever raising funds and, perhaps, to begin fund raising earlier than before, since the contribution limits would remain the same. Proponents of eliminating the checkoff argued that public money has no place in election campaigns. Some of them also concluded that eliminating public funding – an almost certain result of doing away with the tax checkoff – would diminish the importance of the FEC, an outcome welcomed by some critics of the agency.

The proposal to eliminate the political tax credit struck at the heart of campaign finance proposals offered during the 98th Congress, specifically HR 3737, the McHugh-Conable proposal, and HR 4428, authored by Reps. Obey, Leach, Synar and Frost. Supporters of such proposals maintained that the expansion rather than the elimination of the tax credit would be the most effective means of encouraging small contributions to campaigns and preventing further dependence on PAC funds.

When the matter of tax simplification came before the House Ways and Means Committee, committee members voted not to accept the Reagan administration's recommendation to eliminate the tax checkoff, but they voted twice to eliminate the tax credit. In mid December 1985, however, the House voted 230–196 to support Rep. McHugh's amendment to the tax bill (HR 3838) which not only retained a tax credit provision but increased the credit from 50 to 100 percent for contributions up to $100 to House and Senate candidates from the contributing taxpayers' home states. But a tax credit provision was not included in the Senate version of the tax bill, and McHugh's amendment did not survive the deliberations of the House-Senate conference committee that crafted the tax overhaul bill subsequently approved by Congress and signed into law late in 1986. The bill left untouched the tax checkoff procedure for providing money for the Presidential Election Campaign Fund.

It is clear that the campaign finance reforms of the 1970s do not represent a panacea for all the ills that afflicted the presidential campaign financing system before the reforms were enacted. The present campaign finance system has flaws, and some of them are quite serious. Nevertheless, for all its shortcomings, the current system represents a notable improvement over the system in effect only a decade ago. The aims of the reformers were enormously ambitious, and quite probably not all of them can be achieved. Those that are achievable will be reached only step-by-step as new approaches to campaign finance regulation are tested in the crucible of the quadrennial contest for the presidency.

Notes

1 Public Law 92–225, 86 Stat. 3 (1973) (codified as amended in 2 U.S.C. 431 et seq. and in scattered sections of 18 and 47 U.S.C.).
2 Public Law 92–178, Section 701–703, 801–802, 85 Stat. 497, 560–574 (1972) (codified as amended in scattered sections of 26 U.S.C.).
3 Public Law 93–443, 88 Stat. 1263 (codified in scattered sections of U.S.C.).
4 Public Law 94–283, 90 Stat. 475 (codified in scattered sections of U.S.C.).
5 Public Law 96–187.
6 *Buckley v. Valeo*, 424 U.S. 1 (1976).
7 For a thorough analysis of the impact of federal campaign finance laws on the conduct of the 1976 and 1980 presidential campaigns, see Herbert E. Alexander, *Financing the 1976 Election* (Washington, D.C.: Congressional Quarterly Press, 1979), and *Financing the 1980 Election* (Lexington, Massachusetts: D.C. Heath, 1983). Also see Herbert E. Alexander and Brian A. Haggerty, *Financing the 1984 Election* (Lexington, Massachusetts: D. C. Heath, 1987).
8 To qualify as a multicandidate committee, a committee must have been registered with the appropriate federal officer for at least six months, have received contributions for federal elections from more than fifty persons and have contributed to five or more federal candidates.
9 Robert L. Jackson, "Mondale Spending Reaches 60 percent of Limit," *The Los Angeles Times*, March 21, 1984.
10 Michael J. Robinson, "The Power of the Primary Purse: Money in 1984," *Public Opinion*, August/September, 1984, p. 50.
11 "TV Ads Raise Campaign Costs," *The New York Times*, October 25, 1984.
12 Quoted in Jonathan Alter, "How TV Affects Politics," *Newsweek*, March 5, 1984, p. 27.
13 "Spending Limits: A Joke?" *Newsweek*, March 5, 1984, p. 28.
14 Ibid.
15 Ibid.
16 John Dillin, "Labor's Help in Mondale Drive Calls Spending Laws Into Question," *The Christian Science Monitor*, February 14, 1984.
17 Brooks Jackson, quoted in Herbert E. Alexander and Brian A. Haggerty, *PACs and Parties: Relations and Interrelationships* (Los Angeles: Citizens' Research Foundation, 1984), p. 34.

18 "Their Own in 1984 Presidential Races," *National Journal*, June 30, 1984, pp. 1,263–7.
19 Ibid., p. 1,264.
20 "Reagan to Refund $500,000," *The Chicago Sun Times*, September 22, 1984.
21 424 U.S. at 51.
22 Thomas N. Edsall, "More Mondale PAC Money," *The Washington Post National Weekly Edition*, July 16, 1984.
23 Bill Hogan and Alan Green, "Waltergate," *Regardie's*, July 1984, pp. 26–37.
24 See *Federal Election Commission Record*, December 1983, pp. 1, 4–6.
25 Quoted in Richard E. Meyer, "Mondale Will Pay Back Funds Given By PACs," *The Los Angeles Times*, April 28, 1984.
26 Quoted in Brooks Jackson, "Mondale Committees Operated Illegally; Ferraro Violated House Reporting Rules," *The Wall Street Journal*, December 5, 1984.
27 "Reagan to Refund $500,000," *The Chicago Sun Times*, September 22, 1984.
28 Federal Election Commission, AO 1975–1, *Federal Register*, July 15, 1975, p. 26,660.
29 Federal Election Commission, AO 1982–27, *FEC Record*, June 1982, p. 6.
30 Federal Election Commission, AO 1983–29, *FEC Record*, December 1983, p. 3.
31 See Elizabeth Drew, A Reporter at Large, "Politics and Money – II," *The New Yorker*, December 13, 1983, p. 64.
32 Thomas B. Edsall, "Democrats Will Use the Hard Sell to Pull In the Soft Money," *The Washington Post National Weekly Edition*, July 23, 1984, p. 13.
33 Terry Michael cited in Brooks Jackson, "'Soft Money' Givers to Democrats Named in Reports," *The Wall Street Journal*, January 16, 1985.
34 Ed Zuckerman, "'Soft Money': A New Life for 'Fatcats,'" *PACs & Lobbies*, January 16, 1985, p. 1.
35 Ibid., pp. 1–5.
36 See Michael Wines, "Bundlers' Aid Campaigns in Evading Spending Laws," *The Los Angeles Times*, October 1, 1984.
37 See Elizabeth Drew, A Reporter at Large, "Politics and Money – II," *The New Yorker*, December 13, 1983, p. 64.
38 Thomas B. Edsall, "'Liberals' Get-Out-The-Vote Turned Into Get Out Your Knives," *The Washington Post National Weekly Edition*, November 5, 1984, p. 23.
39 "Eye on Washington," *The Conservative Digest*, January, 1985.
40 455 U.S. 129 (1982).
41 *FEC v. NCPAC*, 83–1032, *Democratic Party v. NCPAC*, 83–1122.
42 Federal Election Commission, AO 1983–25, *FEC Record*, February, 1984, pp. 4–5.

6

Party financing in Israel: experience and experimentation, 1968–85

JONATHAN MENDILOW

INTRODUCTION

On February 19, 1969, Israel joined the small group of countries that had pioneered state financing of political parties. Until then, Israeli electoral campaigns had been lengthier than those of almost any other parliamentary system, and were far costlier than most in terms of the amount spent per eligible voter. The combined expenditure of the parties competing in the 1961 parliamentary elections, for example, was estimated at IL 25,000,000 (more than $8 million), or some $6.75 per eligible voter, figures, which according to Guttman,[1] "not only exceeded anything known from other Western countries, but [were] really of an entirely different order of magnitude."

The next parliamentary elections, four years later, were even more expensive. Conducted against the background of Ben Gurion's challenge to the ruling Labor Party, which he had headed for many years, and of the fear of his breakaway party collaborating with the newly united right-wing opposition, its costs constituted an Israeli record. At the lowest estimate, the combined expenditure rose to IL 47,000,000, or approximately $10.40 for each of the million and a half eligible voters. If one includes the costs of the electoral campaign to the Histadrut (the Trade Union Confederation, which also operates several businesses), held between the parties contesting the national elections, the total amount of money spent on elections that year would be about double.[2] Even before the campaign started, voices were raised appealing for emergency regulations limiting the amount each party could spend. Indeed, Ben Gurion's new party (Raffi) included state financing of elections and the auditing of party accounts by the State Controller in its electoral program. After the dust had settled, pressures within the parties, the Knesset (parliament), and the public at large,

124

mounted for some control of the situation. Further, the heavy expenditures caused by the Six Day War added additional meaning to the calls for reform. In a rare instance of cooperation, six Knesset Members from rival parties, ranging from the Marxist wing of the labor movement to the extreme right, introduced the Law for the Elections to the Knesset and to the Local Authorities, 1969 (Financing, Limitations and Auditing), which was passed by a large majority.

The aims of the initiators, as expressed in the preamble to the bill and in the debate on its provisions, were far reaching. First, they intended to curb electoral expenditures. In addition, they hoped to release the parties from the necessity of seeking private sources of money with the attendant danger of attempts by large contributors to influence policy. Further, they sought to enhance the democratic values of transparency, accountability, and open elections by requiring the parties to submit their accounts to the supervision of the State Controller and to reduce the considerable discrepancies between the wealthy, property-owning parties and smaller, less affluent ones. They also hoped to lessen inter-party friction and to forestall the abuse of party prerogatives by substituting state-financed services for the ones offered by individual parties to voters, such as free transport to the polling booths. Finally, the sponsors of the law sought to create a new climate in which competition among the parties as well as the relations between the parties, the electorate and the state would undergo a fundamental change.

The promulgators of the bill were far from being starry-eyed idealists; they did not expect all political evil to disappear at one fell stroke. The law was envisaged from the start as a pilot project, limited in applicability to the approaching elections and thereafter to be adjusted and modified further in the light of practice. As the Chairman of the Finance Committee stated in introducing the bill, "[This] is an experimental law, whose object is to gain experience, to see how matters develop, and to profit from the lessons learned so as to improve from election to election."[3] The appointment of the State Controller, who is not a Member of the Knesset, as the authority charged with promulgating and arbitrating further changes, was another sign that the Knesset expected such changes to be necessary. As one of the bill's sponsors put it: "We shall try an experiment, and receive the report of the State Controller on its effectiveness. If the Controller will find that the law was applied as passed but revealed shortcomings, deviations and the perversion of its intentions, then we shall sit together and try to correct the faults he [has] found."[4]

The law did not come unexpectedly. In what follows, I shall offer a brief summary of the exceptional political conditions that forced the Israeli parties to spend such huge sums on electioneering and on their day-to-day operations. This will be followed by an analysis of intermediate steps that were taken to regulate party financing and which implied a reconsideration of the nature of Israeli parties and of their functions. Next will be presented a closer examination of the provisions of the 1969 Election Law, the changes in the law that were introduced following subsequent elections, and an evaluation of their results. Finally, I shall try to point to some problems which remain unsolved and have given rise to further efforts to plug gaps and tighten the regulations concerning the financing of parties.

THE BACKGROUND: THE ZIONIST PARTIES IN THE YISHUV AND EARLY DECADES OF INDEPENDENCE

Israel was born at the ripe age of about thirty, if one includes its early years as a state-on-the-way which, beginning with the British Mandate over Palestine in 1917, conditioned its entire future. For this reason, an analysis of the role played by money in the politics of the country cannot be divorced from a consideration of the role played by the parties in the Yishuv (pre-state Jewish community in Palestine) and the means by which they financed their activity.

The Zionist parties which came into being in the early decades of the twentieth century were strong rivals despite their shared objectives. They held in common what might be called "Strategic Zionism," namely, the definition of the Jewish problem as a national one calling for a virtually unprecedented revolution involving a clean break in every field with the centuries following the dispersion. Hence, they saw themselves as spearheading a movement to create a new type of Jew, in a new society, in a new-old land. Precisely because they were so conscious of starting from scratch and establishing precedents for future generations, they were fully aware that every step they took was not merely a pioneering venture into unknown territory but also would determine the nature and boundaries of the nation, the society and the land. This made the disagreements among them about what could be called "Tactical Zionism," that is, the nature of the new society and the means by which it was to be realized, so acrimonious. On these issues they adopted – with necessary modifications – virtually the entire range of European ideologies between the two world wars, from the extreme left to the extreme right.

This combination of centripetal and centrifugal tendencies dictated the scope of party activity and the nature of the relationship between it and its members. In the absence of a sovereign Jewish authority, each party aspired to found a semi-autonomous mini-state. Thus, it came about that the Zionist parties, in addition to providing ideological guidance and the kind of services supplied by European mass parties, undertook many administrative and political functions typically carried out by the state. Parties, for example, served as key factors in the promotion of immigration as well as in the subsequent absorption of the newcomers. The first steps of a prospective immigrant would commonly be the result of his or her membership in a Zionist party abroad, or through contacts with party emissaries from Palestine. The contact might include help in obtaining permits and travel expenses. Party involvement would continue with the immigrant's absorption in Palestine within a party framework which would supply most of his or her needs, from work, housing, health, welfare and education to sports, cultural activities and youth movements.

One consequence of this direct party participation in the immigration process was that a heavy percentage of the adult population of the Yishuv were members of a party. Even after the mass immigration of the 1950s, when the newly founded state took over many of the duties connected with immigration, the average ratio of party members to party voters among the veteran parties was about half, and up to a third of the adult population held party membership.[5] This acquired additional significance in light of the special relationship that existed between parties and their individual members. Whereas in the U.S., for example, regeneration in a party usually involves little more than a loose connection, except perhaps in times of elections, party membership in Palestine virtually constituted a way of life. The links were extensive and included active participation in the work of the local branch, acceptance of strong party discipline, and a readiness to serve the community and the nascent state along the lines laid down by it. Indeed, party membership often meant living in the party's urban quarters or rural settlements.

All of this entailed an ever-growing need by the parties for more money to invest in housing, industries, agriculture, and the amenities of life. This, in turn, required growing party bureaucracies to administer these activities and to plan new projects, which necessitated still more money in a self-perpetuating creative process. Such day-to-day party expenditures involved heavy electioneering expenses, not only because party income was linked to the number of votes it could muster. Part of the budgetary needs were covered by heavy membership dues which averaged 0.5 percent of the gross yearly salary of its members, or a flat rate for the self-employed. While not all members paid up regularly, the intimate relationship between the parties and their adherents meant not only that most were conscientious in fulfilling their obligations but that many contributed also to special fund-raising campaigns on the eve of elections. All this, however, was far from sufficient. Additional sums were provided by the counterparts abroad of the Zionist parties of the Yishuv. Monies collected abroad by the National Foundation Fund (Keren Hayesod) also were distributed to the parties, according to the numbers of their voters for the National Institutions, to be used for investment in building the country. Economic enterprises were thus set up, employing large numbers of officials who naturally felt a sense of loyalty to their employers. As these commercial, industrial, financial and other economic institutions developed, they were able to give generously to the parties that had founded – and still controlled – them.

The birth of the State of Israel in 1948 brought in its wake many revolutionary changes, although strong links with the past were maintained. One area that was relatively less affected by the new circumstances was party politics. While many of the state-like functions hitherto fulfilled by the parties were now taken over by the government, what Etzioni[6] called the shift from "particularistic" to "universalistic" services, often was resisted and remained partial. For example, while party military organizations were disbanded and successfully absorbed into the National Defense Force, the nationalization of the educational system still remains incomplete, and health services are largely run by parties to this day. Other vital services, such as employment exchanges, were not nationalized until much later (in this case, 1958), and absorption and settlement were handled by the Jewish Agency in accordance with each party's strength in the Knesset. Moreover, if party functions were restricted in some respects, party resources were stretched to the limit by the need to cope with the mass immigration that trebled the population by the end of the first decade of independence.

Political competition was intensified since many of the newcomers lacked political predispositions and were therefore tempted to shop around for the party that offered them the most. For all these reasons, electioneering expenditures increased, and the introduction of more sophisticated communication media added to the burden. Nor did the legal status of the parties change with independence. They remained Ottoman corporations, that is, voluntary non-profit associations without legal or judicial status. Hence, there were few state controls on electioneering, such as forbidding bribery and intimidation, and few technical restrictions on the modes of propaganda, such as on the size of posters. Even these few restrictions were made law only in 1959. No legal provisions were made to regulate party finance, except for restrictions on the amount of radio time put at the parties' disposal prior to election.

The emergence of the state, therefore, did not contribute formally to party solvency, although the continued link between parties and economic enterprises increased the flow of funds contributed to those parties which were in the government coalition. The practice of government largesse and patronage for the faithful reached its peak in the 1950s and early 1960s, though it usually fell short of the legally permissible lmit. On one of the few cases which overstepped those bounds, a Supreme Court judge commented:

[T]he case before us reveals the disturbing phenomenon of the spoils systems, in which a party in government sees fit to deal out posts and favors to its helpers. One more step . . . and the border has been crossed into the realm of the criminality in the full sense of the term. And never let it be said that this too is customary in our country. We have no reason to believe that our politicians have so blurred the line between the good of the party and that of the state, that even the request for and granting of bribes are acceptable provided that it is done for a worthy cause.[7]

THE TURNING POINT: PARTY FINANCING THROUGH THE HISTADRUT

As the 1960s drew to a close, there were growing signs of a decline in ideological fervor, not a little due to the appearance of large party blocs formed on the basis of the lowest common denominator of the component parties.[8] Among other things, this resulted in decreased party membership and the loosening of the exclusive conditions that entitled members to the various services provided by the parties. Nonetheless, state financing of parties by law would mean a radical departure, not only in its practical effects but even more importantly in its conceptual repercussions. All of the Zionist parties were totalistic in nature. The leading principle was that the member supported voluntarily his or her own party in the belief that it was the truest expression of his or her vision of the future state. The rights of other parties to exist, as well as the pluralistic arrangements reached for the sake of expediency by the Yishuv, were therefore accepted on sufferance and of necessity. State financing of parties, on the other hand, is based on the recognition of the right to disagree and on the desirability of party competition. Hence, part of the taxpayer's money is rightly funneled into the coffers of all parties, irrespective of individual preference.

This change of outlook was put into effect in two stages which followed each other in quick succession. The second was the 1969 Elections (Party Financing) Law discussed above. The first was both in practice and in theory an interim law for party financing through the Histadrut. The idea was broached in May 1968 by the Raffi Party (which had included state financing in its electoral program). It was adopted by the Histadrut Central

Committee, and introduced to the Knesset by the labor-led government on August 5th of the same year. In anticipation of strong opposition in the House – and even stronger among the tax-paying public – the bill was introduced through the back door, as an amendment to the Wage Protection Law. It was rushed through at the end of the summer session, passed the first reading three days after its introduction, and became law six days later.

The law stated that progressive monthly deductions were to be made from the wages and salaries of all Histadrut members earning above a certain minimum, to be used for the financing of the parties according to the number of their elected representatives in that body. The deduction was automatic, but could be cancelled on the submission of a member's opposition given in writing to his employer (contracting out). The law thus offered an element of choice, as its supporters in the bitter Knesset debate were careful to emphasize. However, as its opponents pointed out, there was nevertheless more than a taint of compulsion, for a worker was compelled to take active steps to prevent the deduction and there was always the risk of retribution since most of the employers would be party members.[9] No less important, the fact that the arrangement was enacted by law and that the money was deducted for the benefit of all the parties and not exclusively for the party of one's choice constituted a breach of established practice, clearly reflected in the justifications offered for the bill. The first of these was that experience gained in the twenty years of the state's existence had shown that parties could not function on a budget based only on membership dues. As a result, the parties turned to raising money by deficit financing, what the Chairman of the Finance Committee called "special inducements," or economic institutions set up by the parties, such as construction companies or retail businesses. Therefore, it had become essential to introduce "some order into party financing by new and more suitable methods."[10] The second argument for the law lay in the fact that what was being proposed was in fact a law: "In the light of the prevalent attitude to parties . . . this bill aims at strengthening the realization that party politics is a constructive activity, an essential one, which must be acknowledged by law."[11] The awareness of drastic change was reflected no less in the arguments adduced against the bill. Parties, it was claimed, will be stripped of all pretense of being voluntary organizations. "No longer will the party belong to the member who pays dues out of conviction, as the ideal of participatory democracy demands, but the member will belong to the parties which extort a compulsory tax from him." Worse still, much of his money will go to parties that do not represent him and the old American principle of "No Taxation Without Representation" will be denied.[12]

Both proponents and opponents were agreed that the bill was a portent of things to come. Indeed, an unusual feature of the debate was the consensus between the former and some of the latter over what should follow if the bill became a law. The Minister of Labor, who introduced it, argued that this was only a first step and should be followed by state financing of electioneering expenditure. Moreover, he hoped the bill would help create a situation in which "all political parties would open their books to inspection by the Controller." On the part of the opposition the argument was voiced that contribution to a political party could be compared to buying shares in a company. Both should be a matter of free choice based on the confidence of the shareholder or party contributor in the integrity of those who handled his investment. If, however, it came in the form of a tax imposed by law, then the parties should be made accountable for their expenditure by opening their books to the public. Furthermore, it was claimed that restricting the burden of party financing to Histadrut members was undemocratic and unfair. The least undesirable form of such a law would be its application to the general population and not to trade union members only.[13]

The last point had much logic behind it. While it is true that the absolute majority of Israeli wage earners were Histadrut members, it is no less true that not all members pay dues since housewives, for example, are exempt. Further, the professional classes and the self-employed tended not to join the Histadrut, but what was not openly stressed by the opponents of the bill was that the proportion of the two categories within the various parties was vastly different.[14] It was not a coincidence that it was supported by the large Labor Party and opposed by the smaller parties whose electoral basis was composed largely of non-Histadrut professionals and persons who were self-employed.

Another major weakness noted by both sides in the debate was that the "party tax" could not conceivably suffice to cover party expenditure or even election expenses alone, as events were shortly to confirm. Towards the end of 1968, the estimated annual revenue from the tax was IL 10 million. Some months later it was corrected in the light of the actual monthly collection to IL 6 million. By September 1969, on the eve of the Histadrut elections, it transpired that during the first eight months of the year no more than IL 3.22 million had come in.[15] This may be set against the report of the Labor Party Auditing Institution which ascertained that the expenses of the Labor Alignment's 1969 Histadrut electoral campaign alone amounted to no less than IL 8.5 million.[16] In the years that followed the collection did increase to reach some IL 13 million by the elections of 1973,[17] and in the following decade it came close to doubling further in real terms. However, it was clear almost from the start that additional steps would have to be taken if public financing was to play a part in controlling the sources of party income and party expenditure.[18] The partial consensus that was already apparent in the debate on the Histadrut "party tax" may explain the final wording of the 1969 Elections (Party Financing) Law, as well as the fact that among its architects were some of those who had opposed the previous bill.

THE 1969 EXPERIMENT

The three issues dealt with in the Law for the Elections to the Knesset and Local Authorities, 1969, were specified in its sub-title: Financing, Limitation of Expenses, and Auditing. As regards financing, it laid down that the treasury would allocate to the Knesset Speaker the sum of IL 14,000,000 (somewhat more than $4 million) for distribution among the parties to cover their electoral expenses. Since the number of members in the Knesset is 120, this amounted to IL 120,000 per member (about $34,000). To the total sum the treasury would add another IL 480,000 (four units), thus admitting the Knesset's inability to decide whether the allocation should be based on party strength in the outgoing Knesset at the beginning or at the end of its term. Between the two dates, four members had left their original parties to set up a party on their own. The verdict was not Solomonic: both the brief parents and the recalcitrant children received their full recompense.

In the debate during the readings of the bill two views emerged on how the democratic principle of equality was to be applied to the bill. Should the money be divided equally among the parties so as to ensure equal competition for the next Knesset, or according to their strength in the outgoing Knesset?[19] On this point the large parties won the day. However, all the parties, large and small, cheerfully accepted the provision that the funds would be allocated only to parties already represented in the Knesset and not to new ones that threaten to fight the coming elections. On appeal, the High Court of Justice decided otherwise. This provision, it laid down, violated the basic electoral law of the country which stipulated that elections must not only be secret and free but also equal.[20] Consequently, the law was amended to provide that new parties would be payed retroactively the sum of IL 120,000 times the number of mandates (seats) they received in the elections.[21] One result of this was that money was to be allotted not only according to the beginning and ending of the outgoing Knesset, but also to the beginning of the incoming one.

Regarding limitation of expenses, the law granted each party the right to spend from its own resources up to a third of the equivalant of funds received from the treasury, bringing the amount of each electoral financing unit up to IL 160,000. Also, the state would be responsible for the transportation of voters to and from distant polling booths. Additionally the law defined election expenses as covering only money paid out to cover propaganda and other activities related to the elections. By this definition, services donated by party supporters for electoral purposes such as the use of meeting halls and notices published free of charge in party-owned newspapers would not be included. Nonetheless, the ceiling on total election expenditures was fixed at IL 24,640,000, about half the cost of the previous elections (without taking into account the depreciation of the Israeli currency during the intervening years) and between a third and a quarter of what would have been spent but for the law according to estimates of Knesset Members.[22]

According to the bill, party stipends would be delivered to the parties by the Knesset Speaker in two stages. An advance of 70 percent would be paid to the party after its nominated representatives, one of whom had to be a Knesset Member, had submitted to the Speaker confirmation that the party had officially presented its candidate list, and had formally declared that the party "had made all suitable arrangements for ensuring proper accounting of its election expenses in accordance with the instructions issued by the State Controller."[23] Should he so request, they must submit to him a signed affidavit as to the truth of any facts that, in his opinion, had a bearing on the expenses or on the accounting. The outstanding 30 percent would be paid after he had presented his report to the Speaker affirming that the party had kept its electoral expenses within the permitted maximum. In the event of a party not fulfilling these obligations, its 30 percent would be returned to the Treasury.

Since the law was admittedly experimental and there was no precedent to build on, it is worth dwelling on its implementation in some detail. From an organizational point of view, the most impressive feature of the 1969 electoral campaign was the effort involved in ensuring that the law was carried out as smoothly as possible. Well before polling day, the Controller was at pains to make sure that party officials understood all his regulations concerning the accounting of electoral expenses, and shortly before the actual day he sent his staff to the party offices to check if everything was in order. Immediately after election day he reminded the parties that their accounts must be submitted within six weeks, and offered to conduct the auditing in the offices where the accounts were drawn so as to save time. On the whole, the parties managed to make their returns in time, though many of them had to fill in gaps somewhat later. In view of the fact that party

Table 1. *Campaign expenditures for the 1969 elections by list*
(in Israeli pounds)

List	Actual expenditure	Ceiling
Labor alignment	9,763,937	9,920,000
Gahal	3,540,213	4,160,000
NRP	1,740,909	1,760,000
Ind. Liberals	828,381	800,000
State list	604,797	640,000
Agudat Israel	598,934	640,000
Free center	586,870	640,000
New Communist list	367,784	480,000
Pooli Agudat Israel	329,224	320,000
Progress and development	316,827	320,000
Shituf V'ehava	314,668	320,000
ICP	159,169	160,000
Ha'olam Haze	132,160	160,000
Total	19,283,870	24,640,000

Source: State Controller, *Inspection in Terms of the Law for the Elections to the Knesset and to the Local Authorities, 1969 (Financing, Limitations and Auditing)* (Jerusalem: February 8, 1970).

headquarters were responsible in all for over 600 local branches which were rarely staffed by experts, occasional slips were understandable. In the controller's covering letter to the Speaker of the Knesset he expressed his appreciation of the efforts put in by all concerned, especially "in the light of the absence of models to follow and the lack of experience."[24]

Even more outstanding was the fact that the actual overall expenditure was less than 80 percent of the sum permitted by the law. It is true that the country was in no mood for extravagance after the cost of the Six Day War, and there were even suggestions that the parties reach an agreement to cut down all non-vital electioneering expenses and transfer the money thus saved to the special fund for acquiring Phantom Jets.[25] It is also true that there were instances of less pure-minded attempts to present reduced expense accounts. Some of the branches of one major party, for instance, were found to have recorded only the net and not the gross salaries paid for staff.[26] Nevertheless, the achievements can be seen if one compares the expenses with those of earlier electoral campaigns. Even if we disregard the exorbitant cost of the 1965 elections, we still find that the 1969 campaign cost about $5.7 million as compared with $8 million in 1961. In fact, the picture is more favorable for the electorate had increased from 1,275,000 in

Table 2. *Breakdown of party expenditure for the elections of 1961 and 1969*
In Israeli pounds and percentage of total expenditure (in brackets)

Item	1961	1969
Regular staff	7,000,000	6,478,952
expenditure (including travelling expenses)	(28.0%)	(33.6%)
Special office expenditure	2,000,000	1,066,778
(including phone and postage)	(8.0%)	(5.6%)
Public election meetings	3,000,000	756,750
(including phone and postage)	(12.0%)	(3.92%)
Rent, hiring or buildings	2,000,000	870,880
	(8.0%)	(4.5%)
Advertisement	3,000,000	6,534,388
(including newspapers, TV)	(12.0%)	(33.8%)
Election day	3,000,000	3,022,438
	(12.0%)	(15.6%)
Other expenses	5,000,000	498,014
	(20.0%)	(2.6%)
Total	25,000,000	19,283,870

The sum of IL55,700 paid by the Free Center as guarantees to the Central Elections Committee was not included.
Source: E. Guttmann, "Israel," *Journal of Politics* 25 (1963), p. 716; State Controller, *Inspection in Terms of the Law for the Elections to the Knesset and to the Local Authorities 1969 (Financing Limitations and Auditing)* (Jerusalem: February 8, 1970).

1961 to 1,760,000 in 1969. Moreover, television had been newly intro-duced. Although both radio and television time was allocated free of charge to the parties according to their size, the cost of preparing and producing TV programs added considerably to the campaign expenses. Yet, as Table 1 shows, only two of the smaller parties exceeded the permissible sum, and that by an amount that the Controller considered too insignificant to warrant penalty. As the report of the Labor Party Auditing Institution pointed out, the very fact of state auditing served to deter suppliers of materials and services from overcharging. Although some of the major party branches fought to maintain their independence, and some succeeded in extorting more than their due, on the whole the central party organization managed to keep a tight rein on branch expenditures thereby accelerating the move to greater centralization.[27]

Table 2, providing a breakdown of the main categories of expenditure in the 1961 and 1969 campaigns, helps to throw light on another important effect of state financing on the parties. Whereas there was a reduction in terms on money spent on every item except advertisement (with election day expenses remaining constant), proportionally there were considerable differences. Sundry expenses fell dramatically as did the sums spent on public meetings and rent, chiefly for halls. Staff and election day expenses showed a moderate proportionate increase, but advertisement nearly tripled. This reflects a change in electioneering tactics that became more and more evident as the years passed: from more personal, spontaneous contacts between party leaders and voters, to carefully rehearsed and professionally managed television programs planned and executed by the central party organization. At the end of his covering letter to the Knesset Speaker, the State Controller expressed his general satisfaction with the way the 1969 experiment had worked out. The results called, in his opinion, for the passing of similar laws for future elections. Indeed, the experience had already affected values whose impact would extend far beyond the immediate occasion of the 1969 elections. In retrospect, the truth of his words applied to more than the financial aspects to which he referred.

THE 1973 LAW AND ITS AMENDMENTS

The report of the State Controller gave moral support to the proposals to establish party financing by the state on a permanent basis.[28] Toward the end of 1972, a new bill was introduced and this time the intention was explicitly stated in the title. Whereas the first effort to finance the parties came in the guise of an amendment to the Wage Protection Law, and the second nervously mentioned the purpose only in the brackets added to the official title, the new law was boldly called Law for the Financing of Parties, 1973. It followed broadly the lines of its predecessor but it, and a number of subsequent amendments, addressed some major issues:

A. Method of allocation

One of the difficulties in the 1969 law was the application of multiple criteria in the allocation of money to the parties. This, in turn, related to the question of the status of factions which started in one party and ended in another and the definition of the principle of equality of opportunity between parties in electoral contests. With the 1973 law, it was now laid down that, in the interest of "absolute equality for every contesting party that passed the electoral threshold,"[29] the criterion will be retroactive, based on the composition of the incoming Knesset. This involved a change in the method of allocation. Parties already represented in the outgoing Knesset would get an advance of 60 percent of the finance unit times the number of its representatives on the day of its presentation of its candidate

list. On the publication of the election results the party will get 85 percent of
the adjusted figure less the sum advanced. The remaining amount due (15
percent) would be handed over following the positive report of the
Controller. New parties would receive 85 percent after the results and 15
percent after the report.

The division of the funding of existing Knesset parties into sums paid
before and sums paid after elections, compounded with the retroactive
criterion of allocation, raised an obvious question: how should the law treat
a party which loses so many mandates in a given election that the total
allocation due to it at the end of the election is less than the amount that was
advanced to it based on its expected level of Knesset mandates? Such a
predicament cropped up more than once. The most dramatic example was
the situation of the Alignment in the 1977 elections, which lost 19 of its 51
mandates. This meant that its advance was IL 7 million more than its
rightful share. The answer to such situations was provided by another
innovation in the 1973 law: that the excess sums should be deducted from
the money paid monthly by the treasury to the parties towards their current
expenditure.

B. State financing of current party expenditure

The section of the 1973 law which explicitly provided for state financing of
the day-to-day operations of the parties makes Israel among the first
nations to finance its parties so extensively. This important provision also
provides an interesting illustration of the close interplay between the
prestige and moral authority of the Controller and the legal powers of
Parliament. When the Chairman of the Knesset Finance Committee
presented the bill, he based his case for this provision on a quotation from
the Controller's annual report that had appeared only a few weeks earlier:
"the possibility has been created [by the success of the 1969 law] of the
parties receiving from the treasury allocations towards their general
activities apart from their electoral campaigning, this too subject to the
State Controller's inspection, especially of the sources of their income and
the general scope of their expenditure."[30] These words mention yet another
innovation that was to be introduced in the new bill, namely the inspection
of party income. There can be little doubt that the Controller knew
beforehand of the bill that was being worked out, and, irrespective of
whether or not he was actually involved in its drafting, he lent it his full
support.

While the 1969 law had dealt only with electioneering expenses, the 1973
bill distinguished between expenses incurred by a party in connection with
its electoral campaign and all the party's expenses other than these (current

expenses). To cover the latter, each party would receive a monthly allowance, called the "current financing unit." The amount of these current units would be 5 percent of the electoral financing unit multiplied by the number of that party's Knesset members. In other words, on a four year basis (the period between elections), a party would receive 2.5 times its electioneering allocation for its current expenses. To these amounts each party could add 50 percent from its own resources or, for the benefit of parties with no more than two mandates, 50 percent of three current financing units. Thus, the law established a limit on the day-to-day expenditures of parties. Any infraction against these limitations or of the auditing regulations of the Controller carried the penalty of having three months of grant-in-aid withheld.

After limitations on electioneering and current expenses were put into practice, an unforeseen situation arose which raised the problem whether the two were always mutually exclusive. The Controller's inspection, now carried out annually, revealed that a party had gone beyond the ceiling for current expenses during the year preceding an election, whereas its electioneering expenses fell short of the ceiling by an even greater amount. Among the current expenses were those incurred for its quadrennial pre-election convention. According to the law, expenses falling outside the official campaign period did not count as such. But neither could they be included as current expenses, defined as excluding electioneering cost. On the recommendation of the Controller an amendment was passed, defining electioneering expenses as covering "special expenses of a party during the electoral campaign or in relation to it."[31]

C. Limitation of party income

The 1969 law concerned itself only with party expenditures, on the supposition that state financing would drastically reduce party dependence on doubtful sources of income. Those who drafted the 1973 law were perhaps less naive, and took up the matter of such dependence. The new law forbade contributions, whether direct or indirect, from local corporations or registered companies. In so doing, it opened a Pandora's box, affording the student of politics a clear illustration of the Controller's role in everything pertaining to the regulation of party finance in Israel.

In his first reports following the enactment of the Law, then-State Controller, Dr. Itzhak Neibenzal, broached a number of problems that required attention, and suggested means to solve them. Some of these aroused little controversy, such as the status of contributions given by corporate bodies set up specifically to serve the parties (e.g., companies maintaining meeting halls for the free use of a party and which could be hired to others on occasion to finance the cost), or those given by party-affiliated communal settlements and cooperative villages, or given by the Histadrut. All of these were permissible, in his opinion, since they were not given in the hope of extracting benefits or influencing policy, and the Law was amended accordingly. More debatable in light of intensive party activities in the diaspora, dating from long before the state came into being, was the issue of contributions from corporate bodies and "legal persons" abroad. These, the Controller argued, provided dangerous loopholes and opportunities for getting around the Law and should therefore be expressly forbidden.[32] This also was approved by the Knesset, although soliciting funds from individual foreign nationals remained permitted.

However, other issues touched a raw nerve, for they concerned the very structure of the party system that had been in operation ever since the days of the Yishuv. The real point in question, the Controller claimed, was how a party should be defined. In the narrower sense, it is a political body whose objective is the propagation and promotion of certain social and political tenets, and the increasing of its power in parliament and government. "But over and above party in this sense," he wrote, "in the context of Israeli society and politics there [are] a wide variety of bodies identified with parties and which pursue the parties' aims [through activities which] . . . maintain organizational and ideological liason with the public, but which conduct their financial affairs separately." Such bodies, he continued, should be regarded as integral parts of the party and their sources of income should hence be as open to inspection as are the party's. Moreover, this is desirable because they are liable to serve as means by which doubtful contributions can be channeled into the party's coffers. Not only their income but also their expenditures must be considered as part of that party.[33]

D. Control of party expenditure

Except for the items mentioned above (sections A,B), the law in its original form did not take any innovative steps with regard to party expenditures. Yet, the Controller's crusade for a redefinition of the scope of his inspectional powers led him, as we noted, to demand a thorough going reexamination of the scope of the Law for Financing of Parties in all that pertains to limitations on party expenditure. As he put it, "Inspection according to the law as it stands is of necessity partial and of limited significance . . . [T]he aim should be to define clearly and explicitly to whom the limitations [on expenditure] should apply – to the parties in the narrow sense or to the entire, broad and complex system in the framework of which Israeli party activity operates."[34]

In January 1975, the Controller submitted a list to the Knesset Finance Committee of proposed amendments to the Law for the Financing of Parties. A sub-committee was formed to examine them. The sub-committee debates were protracted and, despite the constant reminders – and even rebukes – of Dr. Neibenzal, were not concluded until more than six years later. In the meantime, a new, but related, problem assumed sudden importance. The report on the elections of 1974 had already drawn attention to the publication of some advertisements in favor of parties by groups of private sympathizers or by unidentified persons. What aroused the Contoller's additional suspicion was the possibility that such advertisements constituted a way of getting around the ban on contributions by corporate bodies. In 1977, this issue remained marginal, but in the 1981 campaign – one of the bitterest and most intensive in the history of the state – it grew to enormous proportions. All of the major parties enjoyed the benefits of extensive propaganda publications appearing over the names of hitherto unknown bodies and employing even the slogans of the parties they favored. While the parties disclaimed all responsibility, the Controller, admitting he could not adduce definite proof, was nevertheless convinced that they were not telling the truth. "The parties did not include the costs of these advertisements in their accounts," he wrote in his report, "and therefore the exact amounts involved cannot be verified. Nevertheless, as far as one can judge, we are dealing with sums . . . of such proportions that the ceiling fixed by law has lost all meaning."[35]

This practice continued in the 1984 campaign. An extra twist was given to it by the organizing of free excursions to the West Bank to demonstrate the settlement achievements of the right-wing Likud Bloc. By then, however, the Finance Committee had concluded its deliberations, and a number of amendments in the spirit of the Controller's proposals had been added to the Law. The amendments broadened the definition of a party to include "any body of people, whether corporate or not . . . that in the State Controller's judgement should be seen as an extension of a party in the light of any or all of these factors: its aims, activities, identity of owners, administrators and members, the use to which its profits were put, and the sources for covering its deficits."[36] The provisions covered all national elections, Knesset and Histadrut alike. Special attention had been paid during the auditing to ensure that all activities of the anonymous groups were entered in the party accounts, and where they did not appear they were added by the inspectors themselves.[37] Consequently, the report on the electoral campaign could note with satisfaction that the hole in the dyke had been plugged. However, the inclusive definition of "parties" still applied only to periods of electoral campaigns. The fact that the Controller saw fit to stress that it was not yet applicable to current party activities and accounts[38] may indicate that the final word has not yet been said.[39]

TRENDS OF BACKSLIDING FROM THE LAW

The 1969 law was promulgated as a one-time experiment, and hence the amount of the subsidy to the parties could be specified. The 1973 law, on the other hand, was intended to be permanent and therefore charged the Knesset Finance Committee with the responsibility of determining the yearly allocation, which would then be included in the National Budget to be approved by the plenum. The underlying assumption behind this arrangement was that it would be necessary to bring the sums up to date from time to time.[40] In hindsight, this assumption was fully justified. For example, an adjustment was necessitated by the rapid escalation of inflation after the Yom Kippur War of 1973. In order to maintain party income in real terms, it was decided in 1975 to raise the financing unit every three months by 70 percent of the rise of the cost of living index, and this was raised to 90 percent in 1980. In addition, from that year on it was enacted that a party which surpassed the current expenditure ceiling as a result of a rapid rise of the index between the three monthly adjustments would not be subject to penalty, and that parties would be entitled to a reimbursement of financial expenses incurred on loans taken during the electoral campaign to cover the difference between the 60 percent advance and the total sum due in light of the election results.

Another kind of adjustment came in the form of amendments to the law in 1980 – and again in 1982 – raising the ceiling on expenditures by allowing the parties to spend more from their own resources. From 1980 on, the parties were allowed to spend 50 percent more than their subsidy on electioneering (one third by the 1969 and 1973 laws) and 80 percent more for their current outlays (hitherto 50 percent). Since from the outset a main purpose of the law had been to put a rein on party expenses, this development demonstrates that there were still those who did not agree with the original intent of the law. As one Member of Knesset argued, "[I]t's our own money. What right does anyone have telling us what to do with it?"[41] But the most blatant reverse of course came after the 1981 electoral campaign which, as noted above, marked a veritable explosion of expenses. In an effort to legitimize the lapse into electoral riotous living and to escape the penalties due on their excesses, the party representatives in the Finance Committee were instrumental in having two retroactive amendments passed. The first of these raised the ceiling for expenditures from the parties' own resources from 50 percent to 100 percent of the current financing unit and linked the number of units per party to its representation in the outgoing or incoming Knesset, whichever was the higher. The second amendment considerably reduced the penalty on expenditures greater than the new ceiling. On appeal, the High Court of Justice declared the retro-active provisions null and void, arguing that they were contrary to the Basic Law of the Knesset which laid down that elections must be equal. Their effect would have been to penalize those who acted according to the law and to reward those who transgressed it. As the judge put it, the retroactive aspect of the law "means a sort of amnesty to some of the contestants: what was hitherto forbidden becomes for them (and only for them) permitted."[42]

If the first kind of adjustment was intended to maintain party expenditures in real terms, and the second at increasing it at the parties' expense, the third was at once the simplest and most problematic from the point of view of the original intent of the law: it increased party expenditures in real terms by increasing the state allocation. From the time the financing unit was first fixed in 1973 to the end of 1985, it has more than doubled, from the equivalant of $42,857 to $87,573. As a result, each party receives – at the time of this writing – the monthly subsidy of $4,379 per Knesset member.[43] In brief, taken together, the amendments pulled in two directions. On the one hand, they broadened the inspection of – and tightened the regulation of – party finance. On the other hand, they added considerably to the sums the parties were permitted to spend.

A similar ambivalence is revealed by the changing degrees to which the parties complied with the law over the years. Table 3 shows that throughout the entire period between 1973 and 1985, the total sums expended on current party activities was somewhat less than the permitted ceilings, though slightly more than the state allocation. A similar pattern is discernible with regard to the individual parties. Throughout the period, there were only two cases of parties exceeding the ceiling, and minor instances of slips in the methods of auditing. None of these, however, were of major proportion or of real significance. Only twice did parties have to be penalized, and even then the Controller reduced the fine in one case.[44] A very different picture emerges when we examine the expenditures for electoral campaigns conducted under the Public Funding Law of 1969. These fall into two distinct groups: the campaigns of 1973 and 1977, and those of 1981 and 1984. In the 1970s, there was little expectation of a major electoral shift: Labor-led coalitions had governed the country throughout its history. In 1969, the first election conducted under the Public Financing Law, the cost of the elections was well below the permitted maximum. However, the surprise reversal of electoral fortunes in 1977 made elections more competitive and hence more expensive once again. In both 1981 and

Table 3. *Sample of total "current" party expenditures*
(in Israeli pounds for the years 1973–9, in shekels for 1983–4)

Period	Actual expenditures	Ceiling	State subsidies
1.1.73–31.12.73	29,536,206	31,460,000	20,973,332
31.1.75–1.2.76	24,713,046	31,776,000	21,184,000
1.6.77–31.5.78	53,249,552	75,875,945	45,648,734
1.6.78–31.5.79	69,741,575	96,403,590	56,895,420
1.4.83–31.3.84	337,703,294	355,824,000	296,520,000
1.4.84–31.8.84	538,000,000	605,304,000	446,000,000

Source: State Controller, *Inspection in Terms of the Law for the Financing of Parties* (Jerusalem, July 4, 1975; November 1, 1978; October 6, 1979; August 27, 1984) and the Knesset Treasurer.

1984, campaign expenses (including the use of foreign consultants) soared and the violations of the law reached serious proportions.

The total cost of the 1981 campaign reached IS 181,391,116 ($17,624,476), surpassing the legal limit by 44 percent. Table 4 shows that of the ten parties which secured representation in the Knesset, five exceeded their ceiling. No less remarkable is the fact that the expense per eligible voter was just over $7 – more than the cost per voter of the 1961 campaign. The nadir, however, had not yet been reached. Table 5 shows that the cost of the 1984 campaign reached the stupendous sum of $20,760,643 or $7.82 per eligible voter.[45] As in the 1981 elections, five lists exceeded their maximum. But what is of greater moment is the nature of the violations committed by some of the contestants. One party, for example, overstepped its maximum as stipulated by the law by no less than 1,447 percent. Three parties received contributions from local and foreign corporations, donations which amounted to about $2 million. Others received large sums from individual donors, in one case no less than $500,000. These extremely large individual contributions could, the Controller argued, possibly serve as cover for corporate contributions. In any case, they create a state of dependence that could influence party policy. The worst abuse was perhaps that of the Kach party (associated with Meir Kahane), which refused altogether to submit its accounts to the Controller, yet received the full subsidy due to new parties which gain representation in the new Knesset.[46]

This does not mean, however, that when it comes to electoral campaigns the law has lost complete influence on the behaviour of the parties. In cases where a law is passed with the intention of changing long-established

Table 4. *Violations of electioneering expenditure in the 1981 campaign*
(in IS. and $)

List	Ceiling	Actual expenditure	Excess spending
Alignment	IS32,482,444	IS89,835,953	IS57,353,509
	$3,156,700	$8,730,413	$5,572,630
Tami	IS2,866,100	IS12,408,162	IS9,542,062
	$278,533	$1,205,847	$927,134
Likud	IS37,259,274	IS45,168,265	IS7,908,991
	$3,620,920	$4,389,531	$768,460
Telem	IS2,866,100	IS8,264,473	IS5,398,373
	$278,533	$803,756	$524,521
Thiya	IS2,866,100	IS3,280,784	IS414,684
	$278,533	$378,832	$40,292
Total	IS78,340,018	IS154,957,337	IS80,617,621
	$7,613,219	$15,251,863	$7,833,037

Source: State Controller, *Inspection in terms of the Law for the Financing of Parties*, 1973 (Jerusalem: The State Controller, March 15, 1982; June 21, 1983)

political traditions, one should not measure its achievements merely by all-or-nothing standards. Norms cannot be altered by the stroke of a pen; they must undergo a process of development and modification. Indeed, the law itself must change as new situations arise. Hence, the assessment of its success should take into account the formation of a normative foundation which determines the range of the permissible and the forbidden. The fact that those who violated the law did so knowingly, and were aware that they would be held accountable, testifies in a sense to the headway made by the law. That is so especially when one bears in mind the crucial importance of the elections with regard to the Lebanese invasion, the issue of the West Bank and the precarious balance of power between the right and left wing blocs which made both the 1981 and 1984 campaigns unique in the history of the country. That there was a general consensus about the value of the law can be demonstrated by the responses to the following question, put by the author to representatives of parties in the Knesset in December of 1985: "What effect do you think an annulment of the law for the Financing of Parties would have on the political system?"[47] For all their differences, often acute, they were at one in their reaction: the parties would revert to more intolerable practices which, in addition, would alienate the public.

Table 5. *Campaign expenditures for the 1984 elections by list[a] in million Israeli shekels and US $ (in brackets[b])*

List	Ceiling		Actual expenditure		Excess expenditure	
Alignment	1,804.3	(6,159,912)	1,847.2	(6,306,373)	42.9	(146,461)
Likud	1,693.8	(5,782,663)	1,476.2	(5,039,773)		
NRP	220.9	(754,156)	462.2	(1,577,959)	241.3	(823,803)
Thiya	184.1	(628,521)	112.7	(384,759)		
N. C. P.	147.3	(502,885)	84.1	(287,119)		
Agudat Israel	47.3	(502,885)	56.5	(192,892)		
Tami	110.5	(377,249)	382.3	(1,305,179)	271.8	(927,930)
M. for change	110.5	(377,249)	97.5	(332,866)		
Raz	110.5	(377,249)	55.7	(190,161)		
Shas	110.5	(377,249)	53.7	(183,332)		
Yahad	82.8	(282,680)	1,198.0	(4,089,993)	1,115.2	(3,807,312)
Morasha	82.8	(282,680)	88.8	(303,165)	6.0	(20,485)
Omez	82.8	(282,680)	82.8	(282,680)		
Renewal	82.8	(282,680)	42.5	(145,096)		
Progressive List for Peace	82.8	(282,680)	40.8	(139,291)		
Total	4,953.7	(17,253,422)	6,081.0	(20,760,643)	1,677.2	(5,725)

[a] Excluding Kach, see above, p. 143.
[b] For the method of calculation, see footnote 47 ($=IS 292.91).
Source: The State Controller, *Inspection in Terms of the Law for the Financing of Parties, 1983* (Jerusalem: January 30, 1985).

In fact, the effects of the law are noticeable at the level of campaign behavior. An example may be found in the comment of a Member of Knesset who, since the 1960s, held a central position in planning one of the largest party's electoral campaigns. "In 1965," he noted, "there were no limitations. I sanctioned whatever I thought necessary. Since the law and inspection of accounts by the Controller, I am not prepared to sign receipts unless I have the express permission of the [party] treasurer. If I did and made a slip, I would be clawed not only by my own party but by the members of competing parties as well."[48] What has set in, as was noted above in connection with the 1969 campaign, is a trend to concentrate campaign decisions away from the local branches and even from leading party individuals to the top echelon at party headquarters.

The indirect repercussions of the law are broader in scope. State subsidies have relegated party membership dues to a less important position as a source of party income. This, in turn, has discouraged efforts to mobilize funds from membership fees. On the other hand, the process of centralization, facilitated by the growing importance of television in the campaigns, has contributed to a diminished need for branch activity and distanced the man in the street from active participation in party affairs. Consequently, party membership has steadily declined from 18 percent of the adult population to 16 percent in 1973, 10 percent in 1981 and 8 percent in 1984.[49] This, in turn, reinforced party interest in the existence of the law as a dependable source of income. In this context, smaller parties, new parties, and those parties that do not have a widespread social and economic infrastructure on which they can rely for manpower and money, are more vulnerable and hence depend on the perpetuation – and even strengthening – of the law. Accordingly, when party representatives were queried by the author as to what the effects of annulling the law would be on their party, there was a wide spectrum of response. Parties that are backed by numerous communal settlements thought that their competitive strength would be unaffected and could theoretically even increase in comparison to others. Others believed that their position would be adversely affected, but that with increased efforts to mobilize funds at home and abroad they could make their voices heard and the public would heed their appeals. Still others, particularly small new parties, felt that they would probably disintegrate.

In sum, one is left with the general impression that the aberrations of 1981 and 1985 do not justify pessimistic conclusions. They were not caused by, nor do they testify to, any systematic circumvention of the law but from one-time decisions of small groups of top party leaders under the pressure of exceptional conditions. The danger lies in the establishment of precedents which, if not dealt with, will lead to more gross violations. This is especially true of a law which, at first avowedly experimental, has not yet emerged from the adolescent stage.

STOPPING THE LEAKS

In most of his reports, the Controller, always on the watch for lacunae, has suggested amendments, most of which have been eventually incorporated in the law. In view of what happened in the 1985 campaign, the lawmakers would be well advised to not only consider his most recently proposed strictures but also to review those earlier comments and suggestions which, as yet, have not reached the statute books. One suggestion that the Controller made as early as 1977 concerns the fixed penalties imposed by the law. In cases where the Controller has given reports that are critical of party accounts, the penalty, according to the current law, is always the same, irrespective of the nature and degree of the violations committed. On the rare occasions when differential criteria were permitted, as in the retro-active amendment of 1981, it was only for greater leniency. On the principle of "as well be hanged for a sheep as for a lamb," this encouraged violations on a grand scale. To respond to this dilemma the Controller recommended in his 1985 report that flagrant transgressions, such as the Kach party's refusal to submit its accounts for review in 1984, should be subject to special punishments.[50] It seems obvious that a complete restructuring of the penalties cannot be deferred if the law is to be respected. This, in turn, must involve a reconsideration of the stages and sums of the allocation to give more leeway for punishment than the present 15 percent.

Other suggestions aim at tightening the regulations pertaining to party income. Hitherto, the law forbade only contributions from corporations and registered companies. However, in light of what occurred in 1984, the Controller suggested a broadening of the ban to include large contributions by individual donors. The model that ought to be followed, in his view, is that of the U.S., where federal law forbids total contributions by an individual exceeding $25,000 per calendar year.[51] No less important was the recommendation, first made in 1977, to prohibit the acceptance of donations from corporations and registered companies even in cases where the party forwent its right to the state subsidy, a proviso which should apply perhaps to large private contributions as well.[52] Since the normal penalty would affect the amount of the state allocation, an additional system of penalties would need to be devised.

Most important of all is the issue of the relationship between parties and their affiliated – but financially separate – bodies. Hitherto, the law broadened the interpretation of the term "party" to include such entities only for the duration of electoral campaigns. Logic demands, however, that the regulations ought to be broadened to apply at all times. The income sources of such bodies and their financial relations with the mother parties must be subject to the same inspection as the parties themselves. In hindsight, one can understand that the apparent illogic of the Israeli lawmakers in failing to enact such legislation from the beginning stemmed from a genuine difficulty in altering at one fell swoop the most deeply entrenched tradition in Israeli politics. Nevertheless, the necessity of eroding such traditions was realized from the beginning. In fact, what was at first considered revolutionary came to be accepted as a matter of course, thereby allowing the process of change to continue. Once the redefinition of "party" was recognized, if only for a limited period, the groundwork for further development had been laid.

CONCLUSION

What gives additional hope that the principles underlying the law will be fully realized is that former Attorney General Itzhak Zamir has recently issued a set of guidelines for the equal allocation of state subsidies to party affiliated bodies.[53] These new guidelines constitute an important step in the right direction. To understand the significance of his new criteria, one must bear in mind that Israel has never been governed except by party coalitions. One of the important, though indirect, methods of party finance consisted of coalition agreements which allocated funds to party affiliated bodies according to the bargaining strength of the coalition partners. As the Attorney General pointed out, this meant the waste of state funds and an invitation to corruption, since "money could be allocated to institutions and purposes of minor and even marginal importance, which would never be entitled to state assistance . . . were it not for political considerations."[54] Further, he argued, such practices could encourage the formation of unnecessary or fictitious bodies whose sole purpose would be to channel state monies directly to the parties. With the increased dependence on coalition partners caused by the almost equal size of the two major contestants in 1981, such arrangements took on unprecedented proportions. Thus, for example, the Controller's general report for 1982 pointed out that in that year religious institutions that were affiliated to coalition parties received – according to the coalition agreements – bloc grants of more than IS 1,400 million out of IS 1,530 million allocated for all religious institutions in the country.[55]

Following appeals by one aggrieved religious movement which complained of discrimination against its institutions, the High Court of Justice forbade in May 1984 the allocation of state funds to any religious institution according to criteria which are not "clear, relevant and equal." The government thereupon decided to draw up a list of the types of religious institutions which conducted activities worthy of state subvention, and to charge the Attorney General with preparing criteria for alloting money to individual institutions falling within the listed categories. At the same time, the Knesset also debated the issue and referred the matter to its Committee for Domestic and Environmental Affairs. The Committee affirmed the criteria prepared in the meantime by the Attorney General, and recommended that the Knesset Finance Committee allot funds not only to religious but to all other "deserving" institutions in education, culture, health, and other areas. Four days later, a ministerial committee, headed by the Prime Minister and his Deputy, decided that "the principle of allocations. . . according to relevant and equal criteria would be applied as from the financial year 1986 to all institutions."[56]

The above story indicates how the process of regulating party finances in Israel could be taken further. A simple legal complaint set in motion a series of actions and interactions involving the High Court of Justice, the Government, the Attorney General, the Knesset and its committees, all of which cooperated in producing a major modification of practices relating to the financing of parties such as none of them by themselves could achieve.

The regulation of party finance, which entered the statute book through the back door as an amendment to another law, has snowballed in less than two decades to a degree that has affected the most central features of political life in Israel. With the increased complexity of the issues, cooperation between lawmakers, the High Court of Justice and the Controller became vital. As the net spreads still wider, the hope is that additional bodies, such as those which participated in establishing the criteria for subsidizing public institutions, will join in the effort. In the words of Dryden:

> Mighty things from small beginnings grow:
> Thus fishes to shipping did impart
> Their tail the rudder, and their head the prow.

Notes

1 Emanuel Guttman, "Israel," *The Journal of Politics*, Vol. xxv, No. 1, 1963, p. 714.
2 *Knesset Minutes*, January 29, 1969, p. 1,364.
3 Ibid., p. 1,351.
4 Ibid., p. 1,355.
5 Guttman, "Israel," pp. 704–5; Benjamin Akzin, "The Role of Parties in Israeli Democracy," S. N. Eisenstadt, R. Bar Yosef, C. Adler, eds., *Integration and Development in Israel* (New York: Praeger, 1970), p. 21.
6 Amitai Etzioni, "The Decline of Neo-Feudalism: The Case of Israel," in Moshe Lisak and Emanuel Guttman, eds., *Political Institutions and Processes in Israel* (Jerusalem: Academon, 1971), pp. 70–87.
7 *Piskai Din* (High Court of Justice), Vol. 18 (1964), Yehuda Spigel against the Attorney General, Appeal 316/64, pp. 19–20.
8 See Jonathan Mendilow, "Party Cluster Formations in Multi-Party Systems," *Political Studies*, V. XXX, No. 4, 1982, pp. 485–503.
9 *Knesset Minutes*, August 8, 1968, p. 3,173; August 16, 1968, pp. 3,346, 3,176–5.
10 *Knesset Minutes*, August 14, 1968, p. 3,348.
11 Ibid., p. 3,348.
12 *Knesset Minutes*, August 8, 1968, p. 3,177; *Knesset Minutes*, August 14, 1968, p. 3,348.
13 *Knesset Minutes*, August 8, 1968, pp. 3,173, 3,181; *Knesset Minutes*, August 14, 1968, p. 3,350.
14 For the party distribution of Histadrut members in the same year see P. Burstein, "Social Cleavages and Party Choice in Israel: a Log-Linear Analysis," *American Political Science Review*, Vol. 72, March 1978, pp. 100–2, 106–8.
15 *Ha'aretz*, October 6, 1969.
16 *Ma'ariv*, March 20, 1970.
17 Leon Boim, "The Financing of Elections," in H. R. Penniman, ed., *Israel at the Polls: the Knesset Elections of 1977* (Washington D.C.: American Enterprise Institute, 1979), p. 203. I would like to thank Dr. Benni Temkin for his current estimate.
18 Beginning in 1970 the Histadrut "Political Tax" was incorporated into the Consolidated Tax, 5.5 percent of which is allocated to the parties according to their Histadrut representation.

19 *Knesset Minutes*, January 29, 1969, p. 1,369.
20 *Piskai Din* (High Court of Justice) Vol. 23 (1), p. 694; also see Leon Boim, "Financing of the 1969 Elections," Alan Arian, ed., *The Elections in Israel 1969* (Jerusalem: Academic Press, 1972), pp. 138–40.
21 *Rashomot* (Law Book), July 22, 1969, p. 201.
22 *Knesset Minutes*, January 29, 1969, p. 1,357.
23 *Rashomet*, February 28, 1969, p. 48.
24 The State Controller, *Inspection in Terms of the Law for the Financing of Parties* (Jerusalem: State Controller, February 8, 1970), p. 7.
25 *Ha'aretz*, October 6, 1969.
26 The authorities, however, declined to defer the flood. The income tax department placed in escrow IS 300,000 of the money due to the party by the 1969 Election Law. The party headquarters lost no time in checking branch accounts, paid out the missing IS 120,000, and thus the matter was resolved.
27 *Ma'ariv*, March 20, 1970.
28 See *Knesset Minutes*, October 25, 1973, p. 143; *Knesset Minutes*, January 1, 1974, p. 1,062.
29 *Knesset Minutes*, January 1, 1974, p. 1,063.
30 *Knesset Minutes*, October 25, 1973, p. 146.
31 *Rashomot*, March 1, 1982, p. 84.
32 The State Controller, *Inspection in Terms of the Law for the Financing of Parties* (Jerusalem: State Controller, November 1, 1978), p. 2.
33 Ibid., July 22, 1977, p. 3; November 1, 1978, p. 2.
34 Ibid., July 22, 1977, pp. 2–3.
35 The State Controller, *Inspection in Terms of the Law for the Financing of Parties* (Jerusalem: State Controller, March 15, 1982), p. 6.
36 See *Rashomot*, March 11, 1982, p. 84.
37 The State Controller, *Inspection in Terms of the Law for the Financing of Parties 1973* (Jerusalem: State Controller, March 15, 1982), p. 6.
38 Ibid., p. 6.
39 Other, less important, amendments following suggestions by the Controller have not been included in this discussion. The more significant of these treat the steps to be taken when a party that received an advance became defunct following the election. Accepting his suggestion, the Knesset provided that an inspection of its accounts be made. If violations of the law are found, the party's representatives will be charged individually and collectively with returning 18 percent of the advance to the treasury.
40 *Knesset Minutes*, October 25, 1972, p. 144.
41 Quoted in Aryeh Rubinstein, "Watching the Ceiling Go Up," *The Jerusalem Post*, December 13, 1985.
42 *Piskai Din*, Mr. Rubinstein versus the Speaker of the Knesset and the Minister of Finance, Vol. 37, 1983, 141/82, p. 162; see also pp. 147, 157.
43 To this, add IS 208.317 ($146.00) per member from the Knesset budget and an extra IS 187,361 as an allocation for each organized faction.
44 The State Controller, *Inspection in Terms of the Law for the Financing of Parties 1973* (Jerusalem: State Controller, August 21, 1983), p. 8.
45 In light of the rapid rate of inflation, these calculations were based on the mean

between the $ rate on the first and last days of the campaign (for 1981 $ = IS 10.292, for 1985 $ = IS 212.91). The number of eligible voters was 2,490,014 and 2,654,613 in 1981 and 1985 respectively.

46 The State Controller, *Inspection in Terms of the Law for the Financing of Parties 1973* (Jerusalem: State Controller, January 30, 1985), pp. 2, 4–5.

47 The questionnaire was answered by parties representing 107 – out of 120 – Members of Knesset.

48 Interview with MK. (member of Knesset) Yossi Sarid, December 11, 1985.

49 Asher Arian, *Politics and Government in Israel* (Tel Aviv: Zamora, Bitan, 1985), pp. 172, 191.

50 The State Controller, *Inspection in Terms of the Law for the Financing of Parties 1973* (Jerusalem: State Controller, August 30, 1977), p. 5 and ibid. (January 30, 1985), p. 3.

51 Ibid. (January 30, 1985), p. 6.

52 Ibid. (August 30, 1977), p. 4.

53 The Attorney General, *Criteria for State Subsidies to Public Institutions* (Jerusalem: Attorney General, December 1, 1985), 1–2. I am grateful to the Press Officer of the Ministry of Justice for permission to quote from the document.

54 Ibid., pp. 1–2.

55 The State Controller, *Report No. 33, 1982* (Jerusalem: The State Controller, 1983), pp. 70–1 and ibid., No. 35 (1985), pp. 19–20. For the allocations to party-affiliated institutions after 1982 see Norit Dovrat, "Money For the Distinguished," *Ma'Ariv*, December 24, 1985. The same procedures operate at the municipal level too. For the situation in Jerusalem see Shahar Elan, "The Coffers of Shosh," *Kol Ha'ere*, December 20, 1985.

56 The Attorney General, *Criteria for State Subsidies to Public Institutions*, pp. 3–5.

7

Public financing of parties in Italy

GIAN FRANCO CIAURRO

During the first period after the introduction of the republican constitutional system in Italy, that is, from 1948 to 1974, no legislation was
passed to regulate the financing of political parties. As it was in the pre-
fascist period, the political funding system was exclusively private.
According to an in-depth survey carried out by the Center for Research and
Documentation, there were five main channels in 1971 through which the
political parties could obtain funds to satisfy their fiscal requirements:

contributions from cardholding members and supporters;
subsidies from external private organizations, including "kickbacks" on
contracts and supplies paid to parties controlling the central and local
administrations;
diversion of public money by means of bureaucratic tricks, "black"
contracts and "black" interest on the bank accounts of state and
parastatal economic agencies.[1]
income from business, industrial and commercial activities controlled
by the parties through cooperatives, financial and trading companies;
financing aid from abroad, either from foreign governments, or from
trade union or private organizations.[2]

This wide range of methods for party fund raising left considerable
leeway to use questionable sources. For a long time, the use of such sources
was rationalized by the state of need in which the parties found themselves
and the absence of suitable legal sources from which to pay their expenses.
In 1961 this state of affairs triggered a wide-ranging political and
cultural debate in Italy. This debate was aimed at solving the problem of
party funds through public financing. To this end, several bills were
presented in parliament: one by the Rt. Hon. Aurelio Curti, a Christian
Democratic (DC), in 1966; another by the Rt. Hon. Luigi Bertoldi, a
Socialist (PSI), in 1968. Finally, in 1974 a draft bill was hammered out

153

between the parties of the government coalition and supported by their respective whips, the Rt. Hon. Flaminio Piccoli (DC), Luigi Mariotti (PSI), Antonio Cariglia of the Social Democratic Party (PSDI), and Oronzo Reale of the Republican Party (PRI). The bill was discussed quickly and then passed by the Chamber of Deputies, becoming Law Number 195 of May 2, 1974, entitled, "State Contribution to the Financing of Political Parties." The relevant regulations governing its implementation, after approval by the chairmen of the two Chambers, were enacted by decree of the Chairman of the Chamber of Deputies on July 10, 1974. In addition, the act governing the public financing of political parties was subjected to a popular referendum on June 11–12, 1978. Approval was expressed by 56.3 percent of the voters (17,663,301), while 43 percent (13,736,577) voted for its repeal. The narrow margin of favorable votes – despite the support of the large mass parties – was concrete evidence of just how controversial the issue was still considered by the Italian public.

Subsequent legislation on the matter made no substantial difference to the decision taken by the Italian parliament in 1974.[3] The 1974 act declared that public financing was to be used not only for the parties' electoral expenses, which would be more explicitly in the public interest, but also for expenditures on permanent party activities. For both types of subsidies, public funds have been apportioned so that all of the parties entitled to them are paid in proportion to the number of votes received at election time.

CRITERIA GOVERNING PUBLIC FINANCING

The system used for public financing of political parties in Italy thus consists in state contributions to defray the costs borne by the parties during regional elections, the election of the Chamber of Deputies, the Senate and the European Parliament, as well as state contributions to cover the costs of the routine work and activities of the parties.

For the election of the regional councils, each region receives a percentage of the funds proportional to its share of the national population. Twenty percent of each region's share is divided equally among the parties which have at least one candidate elected or, in the case of concurrent regional elections, at least one candidate elected in one of the regions. The remaining 80 percent is divided among the parties in proportion to the number of votes each obtains.

For elections to the National Chamber and to the Senate, 20 percent of the funds appropriated for each election is divided equally among all parties which present their own lists of candidates for election in more than two-thirds of the constituencies and which have won at least one seat in one constituency and received a national total of at least 350,000 votes, or no fewer than 2 percent of the total number of votes. Parties and political formations which present candidates under their own banner in the Chamber and Senate elections and have obtained at least a quota in the regions are also eligible for a share of the funds; 80 percent of this sum is divided among the parties and political formations themselves, in proportion to the number of votes obtained in the Chamber election. A special statute provides specific safeguards which protect linguistic minorities.

In addition, for election to the European Parliament, 20 percent of the total appropriation is divided equally among the parties which have obtained at least one representative; 80 percent is apportioned to the parties according to the number of votes each obtains.

Finally, for carrying out the parties' routine work and activities, 2 percent of the annual appropriation for this purpose in the Chamber and Senate budgets is divided equally among all the parliamentary groups; 75 percent of the sum is allocated proportionally and 23 percent by means of a mixed system. Those who chair the parliamentary groups are obliged to pay their respective parties the sum of not less than 90 percent of the contribution received; the remainder may be spent for the group's activities.

RESTRICTIONS AND REQUIREMENTS

All other forms of financing or contributions to political parties, their political and organizational arms or other parliamentary groups by the administration, public agencies or companies whose equity is more than 20 percent state-owned or by companies controlled by them is forbidden by law.[4] Private companies may make such contributions only after a resolution has been passed by their governing bodies and duly entered in their balance sheet. There are heavy penalties for any breaches.

In 1981, these restrictions were extended to cover contributions paid indirectly to Italian or European Ministers of Parliament, to regional, provincial or municipal council members, to candidates standing for election to such offices, to groups inside political parties and to persons holding office in the parties. The ban does not, however, include direct lending by banks on the terms defined by the interbank agreement.[5]

In addition, Italian political finance law requires that the political secretaries of parties which receive public subsidies are required to publish, by March 31 of each year, their party's financial balance sheet for the preceding year, accompanied by a report clearly stating any real estate, shareholdings in commercial companies, the ownership of such companies, any other form of economic activity, the breakdown of state contributions among its central and the peripheral organs and any free contributions amounting to more than 5 million lire per annum made to the party, to its political and organizational bodies, to its interal groupings and to its parliamentary groups. Even if such free contributions consist of the provision of services, it is compulsory for both the contributor and the recipient of the services – or only the latter if the contributions are received from abroad – to make a joint declaration of the contributions to the Chairman of the Chamber. This form of publication, which is aimed at rendering all the financial implications of political activity as transparent as possible, is indirectly completed by the provisions of law number 441 of July 1982. This law makes it compulsory for Ministers of Parliament to declare their personal financial situation, as well as any function they may have as a director or auditor of a company or companies, the content of their annual income tax return and their election campaign expenditures. Similar obligations are laid down by the same law for regional and provincial councillors, and councillors of municipalities which are provincial capitals or have a population of over one hundred thousand inhabitants, as well as for those holding office in public agencies, economic agencies, and in those private companies in which the state owns more than 20 percent of the stock or for the management of which a substantial public contribution is made.

The responsibility for disbursing the public subsidies and enforcing the relevant regulations lies with the Chairman of the Chamber, from whose budget most of the sums allocated for this purpose are drawn, and to a lesser extent with the Chairman of the Senate. The balance sheet is certified by three auditors who must be chartered accountants of at least five years standing and appointed in accordance with each party's internal regulations. The accuracy of the balance sheet is then reviewed by a technical committee made up of standing auditors who are jointly appointed at the start of each legislature by the Conference of the Chairmen of the groups of the two Chambers. The balance sheets are then published, with the report and the technical Committee's statement, in the *Official Gazette*. If it is concluded that a party has failed to comply with the regulations or if there are irregularities in the balance sheet, the payment of all state contributions is to be suspended by order of the Chairman of the chamber and of the Chairman of the Senate, according to their respective responsibilities, until the balance sheet is regularized. If the non-compliance consists in not having declared unsolicited contributions amounting to over 5 million lire, the state contribution for the routine tasks and activities of the party concerned is reduced by double the amount of the undeclared contributions. In cases of non-compliance, the person whose duty it was to make the declaration is fined an amount from two to six times that of the undeclared sum and temporarily banned from holding public office. Any disputes over public contributions are decided by the relevant offices of the President of the Chambers.

THE PARTIES' BALANCE SHEETS

Some concrete observations can be made regarding the first twelve years of public financing of parties in Italy based on the data contained in the parties' annual final balance sheets, published since 1974.[6] These data, however questionable, have the merit of coming from the parties directly over a fairly long period of time; before 1974 only estimates and hypotheses, from research done by experts and journalists, were available. On the basis of such hypotheses, the overall expenditure of the Italian political parties, in the years immediately before the introduction of public financing, has been estimated at about 60–80 billion lire per year.[7] The figures published in the 1974 balance sheet seem to confirm this estimate; the published totals were 65.8 billion. However, as early as 1978 the declared expenditure had nearly doubled – to about 110 billion – and subsequently rose to 246 billion in 1984. This exponential rate of increase is explainable only in part by inflation and by the consequent depreciation of the currency.

The law, however, obliged the parties to publish only the balance sheets of their national apparatus, not those of their local branches. Local funds appear in the balance sheets only as an entry referring to the transfer of funds from the center to the periphery. Therefore, no reference is made in the published balance sheets to the income and expenditures which result from the self-financing activities of peripheral organizations and by supporting groups. The only source of information in this regard is an unofficial estimate made in 1977.[8] To get an overall picture of the cost of party activity in Italy, at least 60 to 80 billion lire, spent by the forty-two thousand party divisions throughout Italy, and about Lit 30 billion, spent by the provincial and regional federations, would have to be added to the Lit 95 million declared by the parties as total expenditure in 1977. This would bring the total figure to more than double that declared in the national balance sheets.[9]

Given the impossibility of checking these figures, this study will be limited to an examination of the revenue and expenditure items taken from the published national balance sheets. However, an investigation of even these figures is made difficult by the various parties' different approaches to their balance sheets. Although the regulations in force recommend the use of a standard format, each party has interpreted this format in their own way, arranging the single items according to criteria which are not always uniform and which often make comparison difficult.[10] In addition, the assets of the parties are not reflected in the balance sheets, which only register cash flow. Nor do the reports refer to the parties initial and final surpluses and deficits. Furthermore, party administrators are reluctant to disclose information that could be used to get a complete understanding of these financial documents, even in the reports accompanying the balance sheets. This attitude seems to be linked to the considerable interest the parties have in concealing at least some of their true financial activities.

Despite the above-mentioned factors and the caution required when examining documents that by and large elude quality control and are subject to possible distortion for political and electoral ends, it can nevertheless be claimed that the reticence and inaccuracy of each party is to some extent canceled out on balance. Consequently, examination of the published balance sheets always provides interesting and essential information for the study of the public financing of parties in Italy.

THE IMPORTANCE OF MEMBERSHIP DUES

The comparison begins with the information contained in the parties' balance sheets for the fiscal years 1974–84, inclusive, from the revenue side.[11] It emerges clearly from the data that membership dues vary over time as a percentage of total revenue for all parties. In addition, dues are seen to be a distinctly greater factor in the Communist and Socialist parties. For the Communist Party (PCI), membership dues – which also include the sum that each Communist Parliament Minister is required to contribute to the party – accounted for 27.2 percent of declared income in 1974. This figure rose to 36.8 percent in 1978 and then remained between 30 and 35 percent between 1979 and 1984. In the PSI, the percentage of total income accounted for by membership dues remained fairly constant during the first few years after the introduction of the law, from 17.6 percent in 1974 to 18.5 percent in 1976, after which it rose sharply to 23.5 percent in 1977 and to 31.5 percent in 1980, and then to 40.6 percent in 1984. This dramatic rise was likely the result of the reorganization efforts of the Craxi leadership. The percentage of yearly membership dues for the DC is lower than for the Communists and Socialists, dropping from 13 percent in 1974 to 8.2 percent in 1977, then rising to 27 percent in 1981 and again decreasing to 6 percent in 1984. The percentage of the membership dues in the smaller "pentapartite" parties is fairly low: the PSDI rose from 9.7 percent in 1974 to 4.4 percent in 1979 and 6.5 percent in 1984; the PRI increased from 0.1 percent to 1974 to 5.8 percent in 1978, leveling out at around 5 percent (4.8 percent in 1984); the Liberal Party (PLI) rose from 2.1 percent in 1974 to 4.3 percent in 1977 and 9.2 percent in 1978, thereafter fluctuating between 5 and 10 percent (7.5 percent in 1981 and 11.1 percent in 1984).

There are considerable variations in the membership percentage for the smaller opposition parties; the Radical Party (PR) dropped from 5.5 percent in 1976 to 1.8 percent in 1977, rising to 5.5 percent in 1980 and to 12 percent in 1984; the figures for the Party of Proletarian Unity for Communism (PDUP) are 17.4 percent in 1976, decreasing to 2.9 percent in 1977 and again rising to 7 percent in 1981; the percentage for Proletarian Democracy (DP) was 1.7 percent in 1984. The percentage for the Italian Social Movement-National Right (MSI-DN) declined from 3.6 percent in 1974 to 0.2 percent in 1977 – corresponding to the breakaway of the "National Democracy" splinter group – and later rising to 9.5 percent in 1980 and 8.3 percent in 1984.

From a general examination of the Italian parties' published balance sheets, membership dues appear to be a very small percentage of total party income. Such income is usually less than the 20 percent of annual expenditures (excluding electoral costs) estimated by Heidenheimer in 1963 for the leading Western European parties.[12] The tendency found in the more recent Italian balance sheets for this item to increase can be interpreted in two ways, either as a means of concealing other sources of income, since this is the least controllable form of all (there is no independent count of party membership), or else as an effective sign of increased popular participation in active political life, which would certainly be positive from the democratic point of view.

THE ROLE OF PUBLIC FINANCING

By far the largest item currently recorded in the balance sheets of all the parties is the government subsidy. But there are significant differences among the party reports in this regard. The balance sheets show that for some parties public financing is only a part, however large, of their mainly independent revenue, while for other parties it is their only important source of income. Included among the former group are the PCI and the PSI. Public financing accounted for 45 percent of the total declared income of the PCI in 1974, 27.9 percent in 1978 and 38 percent in 1981, and barely 23.6 percent in 1984.[13] Government subsidies provided 58.2 percent of PSI income in 1974, 32 percent in 1978, 59 percent in 1981, and 36.5 percent in

1984. The PCI and the PSI were the only two parties to consistently declare that public funding amounted to less than half their income. The balance sheet of the DC however, has moved perceptibly in this direction. In 1974 public financing accounted for 75.7 percent of total income, decreasing in the years that followed until it reached 50.1 percent in 1978, leveling out at around 60 percent (58.5 percent in 1984). If the percentage of public funds used to cover the overall declared expenditure is taken into account, the figure decreases to 47 percent in 1984. But the PCI, PSI, and DC are the exceptions to the rule. Public financing represents virtually the sole or predominant source of income in the balance sheets published by other parties. The highest percentage of total income from the government sources is recorded in the PRI balance sheet: 96.7 percent in 1975, 84.7 percent in 1979, and 8.26 percent in 1984. In fact, in a number of fiscal years, public financing exceeded the total expenditures declared by this party: 196.6 percent in 1974, 120.6 percent in 1980, 154.4 percent in 1981, 109.1 percent in 1982; in 1984 public financing accounted for 75.6 percent of declared expenditure. Public funding also accounts for an extremely high percentage of overall revenue for Proletarian Democracy; in 1984 such income was 86.4 percent of the parties' total income, and was used by the party to cover 79.9 percent of its expenditures.

In the case of the MSI-National Right, public financing accounted for 80 percent of income in 1974, 92.6 percent in 1976, 70.8 percent in 1977, and 83.5 percent in 1984. There was a surplus of public funding over total expenditures in 1981, with the contribution amounting to 114.5 percent of declared expenditures. For the PLI, public financing represented 88 percent of its income in 1974, 72.2 percent in 1978, 88.9 percent in 1981, and 70.3 percent in 1984. Income was in excess of expenditures in 1974 (146.5 percent) and in 1981 (112.6 percent); in 1984 public financing covered 65.6 percent of declared expenditures. In the balance sheets of the PSDI, public financing accounted for 74 percent of income in 1974, 66.3 percent in 1975, 83.5 percent in 1978, 63.8 percent in 1984; it covered 98.3 percent of expenditures in 1981 and lesser amounts in the other years (54.1 percent in 1984). Public financing accounted for 61.8 percent of the Radical Party' income in 1976, 93.5 percent in 1981, and 64.3 percent in 1984. A surplus over expenditures occurred in 1977 (101.7 percent) and 1981 (128.8 percent); in 1984 public financing covered 48.8 percent of declared expenditures.

Despite their heterogeneity, the overall party income data suggest a number of observations. First, the "moral enhancement effect" of replacing questionable sources of party revenue with public financing does not appear to work. The purpose of public financing of parties was to prevent parties from recourse to unlawful or "unmentionable sources," in order to improve the moral dimension of public life. But public subsidies account for half, or sometimes less than half, of total party revenue. Though the balance sheets show public financing as almost completely replacing previous forms of funding for the smaller parties, it does not seem likely that they would have suddenly foregone contribution sources which covered a large proportion of their expenses before 1974. The true facts may differ from those contained in the balance sheets. It can generally be assumed that the parties' expenditures were actually much higher than they admitted and that questionable or illegal sources of income are still a factor in the financing of Italian parties. In addition, it can be concluded that public funding can sometimes act as an inducement for parties to increase their overall expenditure levels, as evidenced by those smaller parties for which public funding exceeded actual expenditures in certain fiscal years.

OTHER SOURCES OF INCOME

The figures declared by the parties under the other income headings in the standard balance sheets are extremely diverse. The same items are found under different headings in different balance sheets and revenue is often quite generically recorded as income from unspecified "other sources." In many balance sheets no entries at all appear under certain headings or the revenue registered there is astonishingly small. In some instances, the reported figures stretch the limits of the observer's credulity. Though it appears as such on the balance sheets, in fact, it is quite unlikely that the economic life of any existing party can take place outside the modern financial system, and that it is unrealistic to believe that a party does not have any dealings with banks or other credit institutions, or that it receives no profits or interest on investment. Nor does it seem likely that income from industrial and commercial activities associated with the parties and carried on in the form of cooperative enterprises (mostly in the cases of the PCI and the DC), or from shareholdings in real estate operations or mediation in trade relations with foreign countries (an important source of income for the PCI in particular) is truly reflected by the low figures appearing in the balance sheets.

Only a few interesting figures can thus be abstracted from a comparison of the income headings in the published balance sheets. These figures include the greater proportion in the Christian Democrat's balance sheet of contributions from members which are greater than their dues, and contributions from non-members and popular collections, which accounted for a total of 33.5 percent of party income in 1984; the financial significance of functions like the "Festival of Unita," which contributed 29.9 percent of the PCI's income in 1984; and the suspiciously small sums declared from interest on financial investments or bank deposits – only in the 1984 balance sheet of the PRI did this item rise to a significant level, 6.2 percent of the total, while the figures for the DC and the PCI are 1.8 percent and 0.04 percent respectively. With regard to external contributions from agencies, associations or private individuals, in 1974, during the first year of application of the law on public financing, only the PSDI (Lit 364 million), the MSI (Lit 275 million) and the PLI (Lit 174 million) admitted receiving such contributions. In the years that followed, the figures declared under this heading decreased progressively until they became practically negligible in the balance sheets of all parties. In 1984 one exception was the Radical Party, which declared Lit 855 million; the DC declared Lit 110 million, the PLI Lit 70 million, the MSI Lit 30 million, the PRI Lit 19 million, the PSDI Lit 2 million, and the others nothing at all.

The unreliability of the balance sheets becomes quite apparent, especially in the light of the numerous cases of evidence produced in court of contributions and "kickbacks" made to parties. In any case, it is hard to deny that the advent of public financing in no way miraculously closed off the sources of funds which has been opened up and painstakingly extended in the years prior to 1974, and from which many parties at the time drew almost all the funds required for their activities.

CENTRAL APPARATUSES AND PERIPHERAL APPARATUSES

An analysis of the cost headings in the party balance sheets is of some interest, even though it is hindered by the lack of homogeniety of the available information. For instance, contributions to parliamentary groups and to the various internal sub-divisions of the parties were entered under different cost headings in the balance sheets before they were grouped together under a single heading in the new standard balance sheet approved in 1982. As late as 1984, the cost of national congresses was still being entered by the DC and the PCI under the headings "Expenditure on Publishing Activities for the Purpose of Information and Electoral Propaganda," by the PSI, PSDI and Radical Party under the heading "Expenditure on Miscellaneous Activities," and by the MSI-National Right under the heading of "Extraordinary Expenditures."

Despite these difficulties, it is possible to gain some insight into the financial actiyities of the parties from a more detailed breakdown of the data. Under the heading, "Allocation of Contributions," it is interesting to note the item which refers to the cost of contributions to local branches and organizations. The largest sums spent for this purpose are recorded in the balance sheets of the PCI; in 1978 it was actually 64.4 percent of total expenditure, with an absolute figure that alone almost equaled the entire budget of the DC. The same year, the DC financed 34.9 percent of the total expenditures of its local organizations. These trends have remained constant with time; in 1984 the sums transferred for this purpose amounted to 54.1 percent of total expenditure for the PCI (more than Lit 58 billion), and 9.7 percent for the DC (just over Lit 6 billion). These figures reflect two distinct political tendencies of the two largest parties, which have peripheral apparatuses' of roughly equivalent size. The PCI supports the activities of its peripheral organizations from the center according to their relative strength and influence; this support takes the form of a share of income from membership dues and press subscriptions, as well as of grants proportional to the number of votes obtained in their area of activity.[14] The DC has tended to accord financial autonomy to the various provincial committees, progressively freeing the central party apparatus from these costs.[15] It should also be noted in this connection that the Christian Democratic provincial organizations are also the centers of the "currents" (factions), which are particularly active in this party. There is no trace in the official balance sheets of the huge sums used to finance this phenomenon, and so it is impossible to ascertain the source of the funds used by the "currents" for their operations, how much they cost and who subsidized them.

In the cases of the other parties, the contribution to the peripheral organizations in the 1984 balance sheet ranges from 31.2 percent of total expenditure in the case of the PRI, 26.6 percent for the PSI and DP and 23.1 percent for the PRI, to 18.7 percent for the PSDI and 9.9 percent for the MSI-National Right. The Radical Party declared no expenditures for this purpose. The apportionment of funds between the central apparatus and the peripheral organizations remains an unsolved problem. Since it has been left to the parties' discretion by the law on public financing, this problem is likely to lead to a heavier concentration of power inside the national executives, thus increasing those forms of oligarchic bureaucratization that have been reported and lamented in several quarters.[16]

PAYROLL COSTS

The data gleaned from the payroll headings of the balance sheets are comparatively homogeneous. These data can be considered more reliable than the others since they can be verified by checking tax and social security payments. An interesting comparison can be made between the two major parties – the DC and the PCI – which are also those with the largest central bureaucracies. The Christian Democrat's payroll accounted for 14.8 percent of its declared expenditures in 1974, 22.2 percent in 1981 and 27.8 percent in 1984. The percentages for the PCI are much lower: 5.2 percent in 1974, 4.5 percent in 1975, 5.8 percent in 1980 and 5.5 percent in 1984. This large difference is not, however, indicative of a greater bureaucratization of the central apparatus of the DC compared with the PCI. The salaries of the Christian Democratic employees are linked to the comparatively high remuneration received by employees of the municipal utility companies; the salaries of Communist Party personnel, on the other hand, are traditionally linked to those of the metalworking and engineering trades, and there is a considerable amount of voluntary work done. In the Socialist Party payroll, costs as a percentage of total expenditure fluctuated between 12.4 percent (1974), 10.4 percent (1980), 19 percent (1981), and 15.3 percent (1984). The percentage is higher for the Social Democrats, rising from 12.7 percent in 1975 to 36 percent in 1978, returning to 15.3 percent in 1979 and again rising to 29.6 percent in 1984. For the MSI-National Right, which has an equivalent organizational apparatus, the figures are 5.9 percent in 1975, 19.3 percent in 1978, 10 percent in 1979 and 9.3 percent in 1984. Cutbacks in the size of the central apparatus of the Republican and Liberal parties recently led to a decrease in payroll costs, which nevertheless still remain comparatively high: for the PRI, 19.6 percent in 1984 (compared with 9.9 percent in 1974 and 26.9 percent in 1980) and 21.6 percent for the PLI (compared with 19 percent in 1974 and 26.6 percent in 1977). Other parties, such as the Radicals and Proletarian Democracy, record much lower expenditures for payroll (0.3 percent and 5.8 percent, respectively, in 1984). However, these parties make extensive use of voluntary workers who occasionally receive small sums to defray their expenses.

GENERAL EXPENDITURES

Under the heading "General Expenses," come fairly diverse items, such as interest paid and bank charges, rents, taxes, and other leavies, maintenance and repair costs and "miscellaneous expenses." In the 1984 DC balance sheet, residual payments on loans were included under this heading; the PCI referred to the cost of running several study and labor organizations, contributions to elderly party members, and national and international "political initiatives"; that of the MSI-National Right included the cost of welfare, decorations, and party defense. The percentage of total expenditure accounted for by "General Expenses" differs considerably from party to party; in 1984, this category amounted to 7.2 percent for the DC, 15.8

percent for the PCI, 21.7 percent for the PSI, 28.3 percent for the MSI-National Right, 18.9 percent for the PSDI, 6.7 percent for the PRI, 9 percent for the radical party, 20.4 percent for the PLI, 20.8 percent for the PD. As mentioned above, however, this comparison is not particularly significant and receives no confirmation from the balance sheets preceding 1982, in which the model used was quite different and the items contained in it even more heterogeneous.

INFORMATION AND ELECTORAL PROPAGANDA

Expenditures recorded under the heading, "Expenditure for the Publishing of Information and Electoral Propaganda," consist largely of subsidies to offset the large deficits of the party organs. The sums involved are considerable, and are indicative of the crisis affecting the political party press in Italy. Generally speaking, the party press consists of expensive dailies with little influence on the public at large, normally running at a loss and which continue to be published for reasons of prestige and political representation. They receive continual subsidies from the parties. The amount spent by the DC to cover the deficits of the party's newspapers – the daily *Il Popolo*, and the weekly *La Discussione* – and for other publishing activities such as the Asca agency and the publishing house Cinque Lune totaled about 12 billion lire in 1984, or 19.3 percent of total expenditures. To this amount must be added Lit 7.8 billion for other propaganda and political information activities, including, as already mentioned, the cost of the 16th National Congress. Overall, this heading absorbed 32 percent of total party expenditures in 1984, compared with 30.9 percent in 1974, 35.5 percent in 1877 and 33.1 percent in 1981. In this sector, the PCI is no better off, even though its official organ, *L'Unita*, is a national daily with a wide circulation that can rely on a vast network of voluntary workers for its diffusion. In 1984, this daily cost the PCI nearly Lit 17 million, or 15.6 percent of its total expenditures, to which a further Lit 2 billion must be added to cover underwriting the share capital of L'Unita S.p.A. Taking into account the costs of the Weekly *Rinascita* and the other party magazines, those for cultural, information and propaganda activities, the total for this area of expenditure comes to 22.3 billion lire, or 20.5 percent of total expenditures, compared with 17.1 percent in 1974, 21.2 percent in 1977 and 23.7 percent in 1981.

The contribution made by the Socialist Party to its official daily, *Avanti!*, in 1984 was Lit 4.4 billion or 12.9 percent of total expenditures. Adding the costs of the magazines, *Mondo Operaio* and *Almanacco socialista*, and for cultural, information and propaganda activities, the total expenditure in this category comes to Lit 6.6 billion or 19.6 percent of the total. In the past, expenditures under this heading had fluctuated widely as a result of the repeated reviewing of PSI publishing policy – 28.5 percent in 1974, 33.2 percent in 1977, 23.4 percent in 1978, 10.7 percent in 1979, and 25.5 percent in 1980.

A considerable amount is spent on publishing also by the MSI, mainly to support its official daily, *Il Secolo d'Italia*. Those subsidies reached 27.7 percent of total expenditures in 1984. In this case also, there had been considerable fluctuations under this heading in the past: 32.1 percent in 1974, 16.8 percent in 1976, 38.7 percent in 1977 and 24.6 percent in 1980. The Radical Party has followed a consistent policy in this field. It has devoted the bulk of its expenditures to its publishing, information and propaganda activities, especially to support its radio and television stations; this category accounted for 84.6 percent of total party expenditures in 1977, 46.4 percent in 1978, 82 percent in 1980, and 61.7 percent in 1984. A considerable sum was spent on publicity by the Republican Party, which publishes the official daily, *La Voce repubblicana*; it spent 20 percent of its total expenditures in this way in 1974, 21.8 percent in 1978, barely 3.2 percent in 1979 and 5.8 percent in 1980 – due to suspension of publications of the party's daily – 16.2 percent in 1981 and 30 percent in 1984. Publicity expenses for the PSDI and PRI are traditionally very small. The PCI does not have an official party daily, and *L'Umanita*, the official daily of the PSDI has only a small circulation. In 1984 the PSDI spent 11 of its total expenditures for publicity as against 8.4 percent in 1974, 11.3 percent in 1977, 7.9 percent in 1978, and 13.1 percent in 1981; the PLI spent 9 percent in 1984, as against 7 percent in 1974, 2.8 percent in 1975, 9.5 percent in 1978, and 8.3 percent in 1981.

ELECTORAL EXPENDITURES

The cost heading, "Electoral Expenditures," is by its very nature subject to large fluctuations from year to year according to the number of elections held. Generally speaking, the balance sheet data confirm that electoral costs are proportionately higher for the smaller parties. In the absence of any permanent organizational structure, smaller parties have to make a greater effort before the election to reach larger numbers of voters. As a significant example, in the year 1979, the year of the general election, the DC declared having devoted 6.4 percent of its overall expenditure to elections, and the PCI declared 5.4 percent. Other parties spent a much higher proportion of their overall expenditure during the electoral campaign: 16.5 percent for the PRI, 24.2 percent for the PLI, 25.1 percent for the PSI, 32.1 percent for the PSDI, 34.1 percent for the MSI-National Right and as much as 43 percent for the Radical Party. It must be added that the cost of electoral campaigns are not borne solely by the parties, but also by the candidates, by means of personal payments and contributions collected by supporters and other groups. These sums do not appear in the balance sheets and cannot therefore be quantified exactly. Also, there are the costs of referendum campaigns, for which the law makes no political contribution. For the electoral campaigns, the public subsidy paid as a "reimbursement of electoral expenditure" seems on average to be greater than declared expenditures in the case of the larger parties and smaller for the others. In 1979, the DC received reimbursements of 3.9 billion lire, as against a declared outlay of Lit 3.2 billion. The PSI, in contrast declared a deficit – 1.2 billion lire received, against Lit 1.9 billion declared expenditures. The other parties had even higher deficits: the PDSI received Lit 598 million and declared expenditures of Lit 1.5 billion; the Radicals received Lit 495 million and spent Lit 1.5 billion; the PLI received Lit 413 million and spent Lit 765 million. Of the smaller parties, the PRI was the exception, receiving 539 million lire and declaring expenditures of Lit 425 million.

THE DEFICIT

With reference to the overall equilibrium of the balance sheets, the published figures show that all parties have had a substantial deficit in most fiscal years. In the case of the Christian Democrat's deficit, already as high as 362 million lire in 1974, rose to Lit 8.2 billion in 1982 and to Lit 11.6 billion in 1984. A positive balance was recorded only in 1980 (Lit 56 million) and in 1983 (Lit 670 million). The Communist Party went from a deficit of Lit 237 million in 1975 to a deficit of Lit 5.6 billion in 1982, dropping to Lit 3.6 billion in 1983; in 1984, for the first time, this party's balance sheet recorded a positive balance of Lit 90 million. The deficit of the Socialists fluctuated between Lit 173 million in 1974 and Lit 2.2 billion in 1984; a positive balance was achieved in 1975 (Lit 12 million) and in 1981 (Lit 300 million). The Italian Social Movement had a positive balance of Lit 1.4 billion in 1974, but the very next year declared a deficit of Lit 1.1 billion, which rose to Lit 1.7 billion in 1979, dropping to Lit 49 million in 1984; a positive balance was again achieved in 1977 (Lit 108 million) and in 1981 (Lit 1.7 billion). The Social Democrats went from a deficit of Lit 647 million in 1975 to a deficit of Lit 1.1 billion in 1979 and Lit 1.4 billion in 1984; it had a positive balance only in 1981 (Lit 933 million). The Republican Party was more frequently in the black. Starting with a positive balance of Lit 1.2 billion it dropped to a deficit of Lit 1.1 billion the subsequent year, returning to the black in 1979 and 1982, reaching a peak positive balance of Lit 2.5 billion in 1981; it was again in the red in 1983 for Lit 2.7 billion. The Radical Party published a positive balance from 1976 to 1978 and again in 1981 (Lit 1.4 billion); it ran a deficit in the other fiscal years, with a maximum debit of Lit 1.7 billion in 1979, probably as a result of heavy spending during the electoral campaign. The Liberal Party balance sheet was in the black in 1974, with a surplus of Lit 1.2 billion, and again in 1980 and in 1981; it showed a deficit in the other fiscal years, the largest in 1983 (Lit 2.5 billion).

CONCLUSION

The overall efficiency of the public financing system cannot be evaluated merely by taking into account the income and expenditure columns of the balance sheets. The parties do not pursue economic goals, the success of which is measurable in terms of profit; their aims are political in nature, and the results must be gauged in political terms.

In this sense, twelve years after its introduction, the following conclusions concerning the system adopted in Italy for the public financing of parties can be drawn. First, while generally adequate for covering the ordinary expenditures of the smaller parties, the system covers only a portion of the expenses of the larger parties. Secondly, the system as adopted does not seem to be particularly effective in discouraging the parties, both large and small, from using hidden or "unmentionable" sources of funds, since it seems to act as an inducement for increased overall spending by the parties rather than as an incentive to eliminate questionable sources of contributions.[17] Thirdly, the existing system prevents any effective internal or external check being made on how the public funds made available are actually used. A more effective system of checks could verify that public subventions are actually used to defray for the costs borne by the parties, and not for private persons' interests, or to favor a peculiar personage or candidate. This kind of checking would require the Auditors of Accounts to closely monitor the expenditure of the concerned funds, and impose sanctions to party administrators in the case of mendacious budgets. Fourthly, the system encourages concentration of power in the central executives of the parties who distribute the funds, to the disadvantage of the minority groups and peripheral organizations.[18] Supporters of public financing counter such observations by arguing that in complex modern democratic societies, the expenses incurred by parties in carrying out the functions assigned to them are, despite all legislative restrictions, so great that they cannot be covered merely by the voluntary contributions of their card-carrying members and supporters.

One solution worth investigating could be to replace cash grants wholly or partly with the provision of certain free services and in-kind donations to the parties, accompanied by a drastic reduction in certain types of expenditures, particularly electoral expenses. Such services and donations could include facilities for printing newspapers and posters, free periods of time on public radio and television, postal, phone, and transportation facilities, office space and supplies. In any case, the overhauling of the present system is still an open question in view of the rather dubious results it has achieved thus far.

Notes

1 The surreptitious and illicit agreements made between public officials, the companies or private persons are generally called, in the Italian political language, "Black contracts." These conventions, which are not reported in that budget of the concerned companies, produce, in practice, two possible outcomes:
> the public official receives benefits, in terms of a percentage on the total return of the business of the firm, which has the formal commitment to him (the so-called "kickbacks");
> the public official can gain, in terms of real money returns, the difference between the bank's rate, established via law, and the actual rate that the banks usually pay for the money on deposit of the public companies ("black interests").

2 Roberto Crespi, *Lo Stato deve pagare i pariti?*, Centro di ricerca e documentazione "Luigi Einaude," Sansoni, 1971.

3 Law No. 422, August 8, 1980; Law No. 659, November 18, 1981; Law No. 22, January 27, 1982; Law No. 441, July 5, 1982; Law No. 413, August 8, 1985.

4 These types of donations were forbidden by Law No. 195, May 2, 1974, and its following amendments (see Footnote 3).

5 For a critical analysis of this system of bans, see Giorgio Oppo, "Finanziamento die partiti e diritto privato," in *Scritti in onore di Salvatore Pugliatti.* (Milano: Giuffré, 1981) I., 2, pp. 1560 ff.

6 This survey is based on budgets up to and including 1984; the budget of the financial year 1984 is actually the latest published in the "Official Gazette" (special supplement No. 66 of March 20, 1986, general series).

7 Roberto Crespi, *Lo Stato deve pagare i pariti?*, Centro di ricerca e documentazione "Luigi Einaudi," Sansoni, 1971.

8 Ibid.

9 "Inchiesta: Nelle tasche dei partiti," *Il Mondo*, June 14, 1978.

10 See Art. 8 of Law No. 195, May 2, 1974, to which is attached the model for drafting the parties' budgets; Art. 4 of Law No. 659, December 18, 1981, according to which this model has to be approved by the President of the Chamber, in agreement with the President of the Senate; and the decree of the

170

President of the Chamber of July 28, 1982, to which is attached a new model for the drafting of the parties' budget.

11 Giorgio Pacifici, *Il costo della democrazia* (Rome: Cadmo, 1983); *Documentazione di base sulla disciplina dell'attività ed del finanziamento dei partiti politici*, a cyclostyled publication by the Study and Research Service of the Chamber of Deputies, September 1985.

12 Arnold J. Heidenheimer, "Comparative Party Finance: Notes on Practices and Toward a Theory," in *Journal of Politics*, August 1963, Vol. 25, No. 3, p. 793.

13 Interpreting the data for 1981, rather anomalous for all the parties concerned, one must consider that in that same year public financing of parties had a substantial revaluation, due to Law No. 659, of November 18, 1981.

14 Giorgio Frasca Polara, "I bilanci dei partiti," *L'Unita*, February 8, 1975.

15 Report accompanying the balance sheet of the DC for the financial year 1978, published in *Il Popolo*, June 19, 1978.

16 See, for instance, Ernesto Auci, "Verità e problemi nei bilanci dei partiti," *Il mondo economico*, n. 17, May 3, 1975.

17 According to the results of a survey published in *Il mondo* on December 1, 1986, 15.6 percent of the sample interviewed considered "all" parties to be unscrupulous in this respect; 15.4 percent regarded the DC as the main offender, followed by the PCI with 9 percent and the PSI with 6.5 percent. All the parties were accused by 17.3 percent of trying to procure "cutbacks" from the building industry; 24.9 percent launched this accusation mainly against the DC, 6.2 percent against the PCI and 3.3 percent against the PSI. The data published in the article cited indicate that between August 1, 1983 and November 20, 1986, some 800 Christian Democrat, Socialist and Communist public administrators were implicated in legal proceedings concerning corruption (368 DC, 284 PSI, 149 PCI).

18 For a general criticism of this system, see Salvatore Valitutti and Gian Franco Ciaurro, *Control il finanziamento publico dei partiti* (Rome; Bulzoni, 1975).

8

Financing of Spanish political parties

PILAR DEL CASTILLO

On November 20, 1975, General Francisco Franco died after having ruled under an authoritarian system for almost forty years. On May 15, 1977, a little less than two years later, the first democratic elections in Spain since 1936 took place. Three months before these elections, the government of President Adolfo Suarez approved a Decree-Law,[1] the objective of which was to set the electoral process down in law. This law also regulated the electoral expenditures and revenues of the political parties and established state subsidies to help pay electoral expenses. The public financing of party expenses incurred in local elections was approved in July, 1978. The Spanish Constitution of 1978 sanctioned a national territorial organization on a regional basis. There are a total of seventeen regions, or Comunidades Autónomas.[2] Each of them has its own political institutions and a certain degree of political and administrative autonomy, the limits of which are set by the Constitution itself and by the Statutes of each Community. The elections for the regional parliaments also receive public financing. The first elections, conducted in the Basque Country and Catalonia, took place in 1980. Normal party activities also are publicly financed. Annual subsidies to parties were established by the Political Parties Law of 1978.[3]

In other words, the Spanish political parties receive, on one hand, state support for electoral expenses on the local, regional and national levels and, on the other hand, public revenues to finance their ordinary activities. This paper will review the different modalities of public financing of political parties, other aspects of the Spanish legislation concerning this matter (prohibition of contributions, disclosure, etc.) and, last of all, the importance and impact the state subsidies are having with regard to party financing.[4]

THE ELECTORAL LAW AND THE PARTY SYSTEM

In 1976 the Cortes (Parliament) still remaining from the Franco regime approved the Law for Political Reform. This norm established the dissolution of the political institutions of the regime and the election, by universal suffrage, of a Constitution-drafting Cortes composed of two chambers: the Congress of Deputies and the Senate. This bicameral system was later sanctioned in the Constitution of 1978. Both chambers are elected by universal suffrage every four years. For the election to the Cortes, the government elaborated in 1977 the above-mentioned Decree-Law in which it was determined that election to the Congress of Deputies would be based on a system of proportional representation, of a simple party-list ballot, conferring the seats corresponding to each party by means of the d'Hondt highest average.[5] The Senate, in turn, would be elected by an adjusted plurality system; each voter casts his or her ballot for three candidates, and the four candidates who receive a plurality of all the votes cast are elected. In June 1985, the Cortes approved a new law which maintains an identical electoral system.

As noted above, the Congress is elected by a proportional system and its seats are assigned according to the d'Hondt formula. The proportionality which results from the application of this system is strongly adjusted given the small size of many of the electoral districts; of a total of fifty-two constituencies, thirty elect seven or fewer deputies (with a minimum of three). On the other hand, it is necessary to obtain at least 3 percent of the vote in an electoral district to be able to participate in the distribution of the corresponding seats. As a result, the Spanish electoral system favors large political formations on a national scale. This encourages the development of electoral coalitions, and parties whose political power is concentrated in one region. As can be seen from the data presented in Table 1, the elections of 1977 configured a multi-party system with two dominant national political formations, the Democratic Center Union (UCD) and the Spanish Worker Socialist Party (PSOE). Two minor parties, also national in character, are situated at opposite ends of the political spectrum: on the left, the Spanish Communist Party (PCE), and on the right, Alianza Popular (AP). Two regional parties, Convergencia I Unio (CiU, Catalonian Nacionalists) and the Basque Nationalist Party (PNV), have received a great degree of popular support in their respective regions, and have obtained significant representation in the Congress of Deputies.

The general elections of 1979, conducted once the new Spanish Constitution was approved by referendum, had similar results to those of

Table 1. Elections for the congress of deputies in Spain in 1977, 1979, 1982, and 1986

Political parties	Votes (in percent)				Elected members			
	1977	1979	1982	1986	1977	1979	1982	1986
Democratic Center Union (UCD)	34.6	35.0	6.3	—	165	168	11	—
Spanish Socialist Workers Party (PSOE)	29.2	30.4	48.4	44.0	118	121	202	184
Spanish Communist Party (PCE)	8.9	10.6	4.0	—	20	23	4	—
Izquierda Unida (PCE + others)	—	—	—	4.6	—	—	—	7
Alianza Popular (AP)	8.3	5.8	26.5	26.1	16	9	106	105
Democratic Social Center (CDS)	—	—	2.9	9.3	—	—	2	19
Catalonian Nationalists (CiU)	2.7	1.8	1.9	1.5	11	8	12	18
Basque Nationalists Party (PNV)	1.6	1.8	1.9	1.5	8	7	8	6
Others*	14.7	13.7	6.3	9.5	12	14	4	11

* In 1977, some seats were attained by diverse regional parties and by the Popular Socialist Party which later joined the Spanish Socialist Workers Party. In 1979, some regional parties also obtained several deputies, notably, the Andaluzian Socialist Party with five deputies and the Herri Batasuna, Independent Basque Coalition, with three deputies. Of the seats under the heading "others" in 1982, three correspond to Basque political formations, one corresponds to leftist Catalonian Nationalists and two to Social Democratic Center (CDS).

1977. The party system which came out of these last elections, therefore, seemed to be consolidated. However, the general elections of 1982 demonstrated that, in the young Spanish democracy, the stability of the party system had not come close to being achieved. The change which took place in the composition of the party system has no comparable precedents in European electoral history. The most remarkable result of these elections was undoubtedly the vertiginous fall of the Democratic Center Union (the government party), which dropped from 159 members in the Congress after the 1979 elections to only twelve. The percentage of UCD votes fell from 35 percent in 1979 to 6.3 percent in 1982. For the Communist Party, the percent of votes fell from 10.6 percent in 1979 to 4.0 in 1982, from electing twenty-three deputies to electing four deputies. In contrast, the rightist Alianza Popular, in coalition with the small Christian Democratic Party, PDP, helped elect 106 deputies, up from nine in 1979, and 26.5 percent of votes, an increase from its 5.8 percent showing in 1979. The Spanish Socialist Workers Party came out the big winner, receiving 48.4 percent of the votes and 202 seats, which gave it the absolute majority. Only the Catalonian and Basque Nationalists obtained similar results as they had in the two previous general elections, thereby representing the only element of continuity with the party system which resulted from the general elections of 1977 and which was replicated in those of 1979.

It is not the objective of this paper to analyze the underlying causes which have determined the evolution of the Spanish party system. If we have pointed out its essential characteristics, through the electoral results from 1977 to 1982, it is, on the one hand, to place the analysis of party financing in context and, on the other, to give evidence to the difficulties posed by a systematic analysis of the principal Spanish parties. In a period of only six years, parties such as the Center Democratic Union, winner in 1977 and 1979, have been born and have disappeared. Others, such as the Communist Party, have seen a significant parliamentary presence reduced to a minimum. In turn, the organization of the Spanish Communists, the most powerful party from an organizational stand-point in 1977, is now on the brink of disintegration. At the opposite end of the political spectrum, the rightist organization, Alianza Popular, which constituted the second most powerful political organization after the 1982 elections, is presently the strongest party in terms of membership. These rapid changes in the party structure pose obstacles for the study of party financing. For example, most parties have had great difficulties in developing a regular financing program. These difficulties are further aggravated by the absence, as we shall see, of an effective system of legal control and by the failure of the parties to disclose their financial accounts. However, this reality does not completely impede an analysis of the financing of political parties in Spain; there exists sparse, yet significant, material upon which an analysis can be based.

FINANCING OF ELECTIONS: LEGAL RULES

General elections

The legal norms which regulated the general elections of 1977, 1979 and 1982 were approved by the government in March 1977. Initially provisional in character, these norms were exclusively intended for the elections of 1977. Once the Constitution was approved in 1978, the government was expected to send the Parliament a bill for electoral law which would result in definitive legislation. This bill, however, was not sent until October 1984. It was passed by the Parliament in June 1985,[6] and was applied for the first time in the general elections of June 1986. The public financing of elections, the prohibition of certain types of contributions and some disclosure requirements regarding electoral finances of the parties were the three most important legal issues with respect to the financing of electoral campaigns. As for prior normative dispositions regulating campaign finances, it should be pointed out that, during the period in which they were in effect, there was practically no opposition to them nor criticism of them by any of the political parties. The 1985 electoral law only slightly modified these provisions of the earlier law.

Financing of elections

The law of 1977 provided state subsidies to political parties for expenses incurred in electoral activities. To have a right to these subsidies, the parties had to obtain at least one parliamentary seat (in the Congress or the Senate). A determined amount of money (15 pesetas in the case of Congress and 45 pesetas for the Senate) was conceded to each parliamentary party for each vote gained in the electoral districts in which the party had obtained at least one seat. In other words, monetary compensation would be allowed only for those votes obtained in the electoral districts where the party won parliamentary representatives, and not for all the votes obtained nationally by that party. By the same token, the parties would receive a sum for each seat won in each of the two Chambers (a million pesetas in each case). The amounts provided for each vote and each seat were the same in the general elections of 1977, 1979 and 1982.

The first and obvious consequence of the law is that the extra-parliamentary parties became marginalized. Although the electoral im-

Table 2. *Official general election subsidies for 1982**

	Spanish Socialist Workers Party (PSOE)[a]	Coalicion Popular (Alianza Popular + Christian Democrats) (PDP)	Democratic Center Union (UCD)	Spanish Communist Party (PCE)[b]
Congress seats	177	105	11	3
Senate seats	125	54	4	—
Congress votes	8,551,791 (8,551,791)	5,403,959 (5,403,959)	512,310 (1,549,447)	247,748 (693,664)
Senate votes	22,479,027	5,301,558	16,965	—
Subsidies for seats	320,000,000	159,000,000	15,000,000	3,000,000
Subsidies for votes	722,016,000	322,701,525	23,308,425	11,148,660
Total subsidies	1,042,016,000	481,701,525	38,308,425	14,148,660

* In parentheses are the total national votes obtained by the parties.
[a] The subsidies obtained by the Catalan branch of the Socialist Party – PSC-PSOE – were 164,818,765 pesetas and are not included.
[b] The subsidies obtained by the Catalan branch of the Communist party – PSUC – were 6,909,130 pesetas and are not included.
Source: "Financiación de los partidos publicos," *Documentacion,* No. 32, Congreso de los Diputados, 1984, p. 259.

portance of these parties in Spain is quite minimal, a party of national scope could theoretically obtain almost 3 percent of the total vote in the elections for the Congress of Deputies, a percentage not to be slighted especially for a new party, and not received the benefit of state subsidies. This would occur since the parties need to win at least 3 percent of the votes in an electoral district in order to participate in the distribution of seats. Compared with the system of public financing of elections in the other European democracies (West Germany, Austria, Italy and Sweden), the Spanish system is one of the most discriminatory in regard to extra-parliamentary parties. Nevertheless, unlike what occurs in other democratic contexts, the Spanish extra-parliamentary parties have not judicially protested the possible violation of equal opportunity due to the application of this system of electoral financing.[7]

The law has negative consequences for the minor parliamentary parties as well. As noted above, the electoral system for the Congress of Deputies produces a highly skewed proportional assignment of seats in numerous districts, granting bonus seats to the parties which obtain the greatest number of votes. Since part of the subsidies are distributed based on the number of seats won, the majority parties also benefit from this provision. For example, in the 1979 general elections the winning party, Center Democratic Union, obtained 35 percent of the votes for the Congress of Deputies, which meant 48 percent of the seats. Also, the second party, the Socialist Workers Party, benefited while groups such as the Communist Party and the Alianza Popular were penalized. The latter group, for example, obtained 5.8 percent of the votes and, as a result, gained only approximately 2.5 percent of the seats (See Table 1). Despite the disfavor which the system of distribution of subsidies implies for the minority parties, they have not yet protested. As in the case of the extra-parliamentary parties, disfavored parliamentary parties did not criticize the system of electoral financing during the entire time that the 1977 norm was in effect. Although all the parties approve of public financing of elections, the majority of the Spanish electorate opposes electoral subsidies. In a 1984 opinion poll, carried out by the Centro de Investigaciones Sociologicas (the Spanish Sociological Research Center), 56 percent of those surveyed were against state subsidies for the parties' electoral expenditures.[8]

The electoral law approved in June 1985 maintains a system of distribution of subsidies which is identical to that of the 1977 law. The only modifications made refer to an increase in the amount of money corresponding to votes and seats (60 pesetas per Congressional vote, 20 pesetas per Senatorial vote and one and one-half million pesetas per seat).

Also the law establishes that these amounts will be periodically adjusted for inflation. Moreover, the new law creates the possibility that one month before the elections, the parties may obtain an advance of the subsidies to which they would be entitled once the elections are held. These advance funds cannot be greater than 30 percent of the amount which the soliciting party would have obtained in the previous elections.

The 1985 action was the first time the Parliament took up the issue of public financing of electoral campaigns – the law in effect since 1977 was a governmental decree, and not subject to parliamentary debate. Nevertheless, there was hardly any debate. The parliamentary groups were almost in unanimous agreement with the system of electoral financing set down in the bill designed by the government. Further, most of the groups ostensibly discriminated against by the criteria for distribution of the subsidies also failed to present amendments to the proposed system. Only one amendment was presented in this regard by a small group, the Social Democratic Center, which had only two deputies. The proposal was that the parties which obtained parliamentary representation would be subsidized for all votes received on a national level and not just those gained in the electoral districts where they won representatives. The amendment was voted down. It can, therefore, be asserted that, in spite of the unfavorable consequences that the Spanish system of public financing of elections has for some parties, there was a nearly complete consensus of all the parliamentary parties regarding the system.

Prohibition of contributions

The 1977 electoral laws prohibited two types of contributions: those coming from the Public Administration and those of foreign origin.[9] The first meant that the parties could not receive donations from the State Administration, local entities, autonomous organisms, parastate entities, and enterprises of national, provincial, municipal or mixed economic character. This measure can be linked to the concrete circumstances of the first general elections. It set strict prohibitions against a possible option of government financing from administration funds (the Central Democratic Union, a party created by the government, was not yet formed). Thus the rules were set down in order to avoid a circumstance in which a party or coalition supported by the government would be suspected of using public funds.

The second limitation dealt with all foreign donations, regardless of who the donor might be. In the three above-mentioned general elections, the media, particularly the press, focused attention on presumed monetary assistance for Spanish political parties from foreign political organizations.

According to media sources, the Spanish Socialists received money for electoral purposes from Swedish Socialists, the Alianza Popular from the German Christian Democrats, and the Communist Party from the Soviet Communists. In all these cases, the parties affected denied having received such help. No public investigation of these matters was carried out. An investigation did take place, however, after a flare up in November 1984 of the so-called "Flick case." According to statements of a German Social Democrat deputy printed in a Spanish newspaper, the General Secretary of PSOE received money for its 1982 electoral campaign from SPD. These funds were contributed to SPD by the Flick Consortium. The inquiry ended in March 1985 after a Congressional Committee investigated the alleged events. The investigation concluded with the approval by Congress of the finding that there was a lack of proof that the accused party – or its Secretary General – had received contributions from the German Social Democrats. However, in the parliamentary debate in which this finding was approved, all the parliamentary groups of the opposition pointed out the significant collaboration which German foundations had been extending to various institutions whose ideology was similar to specific Spanish parties. Such assistance was only considered legitimate by the parties which had benefited from them. The other parties requested that the funding be legally prohibited.[10] Independent of its specific facts, the "Flick case" led to greater interest in the issue of party finance. Until then, the media, the parties themselves and even researchers had paid very little attention to this topic.

The 1985 electoral law maintained the aforementioned prohibitions of political donations. In addition, it set limitations on contributions made by individuals or other entities. In the general elections of 1986, the parties were not able to receive more than one million pesetas from the same person.

Expenditure limitations

While the electoral law of 1977 did not establish an upper limit on electoral expenditures, the 1985 electoral law did establish a maximum amount that the parties could spend on their electoral campaigns in each district where they presented candidates. This amount is calculated by multiplying the number of certified voters in the district by 40 pesetas. To this amount is added a sum of 20 million pesetas for each electoral district. Based on the electoral census of 1982, this means that a party which presents candidates in every district may spend a maximum of approximately 2,100,000,000 pesetas. This figure was updated for the 1986 general elections, since the law states that the spending limit must be adjusted for inflation. The cost of electoral campaigns for the large Spanish parties underwent exponential growth between 1977 and 1982. According to the data offered by the principal parties, the increase of expenditures between the first general elections and the 1982 elections was about 200 percent;[11] these figures, however, are much less than the amounts actually spent, as this analyst has verified. In comparative terms, the expenditures of Spanish political parties in election campaigns are notoriously higher than those of some parties in other democratic systems.[12] When the electoral law was discussed in Parliament, those who defended limitations on electoral expenditures (especially, the Socialist Party) pointed to the urgent necessity of reducing the ever-rising costs of electoral campaigns. As the author sees it, the ceiling which was established is still too high. For this reason, it will be difficult to get the parties to reduce spending, rationalize their campaigns and use their organizational resources to an optimum.

Disclosure

Under the 1977 electoral law, the parties were required to present an account of their expenditures and revenue before the Junta Electoral Central (the spanish election commission) after each general election. This responsibility fell upon the electoral representative of each party. In actual practice, these representatives have only given their formal approval to the reports and the work has been done by party administrators. The Junta Electoral Central (JEC) has the responsibility of verifying the accuracy of the accounts and of disclosing the results of its inspection. In practice, compliance with the disclosure law has been deficient. In the first place, the JEC lacked the organizational resources to function effectively. While it was responsible for the oversight of all aspects of the electoral process, it lacked an adequate budget and staff. In the second place, fines for non-compliance with the norms were so minimal that on numerous occasions the parties preferred to pay the small fines than to submit to the requirements of the law. Thirdly, the JEC itself did not comply with the disclosure requirements set by the law with regard to the inspection of electoral accounting. It merely publicized a report of the 1977 general elections about a year after they took place, and in this document mentioned only the total expenditures declared by the parties in the accounts they presented.[13] After the 1979 and 1982 general elections, not even a report such as the aforementioned was published. Further, the JEC has never allowed investigators or the media access to the financial accounts presented by the parties after each of the three elections. Since the first democratic elections took place, no meaningful documentation regarding electoral financing of the Spanish political parties has been available to the public. The data with which one has to work come mainly from the reports published by the parties for their conventions, from the date offered by leaders to the media at the beginning of electoral campaigns, or from information obtained by researchers in personal interviews with the parties' financial managers. The financing of political parties between 1977 and 1985 has lacked practically all legal control.

The new electoral law of 1985 has attempted to correct major deficiencies in the disclosure of party finances. The penalties for non-fulfillment of the law have been stiffened and control over the reports which the parties must present after the elections has been delegated to the Tribunal de Cuentas, an organ which is responsible for financial oversight of all the organs of the Public Administration. Finally, responsibility regarding electoral spending and revenue, and for the presentation of the corresponding reports, has been centralized. The law created the position of electoral administrator which has a greater domain and responsibility in this matter than that which the electoral representatives had under the 1977 electoral norm.

Further, the 1985 law requires that everyone who makes a donation of any amount disclose personal data. This provision has been one of the most disputed aspects of the debate in the Congress of Deputies regarding the law. The violation of the principle of secret balloting and the possible reduction of the number of contributors were the two basic arguments around which those against the identification of donors articulated their position. The parties which defended the measure (mainly the Socialist Party, the government party) argued from practicality: this measure would be the only way of implementing the prohibitions and limitations on contributions. The second argument used to defend the measure was based on the ideals inherent in the democratic system, namely that it would be in the public's interest to know the true nature of each party's financial backing.

Nevertheless, the new law does not clearly determine the extent of public access to the data presented by the parties in their reports. It will be necessary to wait for upcoming general elections to determine to what extent the new regulation represents an advance over the previous legislation.

Subsidies "in kind"

As in many other European countries, television is a public monopoly in Spain. Under the 1977 electoral norm, political parties received free television time slots for political messages during the electoral campaign. The criteria for the distribution of the slots was established in a 1977 governmental decree and was applied in the general election of that year as well as in those of 1979 and 1982. The assignment of time slots has been based on the following criteria: three ten-minute slots of national programing are allowed for parties which present candidates in twenty-five or more electoral districts; two ten-minute slots in regional programing for those which present candidates in less than twenty-five electoral districts. Finally, one national – and two regional – slots of ten minutes are allowed for those which present candidates in four or more districts, provided that the number of voters in these districts represents more than 25 percent of the national total. These television programs have been of fundamental importance for the parties' political campaigns because television has for many years been the main political information source of Spanish citizens. In addition to television, the parties were allowed time on public radio. This radio time was allotted with criteria similar to those for the television time.

The 1977 electoral laws established three other types of "in kind" subsidies. First, city councils were required to make free space for posters available to the parties as well as public meeting places for gatherings, with a maximum of two meetings per party. Secondly, a reduced postal rate was allowed for campaign mailings.

The 1985 electoral law maintains all the above-mentioned "in kind" subsidies. With regard to television, however, it is probable that its regulation will undergo some type of modification since a law regulating the development of private television in Spain, coexistent with public television, may be enacted.

Regional and local elections

The financing of regional and local electoral campaigns is governed by legal dispositions of basically the same content as those regulating general elections. Since 1977, local elections have been held in 1979 and 1983. Among the Comunidades Autonomas, or regions, some have had two elections and others, one. This difference in the number of elections among the regions is explained by the fact that not all achieved autonomy at the same time. The process of regional organization of the Spanish state, established by the 1978 Constitution, was initiated once the Constitution was approved and not concluded until 1983. That year, all the Comunidades Autonomas held elections to constitute their own legislative assemblies. Since these are elected every four years, those regions which held elections for the first time in 1980 or 1981, such as the Basque Country, Catalonia and Galicia, have already had occasion to hold two elections.

The distribution system of state subsidies which the parties receive for electoral expenses in regional and local arenas is identical to the system which applies to general elections. However, in regional and local elections the distribution of seats among parties becomes more proportional than in general elections since electoral districts are larger. As Douglas Rae has pointed out,[14] under the D'Hondt formula, the larger the number of deputies elected from each district, the more the representation of each party will be truly proportional. As a result, distribution of public subsidies for electoral expenses is more proportional and minor parliamentary parties are less disfavored than in the case of state subsidies for general elections. These subsidies are received by the central organization of the parties, which are very centralized. The local and regional organizations depend financially on a very high degree of national organization and the electoral campaigns have been financed almost exclusively by the party organization at that level. The national regulations regarding prohibition of contributions, disclosure of spending, and "in kind" revenues and subsidies apply also to local and regional election. The only variation, as may seem obvious, is in the territorial scope in which some of these laws are carried out. For example, the television and radio slots were only broadcast in the regional programs. With respect to the financing of these two types of elections, the 1985 electoral law introduces modifications similar to those discussed previously for general elections.

POLITICAL PARTIES LAW

Political parties were officially recognized in the Spanish Constitution of 1978. Following the model rejected by some European Constitutions which emerged after the Second World War (Italy and West Germany), the Spanish Constitution established that parties express political pluralism, work in the formation and manifestation of the will of the people and are basic instruments for political participation. The Political Parties Law of December 1978 was established to regulate the parties. Political parties are defined as those associations which are registered as such by the Ministry of the Interior in an open Registry for this purpose. The statutes by which the party will be governed must accompany the registration application. The law requires that the organization and functioning of the parties follow democratic principles. Further, suspension and dissolution of parties can only be decreed by judicial authority. A party also can be suspended or dissolved in the case that its organization or activities are contrary to democratic principles.

Furthermore, the law mandates that the state will finance the normal activities of the parties.[15] The amount of this subsidy is assigned annually in the General State Budget. The criteria for the distribution of these amounts are the same as those that apply to electoral subsidies. That is, the parliamentary parties receive an annual concession of a fixed amount for each seat obtained in each of the two chambers and a fixed sum for each vote obtained in the electoral districts where the party won representation. This criteria applies to each of the two chambers. In this case, however, the law does not determine the sum which corresponds to each vote and each seat, but rather the government determines an amount which it includes in the annual National Budget bill. A danger of this system is that the parliamentary parties, or as in the current situation, the government party alone if it has an absolute majority, could increase their public subsidy by whatever percentage desired. Until now, however, the annual increase has never been more than the increase in the consumer price index. Nevertheless, with this formula there exists the permanent risk that the parliamentary parties, even just one or a small number, may decide upon a very considerable increase in the budget item earmarked for subsidies. This could become more than a temptation for some political parties, and especially for those which, as we shall see, have not been capable of financing themselves and depend to a high degree – in some cases almost exclusively – on state funds.

Although the law which regulates the political parties is a law and therefore has been approved by the Parliament, unlike the case of the 1977 electoral law which was a governmental decree, the debate in Parliament on its content was practically non-existent. The political parties bill presented by the UCD government immediately had a consensus of all the parliamentary groups of the Congress of Deputies. For that reason, practically no discussion of the dispositions established in that bill was necessary. This unanimous agreement was a consequence of the political consensus among the parties which characterized political life in the new Spanish democracy in 1978, the year that the Constitution was approved. At that time all of the parties made an effort to arrive at an agreement regarding the content of the Constitutional Text. The parties also maintained this attitude in regard to other norms which were enacted at the same time as the Constitution, such as the Political Parties Law, and in regard to norms which were elaborated immediately after this last law was passed. However, the criteria for public financing of parties was briefly discussed in the Senate. One of the groups in this Chamber proposed making extensive subsidies to extra-parliamentary parties and assigning the subsidies on the sole basis of votes obtained. This amendment was defeated but it did produce brief consideration regarding the political consequences of using one or the other type of criteria. The proponents of the amendment argued that the criteria proposed in the bill could bring about a solidification of the party system since the proposed rule did not favor the development of new political formations. This was the only criticism in Parliament of the system of public financing regarding ordinary party activities (and by extension of electoral activities) as established by the Law.

Unlike the legislation regulating electoral financing, the Political Parties Law sets no limitations on either spending or revenues, nor does it impose upon the parties any obligation regarding their bookkeeping. This means that there is no prohibition of foreign donations between elections and that there is no legal control of the parties' ordinary expenditures and revenues. As a result of the Flick case, the government promised to send a bill to Parliament regarding party financing. On June 22, 1986, new general elections took place, in which the Socialist Workers Party received an absolute majority for the second time. On December 3, 1986, all parliamentary groups, with the exception of the Catalans (CiU) and Basques (PNV), signed and sent to the Parliament a new party finance bill.

THE PARTIES' MAIN SOURCE OF INCOME: THE ROLE OF PUBLIC SUBSIDIES

An important characteristic of the Spanish political parties is their extreme structural weakness. This organizational fragility has greatly hampered the development of one of the traditional sources of income for party organizations: membership dues. From the time they were legalized in 1977, the four main parties of national scope – UCD, AP, PSOE and PCE – have been able to affiliate only a very small number of voters (See Table 3). After the general election of 1979, self-denominated "parties of the masses" such as the Socialist and Communist parties had the lowest member/ general voters ratio of all their European fraternal parties. For PSOE the ratio was 0.6 and for PCE, 0.9 the same ratio for the center-right party, UCD, was 0.4 and for the rightist, AP, 0.3. No more favorable were the results of the member/party voters ratio: 1.8 for PSOE and 8.7, 1.1 and 4.7 for PCE, UCD and AP respectively. In this case, the Socialist and Communist organizations also present a lower member/party voters ratio than homologous European parties which obtain similar electoral results. In the 1982 general elections, both relations decreased even further for all the parties cited with the exception of Alianza Popular.

It is not the purpose of this chapter to study the causes which may explain the low membership level of political parties in Spain. But it can be pointed out that, among other factors, the political culture inherited from the previous regime was, as Montero[16] has explained, characterized by demobilization, depoliticization, apathy and anti-partisanship. Moreover,

Table 3. *Evolution of political affiliation in Spain, 1977–86*
Members

Parties	AP	UCD	PSOE	PCE
1977	—	10,000 (1)	51,552 (1)	201,740 (2)
1978	50,000 (3)	61,256 (1)	—	168,175 (1)
1979	—	70,000 (3)	101,082 (1)	—
1981	—	144,097 (1)	97,320 (5)	132,069 (6)
1982	85,000 (4)	—	119,101 (5)	—
1983	128,000 (4)	—	145,471 (5)	84,652 (6)
1984	160,000 (4)	—	153,076 (5)	—
1985	—	—	160,000 (8)	—
1986	202,000 (7)	—	—	—

Sources: (1) Jose Ramon Montero "Partidos y participación política algunas notas sobre afiliación política en la etapa inicial de la transición española," *Revista de Estudios Políticos*, n. 23, 1981, pp. 38–9.
(2) *Noveno Congreso del Partido Comunista de Espana. Informes, debates, actas y documentos*, Madrid, Ediciones PCE, 1978, pp. 470–1.
(3) Richard Gunther, "Strategies, Tactics and the New Spanish Party System: The 1979 General Elections," paper prepared for the International Symposium, *Spain and the United States*, p. 13.
(4) The 1982 figures correspond to December. In March of the same year this party had 44,000 members. *La Alternativa Popular*, VI National Alianza Popular Convention, Madrid, 1984, pp. 22 and 33.
(5) *Memoria de Gestion*, Federal Executive Commission, XXX PSOE Convention Madrid, December 13–16, 1984, p. 48.
(6) *Mundo Obrero* (XI Spanish Communist Party Convention), n. 295, December 1983, p. 16.
(7) According to the data presented by AP in its VII Convention, February 7–9, 1986).
(8) *El Pais*, December 22, 1985.

the parties have not made party membership an essential requirement for obtaining certain economic and social privileges. This type of benefit of party membership was a reality at the beginning of the post Second World War era in those countries which had authoritarian regimes, and permitted the parties in those systems a vigorous organizational expansion.[17]

Neither the process whereby the Spanish political system changed from a dictatorship to a democracy nor the degree of development of Spanish society in 1977 are comparable to the circumstances under which the emergence of democracy came about in Italy and Germany after the Second World War. In 1977, Spain was a country with a high level of economic development, and consequently, with a complex degree of social stratification. The majority of voters, according to all previous studies, were oriented toward the center. Further, this was certainly the picture that the four main national parties had in mind as they broached the first general elections. Consequently, they all developed a "catch-all" electoral strategy.[18] Instead of addressing only one sector of the electorate or offering a specific political sub-culture, they represented their ideological identity in vague terms, each attempting to attract the great majority of the voters. Furthermore, since the beginning, and in ever increasing measure, the electoral campaigns have developed almost exclusively through the media, especially the television, and, in general, through the normal means of commercial publicity. The local campaigns have a minimal importance in the general elections because the parties make their leader the center of their campaign publicity.

Given these facts, what interest can the parties of the new Spanish democracy hold for potential members? It must certainly be very minimal if we consider on the one hand the role traditionally played by members in mass parties. On the other hand, due to their "catch-all" strategy, the Spanish parties do not respond in a totaly satisfactory manner to the needs of those who look for a more rigid ideology and clearly defined class identity in their party affiliation. While the extremely weak development of party membership in Spanish political parties is, of course, not fully explained in the above analysis, the aforementioned factors play an important role in understanding this phenomenon.

The pages which follow will discuss the main sources of income for the Socialist Party, Alianza Popular and the Communist Party, currently the three most important parties of national scope after the dissolution of the Central Democratic Union in 1983. Unfortunately, the data regarding the finances of this last organization, from the year of its creation in 1977 to its dissolution in 1983, are extremely scarce. Of the four parties discussed, UCD has offered the least amount of data regarding its finances. For this reason, there is insufficient basis to study its financing in this study.

The Spanish socialist workers party

With 160,000 party members in December 1985 (See Table 3), the Spanish Socialist Workers Party has an absolute majority in Parliament, having won more than ten million votes in the 1982 general elections. Its organizational structure is federal in character. Its administrative and financial organization is based on a Federal Secretariat of Administration and Finances composed by the Federal Clerk of the Area and the regional Clerks. The provincial organizations of the party have two principal sources of revenue.[19] The first is membership dues of 200 pesetas per

Table 4. *Official total subsidies to political parties, 1979–83*
(in millions of pesetas)

1979[a]	1,651,520,000
1980[b]	1,594,322,000
1981[c]	1,925,000,000
1982[d]	2,081,000,000
1983[e]	2,431,942,000

[a] Ley 12/1979, *BOE*, No. 240, October, 6.
[b] Ley 20/1980, *BOE*, No. 120, April, 28.
[c] Ley 74/1980, de Presupuestos Generales de Estado de 1981. *BOE*, December, 30.
[d] Ley 44/1981, de Presupuestos Generales de Estado de 1982. *BOE*, No. 320, December, 28.
[e] Ley 9/1983 de Presupuestos del Estado de 1983. *BOE*, December, 13.

month. Of each share received by the provincial organizations, 30 pesetas are transferred to the central party organization. Following a resolution of the Party Congress, a part of the annual state subsidy is divided among the provincial organizations. In 1983, for example, of the 1,258,000,000 pesetas which were allocated to PSOE, approximately 310,000,000 were allocated to the provincial organizations. This amount is distributed according to a scale which takes into account the number of party members and the population of the province. The economic needs which are not covered by the funds obtained from these two sources are covered with bank credits or loans which the provincial secretaries of Administration and Finance may request with an upper limit of five million pesetas. Any credit request which exceeds this amount must come from the Federal Secretary.

The financial sources of the central organizations are the following: the funds which the provincial organization contribute; 10 percent of the salaries of its elected officers (following a resolution of the Party Federal Committee); and, lastly, the public subsidies, discounting the amount which is transferred to the provincial organizations. Of the revenues obtained by this party between January 1, 1982 and December 31, 1984, approximately 92 percent came from state subsidies (See Table 5), including those obtained by its parliamentary group. The membership dues make up only a little more than 3 percent of the total revenues. In reference to the membership dues in Table 6, it should be pointed out that they include the salary percentage handed over to the party by its parliamentary members and elected officers. For example, in 1983 this last sum amounted to 55 million pesetas while the funds from the members came to 46 million.

Table 5. *Income and expenses of the Socialist Party, January 1, 1982–October 31, 1984*
(in millions of pesetas)

Expenses		Income	
		Official subsidies	4,103
		Membership dues[b]	246
		Others[c]	67
Total	5,824[a]	Total	4,416

[a] Only the total sum of expenses was facilitated from the Central Party Office to this investigator.
[b] This sum include the salary percentage handed over to the party by its parliamentary members and elected officers.
[c] Most of this income was obtained from the sale of party publications and campaign paraphernalia.

Considering the number of party members in 1983 (See Table 3), this means that the percentage which the members contribute periodically is very low. The expenditures during this time period exceeded revenues by 1.4 billion pesetas. The main reason for this difference was the repayment of credit requested for electoral expenses during those years. In the 1986 party budget, for expenses forecasted at 2.16 billion, a revenue of 1.98 billion pesetas is expected from state subsidies, including those of the parliamentary group, and 96 million is expected from membership dues and salary percentages of parliamentary members and elected officers.[20] The Socialist Party does not receive monetary assistance from its affiliate labor union, the General Workers Union (UGT), as is the case with other socialist parties. While their ideologically affiliated labor unions are one of the major sources of financing for European socialists and communists, in Spain the degree of union affiliation is minimal. With a structural weakness comparable to that of the political parties, the Spanish labor unions barely have sufficient funds for their own activities and, like the parties, also receive public funds.

Spanish political parties have never developed, or developed only very marginally, their own businesses. In the case of PSOE, efforts in this direction have had very little success, for which reason most of them were finally abandoned. On the other hand, the party has stimulated cooperatives with its own funds. It has obtained minimal profits from them, while some, such as the Pablo Iglesias housing cooperative, have been successful with regard to sales, but they have not shown substantial profits.

The electoral financing of this party is very similar to its financing of ordinary activities. For the 1982 general election campaign, it announced a budget of 1.3 billion pesetas. This amount, however, seems to be much lower than the amount that was actually spent, according to statements of the party's financial manager. The amount invested probably was around 2.3–2.4 billion pesetas. The party's share of electoral subsidies was a total of 1,042,016,000 pesetas (See Table 2), of which it directly received about a third. The rest was handed over to the banking entities which had extended credits to the organization.[21] These loans totaled 720 million pesetas and constituted part of the loans obtained by the party for the 1982 electoral campaign. The revenues for extraordinary membership dues and donations from supporters obtained by the sale of bonds did not cover even 10 percent of campaign expenses. As a consequence of these elections and the 1983 municipal and regional elections, at the end of 1984 the party had a debt of 3.48 billion pesetas.

The German Foundation Friedrich Ebert, associated with SPD, has collaborated with the Socialist Party in the capacity of carrying out electoral polls. The German assistance was acknowledged by the socialists during the Flick case investigations. Besides this collaboration, the German Foundation has lent its support to foundations affiliated with the Socialist Party and organized series of speeches and meetings mainly aimed at union-management relations.

Alianza Popular

After two electoral fiascos in 1977 and 1979, this organization ran in the 1982 general elections with magnificent prospects, according to the opinion polls. In great part, this was due to the progressive disintegration of the government party, the center-rightist UCD. Although it ran in coalition with the Christian Democrat Party (PDP), Alianza Popular was the central axis of the coalition, from a political as well as economic and organizational viewpoint. In March 1982, the group had 44,000 members. By January 1984, the number of members had risen to 160,000 and, according to the most recent data offered by the party, in February 1986, its members numbered 200,000 (See Table 3). After the 1982 elections, the organizational structure underwent extensive reorganization, and the group's finances were significantly restructured.[22] Until that time, the annual public subsidies which it received were scarcely more than 30 million pesetas and membership dues were barely regulated. The national organization took charge of a very high percentage of the budget of the provincial organizations, and 80 percent of the 1982 electoral campaign of the provincial organizations was financed by the national organization.

Table 6. *Income and expenses of the Alianza Popular, 1983*
(in millions of pesetas)

Expenses		Income	
Salaries	250.3	Official subsidies	576
Real Estate	82	Parliamentary Group and	
Management	150	elected officers	81
Offices	50	Membership dues	190
Publications	60	Contributions	103.3
Legal services	10		
Transfer to party			
associations	330		
Total	932.3	Total	950.3

Source: La Alternativa Popular 1984–1986, VI AP Convention, Ed., Publicaciones Alianza Popular, Madrid 1984, p. 40.

According to the 1983 balance sheet presented at the party's Fifth National convention (See Table 6), 68 percent of the revenues were made up of subsidies obtained by the party and its parliamentary groups (Congress and Senate)[23] in addition to the amount contributed by its elected officers who receive official salaries. Such officers contribute 10 percent of their salaries. Its membership dues amounted to 20 percent of the total revenues and donations to 11 percent. In the 1982 electoral campaign, the party declared expenditures of 800 million pesetas (See Table 8), a figure which seems excessively low considering the sum invested by the Socialists and Communists. In turn, the party shows revenues of the same amount. Of these revenues 62 percent correspond to electoral subsidies and 36 percent to donations and contributions including extraordinary membership dues collected by some provincial organizations.

This party has not developed any type of business interests because it fears that the voters may come to criticize this kind of activity on the part of political parties. Regarding possible foreign assistance, party President Manuel Fraga admits that the party received a small amount of assistance from the Bavarian Social Christian Union (CSU) in 1977. Also, the German Foundation Hans Seidel collaborates with Spanish foundations ideologically close to AP.

Spanish Communist Party

During the Franco regime, the Spanish Communists were the most active and best organized of all the present national parties. After the death of

Table 7. *Income and campaign expenditures of the Alianza Popular, 1982 general elections*
(in millions of pesetas)

Campaign expenditures		Income	
Transfers to party organizations	180	Official subsidies	498
Publicity	545	Contributions	302
Salaries	25		
General expenditures	50		
Total	800	Total	8,000

Source: La Alternativa Popular 1984–1986, VI AP Convention. Ed., Publicaciones de Alianza Popular, Madrid 1984, p. 40.

Table 8. *Income and expenses of the Communist Party, January 1–November 3, 1983*
(in millions of pesetas)

Expenses		Income	
Commissions depending on Central Committee	120,743	Membership dues	16,558
		Contributions	294,096
Central Committee service	46,143	Annual official subsidies	20,461
Election campaigns[a] (local and regional)	229,067	Parliamentary group and elected officers	21,705
Special campaigns	7,382	Official election subsidies[c]	28,493
Transfers to party provincial organizations	61,075	Recuperation of private loans[d]	59,371
XI convention expenditures	5,596	Private credits	123,493
Others[b]	114,682	Real estate sales	2,062
Total	584,690	Others[e]	7,822
		Total	574,041

[a] Most of this expenditure is due to local and regional elections held in 1983. Only 25, 167, 716 pesetas are due to the 1982 general elections.
[b] Most of these expenditures are due to the repayment of bank credits.
[c] This includes electoral subsidies for the 1982 general elections and for the 1983 regional and local elections.
[d] Loans given to the party newspaper *Mundo Obrero*.
[e] Income obtained mainly from the sale of party publications and campaign paraphernalia.
Source: Mundo Obrero, Supplement 1, (XI, PCE Convention), Madrid, December 1983, pp. 8–9.

Franco, and during the period of permissiveness up to the time of the parties' legalization in 1977, many Communist party sympathisers enrolled officially as members of the party. In 1977, the Communist Party had 201,740 members, according to party statistics, and was undoubtedly the most firmly implanted and best organized group. In the elections of 1977, the party obtained 9 percent of the votes and in 1979 the results were slightly more favorable. These results were undoubtedly discouraging for a party which for many years constituted the most articulate and important clandestine political force confronting the Franco regime. From 1977 on, the number of party members progressively decreased. By 1978, the number of party loyalists had dropped to 168,175. In December 1983, after the party's catastrophic 1982 electoral results and the intensification of an internal crisis which first flared up toward the end of 1981,[24] its members numbered 84,652.

Until 1982, state subsidies for ordinary party activities played an important role in financing the party's Central Committee. In 1981, for example, 50 percent of the revenue obtained by the organization for use at this level came from public subsidies (including those received from its parliamentary group). This covered 58 percent of their expenses.[25] In 1983, as a consequence of the party's unfavorable electoral results, the state subsidies were drastically reduced.

Membership dues also play a relevant role in this party's financing, especially for its provincial organizations. These organizations transferred 25 percent of each share to the Central Committee. This last sum amounted to 16,558,063 pesetas in the first eleven months of 1983 (See Table 8). Using the December 1983 data as a reference, this means that the members contributed a total of 64,232,000 million pesetas to the party.

Some agricultural cooperatives have been developed by the provincial organizations of the party, but their profits have been minimal. Regarding foreign economic assistance, rumors implicating Yugoslavia, Romania and Communist Korea have never been confirmed.[26] As in the case of the Socialists, and for the same reasons, this party has not received economic assistance from its affiliated labor union, Comisiones Obreras.

In respect to its electoral financing, the Communist organization has been more successful than the other parties in receiving assistance from its members and supporters. It invested 505,852,920 pesetas in the 1982 electoral campaign. Of this amount, 282 million came from bank loans and 316 million from donations and from the sale of bonds. Subsidies received after the election amounted to slightly more than 14 million pesetas, (See Table 8), covering only 3 percent of campaign spending. Due to its failure in these elections – as well as in the 1983 municipal and regional elections – the party had accumulated a debt of 412 million pesetas by December 1983.[27]

The report which its Central Finance Commission presented in the Eleventh Party Convention (December 1983) stressed the party's financial difficulties after these elections and advocated a policy of austerity, optimum use of resources and special contributions from its members. One imagines these plans would be difficult to carry out with the acute crisis and splintering which the party has undergone since then.

CONCLUSIONS

Spain is the first democratic country which adopted public financing of parties before the emergence of a party system. The concession of subsidies, initially electoral and later annual, was justified in the name of democratic principles. It helped newly formed and very weak parties with scant economic resources to begin to develop their activities in the new democratic system. It also favored equal opportunities among the parties. However, the consequences of the extremely important role which public funds play in the financing of Spanish political parties, especially for parties such as the PSOE and UCD, remain undetermined. To what degree, for instance, has state monetary assistance contributed to the meager implantation of parties in Spain? Further, in what measure has public financing of parties been weakening the party-society relationship? It is important to note that irrespective of the importance which state subsidies have had for each of the parties, all have very low membership levels compared with their European fraternal parties. Nevertheless, it is interesting to point out that precisely the group which has been receiving the greatest amount of state support due to its excellent electoral results, PSOE, has been the least successful in obtaining economic resources from its members and sympathetic social sectors. It could be contended that Alianza Popular has obtained greater economic assistance from these two latter sources because it represents wealthier sectors of society than PSOE. The Communist Party, on the other hand, depends on the support of a more highly politicized sector which has a greater economic commitment to its party. Also, it must be kept in mind that the AP and PCE have needed to raise a greater percentage of their own funds than PSOE. This fact has probably forced them to put forth a more sustained effort than the socialists to obtain economic support from the sectors they represent.

The electoral subsidies to parties have undoubtedly helped the Spanish party system in its early growth and development. For this reason, they have played a valuable role in the stabilization of the young Spanish democracy. It is questionable, however, whether public financing of day-to-day party activities has had equally positive results.

The study of political finance in Spain, like democracy itself, is still in its early stages. There are many obstacles which impede the process of gathering complete and accurate information. As a result, indepth knowledge about the financing of political parties and its consequences for both the party system and for the Spanish political system as a whole is difficult to obtain. For this process to move forward, it will be necessary for the party system to become more settled. In addition, the revenue and expenditures of political organizations must be fully disclosed to the public. Otherwise, the study of political finance in Spain will become a task more suited to private investigators than political scientists.

Notes

1 A "Decree-Law" is a government decree with the same force of law as a parliamentary statute. For the text of Suarez' Decree-Law on the electoral process, see "Real Decretoley 20/1977," March 18, *Boletin Oficial del Estado*, n. 70, March 23, 1977.
2 The Comunidades Autónomas were established by the Spanish Constitution of 1978. In geographical terms, most of them correspond to the region in which Spain was administratively divided before the Constitution. Throughout the text, we use the phrase "Comunidades Autónomas" although with regard to elections the words "regional elections" are used since the Spanish word "elecciones autonómicas" has no meaningful translation.
3 "Ley de Partidos Políticos" 54/78, December 4, *BOE*, n. 293, December 8, 1978.
4 See Pilar del Castillo, *Financiación de partidos y candidatos en las democracias occidentales*, (Madrid: Centro de Investigaciones sociológicas, 1985). Spanish political party finance is discussed in detail in the second part of this book.
5 The d'Hondt formula is a method of distributing parliamentary seats among competing parties; for more on the d'Hondt formula, see Douglas Rae, *The Political Consequences of Electoral Laws* (New Haven: Yale University Press, 1971), pp. 31–3.
6 "Ley Orgánica del Régimen Electoral General," 5/1985, *BOE*, June 20, 1985.
7 For example, the extraparliamentary German parties brought the 1967 Law of German Parties before the Constitutional Court which in turn required the Parliament to modify the law, decreasing to 0.5 percent the votes required on a national level in order to receive public subsidies.
8 *Centro de Investigaciones Sociológicas*, study n. 1430, 1984.
9 Contributions from the Public Administration are different from those that parties receive for electoral expenses according to the electoral law. This prohibition was inspired by the Italian Law of State Contribution to Political Parties of 1974. The goal of the law is to avoid the possibility of public enterprises or enterprises of a mixed economic character becoming sources of finance for parties. This was the case, for instance, in Italy for some period of time for the Christian Democratic Party. See Donald Seasson, "The Funding of Political Parties in Italy," *Political Quarterly*, Vol. 46, January–March, 1975, pp. 94–8.

10 This report is discussed in detail in Pilar del Castillo, "Ley Electoral y financiacion de las campañas electorales," Madrid, 1985 (unpublished). This study was supported by the Centro de Estudios Constitucionales.

11 Pilar del Castillo, "Financiación pública de los partidos en España." *Revista de Derecho Político*, n. 22, 1986, pp. 149–74.

12 For example, in 1979 the election campaign expenditures of UCD, AP and PSOE were substantially higher than those of the British parties at the General Election of 1979 and those of the Canadian parties at the General Election of 1980. See Michael Pinto-Duschinsky, "Financing of the British General Election of 1979," in Howard R. Penniman, ed., *Britain at the Polls, 1979: A Study of the General Election* (Washington D.C.: American Enterprise Institute, 1981), p. 234; and F. Leislie Seidle and Khayyam Zev Paltiel, "Party Finance, The Election Expenses Act, and the Campaign Spending in 1979 and 1980," in Howard R. Penniman, ed., *Canada at the Polls, 1979 and 1980: A Study of General Elections* (Washington, D.C.: American Enterprise Institute, 1981), pp. 254 and 269. For a review in detail of this matter, see Pilar del Castillo *Financiación de las elecciones generales de 1982*, (forthcoming).

13 "Resolución de la Junta Electoral Central," July 13, 1978, *BOE*, July 18, 1978.

14 Douglas Rae, *The Political Consequences of Electoral Laws* (New Haven: Yale University Press, 1971).

15 Parliamentary Groups also receive subsidies covered by Congress of Deputies and the Senate budget.

16 See Jose Ramon Montero, "Partidos y participación política algunas notas sobre afiliación política en la etapa inicial de la transición española," *Revista de Estudios Políticos*, n. 23, 1981, pp. 38–9.

17 Ibid., pp. 40–1.

18 See, for example, Richard Gunther, "Strategies, Tactics and the New Spanish Party System: The 1979 General Elections," paper prepared for the International Symposium, *Spain and the United States*, held at the Center for Latin American studies, University of Florida, Gainesville. Florida, December 3–7, 1979.

19 All the information regarding PSOE was provided to this investigator by the Federal Offices of Administration and Finances of this party, unless otherwise indicated. I would like to acknowledge my gratitude to Emilio Alonso, Federal Secretary of the Office, for his assistance.

20 *El País*, December 22, 1985.

21 However, the money from the subsidies which the party receives directly is, by best assumptions, greatly reduced. In most cases, all the money received as a public subsidy is directly handed over by the state to the financial entities which have extended credit to the parties for the financing of their campaign. All the political formations have an extremely large portion of their electoral expenses in bank credits. Both the 1977 electoral norm as well as the new 1985 law establish that parties may disclose to the Central Electoral Commission the number of credits obtained, their value and the entities which granted them so that the subsidies to which they have a right may be directly handed over to the banks. In each of the elections, the parties have disclosed most, but in some cases not all, of the credits obtained. For this reason, the central organizations

of parties only receive, in the most favorable of cases, a reduced part of the subsidies to which they are entitled.

22 All the information regarding Alianza Popular was provided to this investigator by the *Tesorero Nacional Adjunto* of this party, Luis Gerardo López Delgado, to whom I would like to acknowledge my gratitude for his assistance.

23 As pointed out in Note 15, Parliamentary Groups also receive state subsidies.

24 The crisis seemed to be resolved with the expulsion of some Central Committee members as well as several elected officials of the party. Nevertheless, the crisis flared up again after the 1982 election when Santiago Carrillo, longtime party leader, resigned as General Secretary. At the present time, along with PCE, two splinter groups of the same are trying to attract the voters with communist sympathies.

25 *Mundo Obrero* (PCE newspaper), supplemento No. 1, XI Party Convention, Madrid, December 1983, p. 7.

26 *Tiempo*, No. 61, July 11, 1983.

27 *Mundo Obrero*, December 1983, pp. 6–7.

9

The "modesty" of Dutch party finance

RUUD KOOLE

THE DUTCH PARTY SYSTEM

This chapter explores the specifics of Dutch party finance. Relatively cheap election campaigns, quasi-absence of business donations and reluctance to grant state subventions to parties can only be explained in terms of a Dutch political system in transition. Dutch society is and has always been highly segmented, which was also reflected on the political level. This situation was most often compared – at least until the 1960s – with the structure of an ancient Greek temple. From 1920 onwards, several "pillars" of ideological or religious groupings existed side by side without knowing each other very well. Thus, it was possible that, within the same village or town, Catholic, Protestant, Socialist or Liberal "societies" (including soccer clubs, trade unions, churches, and political parties) were present almost without having any contact with comparable organizations in the other "societies." This also was the case at the provincial and national level; broadcasting organizations are but one example. So, it was not a specific common policy area or interest that defined the relations between organizations, but their common religion or ideology.

The vertical organization of the "societies" is illustrated by the metaphor of the "pillars": side by side, but at a certain distance. Only cooperation by the political elite at the top of these pillars (the roof of the temple) guaranteed a rather stable political system in spite of a very segmented society. This paradox of "pillarization" or "consociational democracy" is amply dealt with by Lijphart and Daalder.[1] Between approximately 1920 and 1960 four main currents or "pillars" could be distinguished: the Catholics, the Protestants, the Socialists and the Liberals. Sometimes these pillars could contain more than one political party within the same ideological family. The first two were pillars in a broad sense, because all socio-economic strata were represented. The Socialist and

200

Liberal pillars were based on ideologies, articulating the interests of the blue and white collar segments and the more well-to-do respectively. No pillar has ever been able to win a majority in Parliament. Hence, the need for cooperation in coalition cabinets. This may explain also the relative "tolerance"towards other pillars: one had to allow other groupings to have a certain internal sovereignty in order to be accepted by the others in the same way.

The fact that even within one pillar several parties could exist is mainly due to the system of extreme proportional representation, which was introduced in 1918, along with the universal franchise. Under this system, the Netherlands is considered to be one constituency comprising nineteen electoral sub-districts. So, at the national elections for the Second Chamber, about 55,000 votes (0.67 percent), sometimes scattered all over the country, guarantees a seat in Parliament. However, until the 1960s, the electors were rather faithful to the political exponents of their social group. Most of the Calvinists voted in accordance with their specific branch of Calvinism for the Anti-Revolutionary Party (ARP) and the Christian Historical Union (CHU) or for the smaller orthodox parties, the Political Reformed Party (SGP) and the Reformed Political League (GPV). The Catholics voted for the Catholic People's Party (KVP), the Social Democrats for the Labor Party (PvdA), the Communists for the small CPN and the Liberals for the right wing People's Party for Freedom and Democracy (VVD).

During the 1960s, this pillarized system began to fall apart. Especially within the Catholic stream "deconfessionalization" or secularization gained momentum. Catholics no longer voted for the Catholic party as a matter of course. Changes in the church and the impact of the mass media, through which the individual elector was able to receive easily information about other pillars, may have contributed to the enormous electoral decline of the KVP in the 1960s and the 1970s. But also other established parties could no longer count on their electoral social base. A growing number of voters changed parties between one election and another. This phenomenon of electoral nomads directly influenced the Dutch party system. First, the traditional ties between political parties and their congenial social organizations were loosened. Secondly, new parties could penetrate the market easier than before.[2] Some of them disappeared soon after their initial success. But others managed to become a more constant part of the political spectre. In 1957, the Pacifist Socialist Party (PSP) was established in order to offer an alternative to those who refused to join the PvdA, which supported the Atlantic Alliance, or the CPN, which had a Stalinist orientation. In 1966, a year of political turmoil in the Netherlands, a progressive liberal party, the Democrats 1966 (D66), was founded; it stressed the necessity of constitutional reforms. In 1968, left-wing members of the KVP set up the Political Party of Radicals (PPR), which dropped religion as a guiding principle in politics and adopted a leftist, ecological approach.

    A third result of "depillarization" was the merger in 1980 of the three largest religious parties, the Catholic People's Party (KVP), the Christian Historical Union (CHU), and the Anti-Revolutionary Party (ARP), into the Christian Democratic Appeal (CDA). This fusion of the political exponents of two pillars succeeded in slowing down the electoral decline. Nevertheless, the CDA-electorate in 1982 was only 60 percent of the combined totals of the constituent parties in 1963 (29 percent for the CDA in 1982; 45.6 percent for the ARP,CHU and KVP together in 1963). But due to its center position the CDA continued to play the pivotal role in government coalitions as the KVP had done before. Moreover, due to the popularity of its leader, Prime Minister Ruud Lubbers, the CDA managed to win for the first time in the history of religious parties a considerable amount of secular votes at the 1986 national elections, which fostered this role. The elections of 1981 and 1982 showed very clearly the result of the depillarization of the last two decades. Whereas before the 1960s political fragmentation was limited by the strong organizations of the pillars, at the beginning of the 1980s the voters could choose among more than twenty parties. Twelve among them entered Parliament. The fate of D66 is illustrative. This party's share of the electorate jumped from about 5 percent in 1977 to 11.5 percent in the elections of 1981. One year later, when new elections were held because of the fall of the government, D66 fell back to 4.3 percent.

    This phenomenon forced the parties to address themselves more directly to the electorate. Where a growing number of voters began to play at hide-and-seek in a landscape with old and new parties, surrounded by the remnants of the former pillars, these parties were obliged to go and find the electors. Hence, a fourth result of the changes in the Dutch political society: an increasing effort to bind the electorate to the party and to win new voters. Election campaigns were intensified but – as in West Germany – the inter-election organizations of the parties also became more and more involved in so-called "permanent campaigns." Although the old established parties still receive sympathy from the (formerly) congenial organizations within their pillar, they can no longer really count on them. Moreover, new social organizations have come to challenge the impact of the old "pillarized" ones.

    Thus the Dutch political parties of the mid 1980s are more than ever confronted with tasks of educating members and citizens and persuading voters in a very competitive environment. Whether the process of secularization and depillarization will continue is a difficult question to answer. Dutch society seems to be in a period of transition; the direction is hard to predict. But the changes have had – and will continue to have – an impact on Dutch party finance.

PARTY MEMBERSHIP

Whereas the role of the Dutch political parties has changed, their legal status has remained the same. Officially, political parties do not exist as such. They are treated as ordinary voluntary associations, amenable to civil law. Therefore, one would expect the parties to depend completely on dues-paying members and on other contributions, without special state subvention.

Since 1970, however, the practice is different. Foundations affiliated with parties can obtain financial aid from the state for specified purposes. Yet, as we shall see, the total amount should not be exaggerated. The main source for Dutch political parties has always been and still is the membership dues. In 1984, for instance, 61 percent of the combined expenditures of the national organizations of the largest party, the PvdA, was covered by membership dues. Twenty-five years before this share was more than 90 percent.[3]

Thus, knowing the number of members is very important to an understanding of the expenditures of the parties. All Dutch parties are more or less mass organizations. Skeleton parties, as the old Liberal or Conservative parties in Europe or the present U.S. parties, have been almost non-existent in post-war Holland. Centralized party organizations collect the dues and receive other contributions directly from the individual members. Indirect membership, as in the case of the Labor Party in Great Britain, is not known.

Table 1 shows the number of members. It also shows that the "massiveness" of the mass parties should not be exaggerated. On average, just over 5 percent of the voters is a party member and, if we include the non-voters as well (about 20 percent of the electorate) this percentage goes down to a little more than 4 percent of the total electorate of 10,200,000. In the heyday of pillarization in the 1950s, the number of party members was considerably higher. The KVP is reported to have had 400,000 members in 1950, which is about the same as the total membership of all parties in 1980! Most of this decline can be attributed to the fall of the membership of the religious parties (except for the small orthodox SGP and GPV), but also the

Table 1. Members and voters in 1982 and 1985; the percentage of voters and the members/voters ratio of Dutch political parties, 1982

| Party | Numbers of members | | Number of voters | | |
	September 1982	January 1985	1982	Members/voters (Percent)	Ratio-1982
CDA	153,490	131,627	2,414,176	29.3	6.2
PvdA	105,306	99,465	2,499,562	30.4	4.2
VVD	101,309	89,120	1,897,986	23.1	5.3
D66	15,000	8,774	355,830	4.3	4.2
PPR	9,500	7,848	136,095	1.6	7.0
PSP	10,297	7,767	187,150	2.3	5.5
CPN	17,000	10,966	147,510	1.8	11.5
EVP	1,800	2,500	56,363	0.7	3.2
SGP	20,760	21,400	156,782	1.9	13.2
RPF	9,800	8,970	124,018	1.5	7.9
GPV	13,047	12,909	67,234	0.8	19.4
CP	n.a.	n.a.	68,363	0.8	n.a.

CDA – Christian Democratic Appeal
PvdA – Labour Party
VVD – People's Party for Freedom and Democracy (rightwing liberal)
D66 – Democrats 1966 (progressive liberal)
PPR – Radical Political Party (leftwing, ecological)
PSP – Pacific Socialist Party
CPN – Communist Party of the Netherlands
EVP – Evangelical People's Party (leftwing christian)
SGP – Political Reformed Party (orthodox calvinist)
RPF – Reformed Political Federation (orthodox calvinist)
GPV – Reformed Political League (orthodox calvinist)
CP – Centre Party (extreme right)

PvdA has had better years in this respect: 143,000 members in 1960, which is about one third more than in 1985. Since 1970, however, the total membership of all parties seems to fluctuate around 420,000.

The exodus of members in the 1960s within the old major parties (except the VVD), together with the growing number of tasks of political parties (also due to the depillarization), called for a rationalization of the use of the available funds as well as for new resources. The administrative bodies of the parties became more and more centralized. A debate was opened whether or not the state should come to the assistance of the parties. A shift toward greater reliance on financial aid coming from business circles was not considered seriously since the 1960s. It was the parliamentary leader of the KVP, Norbert Schmelzer, who persuaded the government in 1968 to study the possibility of state subventions.[4]

This debate led to the introduction of subventions to affiliated party foundations. These were extended to research institutes in 1972 (with retroactive effect to 1970), to educational institutes in 1975 and to youth organizations in 1976 (first temporarily, from 1981 onwards more permanently). Before describing these kinds of subventions we will first throw more light on the non-state financial resources of parties in the Netherlands.

MEMBERSHIP DUES

In order to understand the extent to which parties depend on their different financial resources, we roughly calculated for the four major parties (PvdA, CDA, VVD and D66) the total sum of the expenditures of the national parties and their affiliated national organizations based on the data of 1980.

Table 2 shows how these expenditures were covered by the income from membership dues, state subventions and other resources. In recent years, these percentages have changed slightly, due to some cuts in state subventions. But it is clear that membership dues are still the main resource of Dutch political parties. For example, in 1984 the total expenditures of PvdA organizations were covered for about 61 percent by membership dues. Most of the parties have their members pay an annual fee depending on income, sometimes on a very progressive scale. The VVD, however, uses a system based on age groups. The average membership fee in 1984 was the lowest for the small Orthodox-Calvinist SGP (Dfl. 16), and the highest for the small left-wing PSP (Dfl. 105). Of the larger parties, CDA and VVD members paid about Dfl. 50 whereas the average PVdA and D66 member had to pay Dfl. 86. (Dfl. 1 = U.S. $0.30)

Table 2. *Total expenditures of Dutch national party organizations and affiliated organizations; coverage by membership dues, state subventions and other resources, 1980*

Party	Total expenditures (Dfl.)	Membership fees (Percent)	State subventions (Percent)	Other (Percent)
CDA	7,350,000	60	15	25
PvdA	9,420,000	65	14	21
VVD	4,000,000	61	20	19
D66	1,750,000	43	20	37

Dfl. 1.00 = U.S. Dollar 0.47 on 31 December 1980.

According to Dutch tax law, membership dues and other contributions to a party are tax-deductible as long as they are at least 1 percent of the gross annual income of a citizen, up to a maximum of 10 percent. No legal limits are put on the amount of the total contributions. Therefore, parties with wealthy members could be in a more favorable position to raise funds. The "equality of opportunities" (*Chancengleichheit* in Germany) may be in question here.

CONTRIBUTIONS AND OTHER RESOURCES

Skipping the column of state subvention in Table 2, we see that all parties depend to a certain degree on "other resources." Most of them consist of contributions from members for special purposes, often election campaigns. In the last section, we mentioned the possibility of tax relief for individuals. This also is true for business enterprises. They can distribute funds to political parties if the amount is at least Dfl. 500 to a maximum of 6 percent of the profit made by the enterprise. In practice, however, this kind of contribution remains rare. Some parties have enacted their own regulations which strictly limit the acceptance of funds coming from non-natural legal persons. After a minor scandal in 1977, the CDA accepts money from non-natural persons only if they are non-profit organizations and they are not linked with business enterprises. Natural persons can contribute a maximum amount of Dfl. 5,000 provided they permit their names to be published. The Labor party does not receive any money from private enterprises or from labor unions. The right-wing VVD only rarely receives some donations from enterprises. But, according to the treasurer of the party,[5] they do not exceed the amount of Dfl. 5,000. Some party-affiliated foundations may have received these kinds of funds, but the available audits over 1984 indicate that this "roundabout-financing" was almost absent.[6]

In the past, however, some minor "scandals" did occur. In 1968 the Catholic KVP asked for money from business circles; the small DS'70 did the same in 1972. These events were negatively reviewed in the press. In 1977, there was some discussion about very small gifts from industrial enterprises to CDA and VVD.[7] The available data and these "scandals" suggest that enterprises do almost completely disregard the importance of donations to Dutch parties. In recent years, it also is the parties themselves that are rather strict in refusing such donations.

Another form of financing is practiced by left-wing parties in the Netherlands as elsewhere in Europe; they demand from their members who hold an elective or appointed public office to contribute a fixed share of their salaries to the party. The PvdA demands 2 percent, which is little compared to its sister party, the German SPD, which requests 20 percent, according to the treasurer of the party.[8] PPR requests 3 percent, while PSP asks 25 percent. The Communist Party allows their representatives the equivalent of the salary of a qualified industrial worker and transfers the rest to the party chest. Some parties have rather high "pseudo-resources," that is, "donations" to parties from party cadre of non-claimed travel expenses. In these cases, the party does not receive money in reality, but is able to book the "donation" on the credits side of the budget of an affiliated foundation. Since – as we shall see – the amount of state subventions depends directly on the quantity of the foundation's own resources, it is important to have the credits side as high as possible. What is registered as "travel expenses of the party cadre" on the debits side, is noted as a "donation" on the credits side; thus, it is only a paper transaction. The party cadre in this example gets a part of his "donation" back through tax relief, while the party foundation itself can claim more state subvention because of a higher amount of its own resources though these "donations." So, in 1980, the research institute of D66 "received" Dfl. 100,000 in "donations" of this kind, whereas its total budget was Dfl. 360,000. This explains to a large extent the high percentage of "other resources" for D66 in Table 2. The practice is not illegal.

Moreover, interest constitutes a modest financial source. The PvdA received Dfl. 526,000 in 1983–4; CDA, VVD and D66 Dfl. 325,000, Dfl. 45,000 and Dfl. 18,000 respectively in 1984. Even smaller are the returns from the sale of propaganda material (to local branches, for instance) and from advertisements in party periodicals. Dutch parties are not engaged in "party business enterprises," as Paltiel called them.[9] Only the Communist Party owns a daily newspaper, which is currently undergoing serious financial problems.

Thus the party members furnish the bulk of the "other resources" mentioned in Table 2. Most of these donations are elicited during special fund-raising campaigns by the party for electoral purposes. In addition to their membership dues, many members are willing to pay considerable "incidental" amounts of money. We will deal with the election campaigns more extensively below.

PUBLIC FINANCING

The last main category of party income consists of the resources coming from the state. Between 10 and 20 percent of the expenditures of the party organizations are covered in some way by state subventions (excluding tax relief). Only one kind of state subvention is direct (radio and television time), while the others are indirect.

Since 1925, political parties have had direct access to radio; since 1959, they have had access to television. An exception was made for the Communist Party from 1948 through 1956 at the height of the Cold War. Another exception is the orthodox Calvinist SGP which voluntarily refrains from the use of television time on ethical grounds. All parties that are represented in the Second Chamber are allotted free broadcasting time: ten minutes every two weeks on radio and ten minutes every three months on television. To meet the production costs of these programs, each party could claim about Dfl. 28,000 from the government in 1984.

It is important to note that the size of the party does not affect its allocation. This is equally true for the specially allotted time during the election campaigns for the Second Chamber or the European Parliament. In this period the normal broadcasting time is suspended; instead, the parties get twenty minutes on radio and the same on television. During these campaigns even parties that are not represented in the Second Chamber have the right to go on the air, but since 1981 they have to present themselves in all nineteen electoral sub-districts to receive broadcasting time. This is a cheap way to get access on television, since a party only needs Dfl. 19,000 to present itself in all these sub-districts!

Indirect access to radio and television is hard to measure. But the unique Dutch broadcasting system based on associations of listeners and spectators – originally within the framework of the social pillars – still facilitates the access of parties to the mass public. The ties between parties and congenial broadcasting associations are less formal now than before the "depillarization," but still survive to some degree.[10] Until now the need of the parties for publicity has been met sufficiently by the existing broadcasting system, although larger parties tend to be favored. So far the parties do not need large sums of money in order to buy time on the airwaves.

One could consider the allocations to the parliamentary groups and individual Members of Parliament to be a form of direct state subvention. But, since these relatively small grants are limited to the administrative support of the members themselves and not of the party organizations, they are omitted from consideration here. Further, space provided by the authorities for the posting of signs during election campaigns could be seen as a case of very limited public financing.

Indirect state subvention is more important. Since the 1970s, the parties that are represented in the Second Chamber can claim subsidies for their research institutes, their educational institutes and their youth organizations.[11] The research institutes are entitled to public money up to a certain maximum that depends on the size of the parliamentary group in the Second Chamber. But to receive the subsidies they have to prove that their own income is equally high. The justification of this "matching fund" system is twofold. First, institutes affiliated with larger parties need more money for their larger organizations. Secondly, institutes that are unable to raise money from other sources should not be kept alive artificially. The same principle applies to the educational institutes and the youth movements. But the educational institutes have to finance only 30 percent of their expenditures. The youth movements need to have enough resources to pay 10 percent of the staff salaries and 30 percent of other expenditures. In this case, the maximum amount depends not only on the size of the parliamentary group, but also on the membership of the youth movement. The resources listed as their "own" by the foundations are in most cases largely donations from their affiliated parties.

In 1983 and 1984, the state subventions for research institutes and educational institutes were lowered by 16 percent and 10 percent respectively due to the retrenchment policy of the government. Thus in 1984 the largest party, the PvdA, received Dfl. 319,000 and Dfl. 370,058 respectively for its research institute and its educational institute. Plans of the Cabinet to cut the budgets of the research institutes still further and to stop completely the subventions for the educational institutes were rejected by Parliament, however. In 1985, the Minister of Domestic Affairs agreed reluctantly with the idea that these subventions should continue to exist in the future. Moreover, these subventions will be based on a special law that gives the institutes a stable financial basis.[12]

Further, there have been other cases of indirect but goal-oriented subventions: the government allocates funds for the emancipation of women, which to some extent also benefits the political parties; the NCO (Nationale Commissie Voorlichting en Bewustwording Ontwikkelingssamenwerking), a state-financed commission set up to inform the public about development cooperation, spends a part of its annual budget on parties. For instance, a special Third World-oriented foundation of the PvdA received almost Dfl. 100,000 of government funds in 1984.

A new method of state subvention was proposed in 1980 by the Minister of Cooperation with the Developing Countries. Under this plan, projects in which Dutch political parties and parties in the Third World were to cooperate would be eligible for state aid. One million guilders would be available from 1981 onwards. The plan of Minister De Koning, which resembles to some degree the German practice of party foundations dispensing aid to developing countries, encountered many objections. This "politicization of development aid" (VVD) or "export of Dutch political disagreements to the Third World" (PPR) appeared to have been suggested by the CDA-executive, but the idea was abandoned soon afterwards.[13]

Another example of public finance is the special funding of the campaigns for the European elections. In 1979 and 1984, various countries received a certain amount of money from the European Parliament which was distributed among the political parties. It has to be noted, however, that this kind of "state-subvention" is rather alien to the spirit of the Dutch practice. Moreover, the amount of European subventions is very high compared with the Dutch standard of relatively inexpensive election campaigns. In 1984, the subventions covered almost completely the total costs of the rather boring campaign. For example, the VVD received Dfl. 891,000 and spent Dfl. 916,000 for the elections; the PvdA got Dfl. 1,435,685 and spent Dfl. 1,865,035.

The official attitude toward public funding in the Netherlands is still based on the assumption that direct subsidies to parties are undesirable for several reasons. First, public subsidies are thought to reinforce the status quo of the party system. Secondly, the danger of manipulation and control by the state would be enhanced. Thirdly, the distance between elite and grassroots would increase because the parties would no longer have to rely financially on their members. In brief, democracy would be endangered.

But practice is different. The so-called "indirect" subsidies are often used for normal party activities. Several parties had research institutes long before the state made money available for these tasks in 1970. The educational task has been a common feature of all mass parties since their establishment in the nineteenth century, and party youth organizations have always existed, often as recruitment schools for the party elite.

Moreover, during the debate in the Second Chamber in 1971 about the possibility of granting state subventions to research institutes, it was already admitted that it would be impossible to draw a clear line between the parties and their affiliated foundations.[14]

Then why this discrepancy between fact and norm? As stated elsewhere,[15] the present ambiguous situation of public finance in the Netherlands is rather an escape from the problem of recognition of political parties by public law than the result of a decision in principle. In the political arena, it is impossible to create a consensus on direct subvention by the state. The traditional emphasis laid on "sovereignty within one's own circle" by the Christian Democrats or on "state abstinence" by the Liberals still makes it impossible to finance parties directly. The actual practice of subsidizing affiliated foundations was set up to meet the growing needs of political parties without making a statement in principle, but the decision of the Cabinet in 1985 to make a special law for these subventions comes close to it.

EXPENDITURES FOR PARTY BUREAUCRACIES AND ELECTION CAMPAIGNS

In this section, data will be presented concerning the two main areas of party expenditure, bureaucracies and campaigns.

In the Netherlands, as elsewhere on the European continent, political party organizations play an important role between elections, and the national party secretariats are at the center of these efforts. Most of these national party offices have professional staff members. Table 3 shows the degree of bureaucratization of the national party offices – not including the affiliated foundations – in 1980.

Three small right-wing parties (SGP, RPF and DS'70) relied almost exclusively on volunteers. In general, left-wing parties were more bureaucratized than right-wing parties. Available data on the three major parties confirms this phenomenon also for the year 1984. The average cost of salaries per member was about the same in 1984 as in 1980 for the CDA and the VVD; the PvdA-average in 1984 was still considerably higher than those of the CDA and the VVD, but less than in 1980 (Dfl. 23.40 instead of Dfl. 28.07). One can only guess at the reasons for these differences between the various parties. Left-wing parties probably have more centralized party organizations and they may have a more active rank-and-file that require more bureaucracy. On the other hand, staff members and leaders of right-wing parties may have other sources of income, such as private businesses, to which their left-wing counterparts do not have access.[16] This would be

Table 3. *Bureaucratization of national party bureaus, 1980*

Party	Salary expenditures (Dfl.)	Average per member (Dfl.)	Party members per staff member
CDA	1,800,000	12.25	3972
PvdA	2,697,000	28.07	2328
VVD	845,000	9.83	3654
D66	350,000	15.81	2202
PPR	190,000	18.09	2333
PS	185,000	19.91	2545
CPN*	902,583	56.00	n.a.
SGP	7,500	0.37	(67666)
RPF	4,000	0.72	n.a.
GPV	122,220	9.45	4907

* figures from 1978/1979.
Source: Ruud Koole, "Politieke partijen: de leden en het geld," in *Jaarboek 1981 DNPP* (Groningen: University of Groningen, 1982), pp. 20–2; for DS'70 (right-wing Democratic Socialists), no accurate data were available.

an indirect form of business support to parties, but it is hard to substantiate.

The election campaigns are another important area of party expenditure. But compared with other countries they do not cost extremely large amounts of money. In 1981, the regular elections for the Second Chamber were about as expensive as the annual salaries of the professional staff members of the national secretariats. Table 4 shows how much the parties spent during the campaigns for the Second Chamber in 1981 and 1982. The 1982 elections were necessary because of the fall of the center-left coalition, formed in 1981. One has to note that in Dutch practice electoral campaigns are completely run by the party organizations, not by individual candidates. The latter have to adapt themselves to their party's electoral strategy and do not need to raise funds for their own election. All the expenditures are to be paid by the party. The organization of the election as well as the registration of the voters are totally financed by the state. Perhaps this could be considered another form of state subvention.

Somewhat more than 8 million guilders spent in 1981 and less than 5 million spent in 1982 indicate the rather modest financial scope of Dutch election campaigns. A Belgian scholar calculated that the national elections in 1977 in Belgium cost the equivalent of about 30 million guilders, whereas

Table 4. Expenditures by the national parties during the campaigns for the elections for the second chamber, 1981 and 1982*

Party	1981				1982			
	Expenditure (× 1000)	%	Average per Member	Average per Voter	Expenditure (× 1000)	%	Average per Member	Average per Voter
CDA	1.500	18	9.5	0.6	1.150	24	7.5	0.5
PvdA	2.862	34	26.0	1.2	1.391	28	13.2	0.6
VVD	1.162	14	12.7	0.8	962	20	9.5	0.5
D66	510	6	30.6	0.5	250	5	16.7	0.7
PSP	270	3	29.1	1.5	200	4	19.4	1.1
PPR	450	5	42.0	2.6	206	4	21.7	1.5
SGP	400	5	19.5	2.3	200	4	9.6	1.3
RPF	282	3	39.7	2.6	130	3	13.3	1.1
GPV	329	4	25.4	4.6	160	3	12.3	2.4
CPN	461	6	28.6	3.2	**	**	**	**
DS70	104	1	32.5	2.1	**	**	**	**
EVP	**	**	**	**	250	5	138.9	4.4
Total/ average	8.329	99	18.3	1.0	4,900	100	11.2	0.6

* In Dutch guilders: Dfl. 1.00 = U.S. $0.40 per December 31, 1981.
** The data for CPN and DS'70 in 1982 and of EVP in 1981 are missing. Therefore, the totals and average at the end of the table are not 100 percent accurate, but they may indicate the size and the direction of the expenditures.

the expenditures for 1981 would be about 45 million guilders.[17] The Netherlands, so close to Belgium in size and geography, spent about seven times less: one guilder per voter in 1981. A year later, the elections were even cheaper (Dfl. 0.60 per voter). The parties were not able to fill their campaign chests to the same level, just a year after the 1981 national elections. Moreover, in 1982 there also were local and provincial elections. One guilder per voter also was inexpensive compared with election costs in the United States, Canada, or Germany. The North American countries spent more than seven times more than the Netherlands; the Federal Republic of Germany spent twenty times as much.[18] In 1982, the party members who "bear" the financial burden of the parties in the Netherlands had reached their donating capacity. The 1982 election campaign was somewhat shorter and perhaps less intense than the one in 1981. But more money does not guarantee better election results.

CONCLUSION: THE RELATIVE "MODESTY" OF DUTCH PARTY FINANCE

As we have seen, Dutch election campaigns are relatively inexpensive. But on the European continent, parties play an important role as inter-election organizations as well. We saw that the salary costs of the professional staff members tend to be as high as the expenditures for a national election. But they are paid by the parties every year, whereas regular national elections are to be held every four years, although in reality, an election has been held about once every three years since 1945. Moreover, in the Netherlands, as for instance in Germany or France and unlike the United States, different elections (local, provincial, national or European) are held at different times, which puts extra pressure on the parties' budgets. A comparison over a complete election cycle of all the expenditures made by parties would allow a more accurate approach. While the available data are not fit for exact calculation, a rough comparison of the Dutch situation with the activities of political parties in the United States, Canada and West-Germany may give an indication.[19] This comparison shows that the estimated expenditures at the national level of the Dutch party system are somewhat higher – in relative terms – than the U.S. "costs of democracy," as Heard (1960) called them.[20] Thus Alexander's statement that "money – lots of it – is essential to the smooth conduct of our system of free elections,"[21] is equally true for the Netherlands, although in the latter case the statement is true for the whole system of party democracy, rather than for elections only.

But compared with Germany, which has equally important inter-election party organizations and also holds different elections scattered over time, Dutch party finance is indeed very modest. In Germany, 31 percent of the total expenditures was financed by the state.[22] In the Netherlands this percentage was about 20 percent in 1980 and even lower in the years after. The rest of the costs were almost completely covered – as we have seen – by membership dues or other contributions from individual members. This phenomenon, the heavy reliance on individual members and the near absence of funds from business circles might be called the main feature of Dutch party finance. The Dutch reluctance to accept direct state subvention is a partial reason for this phenomenon. We can only suggest a tentative explanation of this feature. Owing to the tradition of "pillarization," Dutch citizens have learned to support their own organizations and not to rely directly on the state. Most of the pillars were, in principle, against state interference when their own organizations could accomplish their appointed tasks without outside aid. At the beginning of the twentieth century, the Calvinists argued for "sovereignty within one's own circle," and the Catholics defended the "principle of subsidarity." Liberals called for the largest possible degree of state-abstinence and the Socialists did not have much faith in a bourgeois state. No pillar wanted to be deprived of established rights or to be over-ruled by the other pillars by means of a greater influence of the state. The pillars did allow the state a referee role. But, in order to prove the legitimacy of their organizations, the pillars had to be able to show the readiness of large numbers of citizens to make sacrifices. Hence the need for mass organizations in many areas, such as parties, as well as school – or broadcasting – associations. The only way for one pillar to have a higher degree of influence in a certain area and be recognized by the other pillars was to prove its popular support.

This rigid system no longer exists. "Depillarization" has loosened many traditional ties since the 1960s. But the social and political climate is still determined to a large extent by traditional phenomena. Practices that clash with the idea of reliance on the readiness of citizens to sacrifice money and/or time continue to be rejected. The movement for democratization of society at all levels at the end of the 1960s and the beginning of the 1970s may even have fostered this climate. So business financing of political parties, although not officially prohibited, is still taboo. And state subvention has been accepted only very reluctantly and always on the condition that the dependence of a party or foundation on its rank-and-file membership would not be endangered.

Whether this "serene" climate will continue to prevail is hard to predict. The "commercialization" of social activities does take place now in areas where these activities had already been taken over by the welfare state.

"Deregulation" and "privatization" are popular catch-words in the mid 1980s. Although the plans of the Cabinet to cut – or even to stop – state subventions to party foundations were rejected in 1985 and a special law regulating these subventions was announced the same year, a positive decision to grant parties more state subventions seems very unlikely in the near future. Growing dependence on the state through a slow and hidden process of bureaucratization remains possible, however. Large-scale business interference in the finances of the parties should not be expected in the near future. Until the present time parties have managed to raise enough funds without business donations to be able to function more-or-less satisfactorily. Direct interference on a large scale in election campaigns by interest groups is something else. For example, the largest trade union, FNV (Federatie Nederlandse Vakverenigingen), spent about DFl. 3 million during the campaign of 1986 in order to "inform the voters about the socio-economic paragraphs of the platforms of the three major parties" and to prevent the return of the actual centre-right coalition cabinet after the elections.[23] While such spending did not constitute a direct donation to a political party, it was clear that – if successful – the PvdA especially would profit from this activity. The FNV activity may indicate a tendency toward a role for Dutch interest groups similar to that already performed by the U.S. political action committees (PACs), rather than a simple return to the "pillarized politics" which predominated before 1970.

Finally, the fall of one of the last bastions of the pillarized society, the mass media, may change party finance in the long run. New technological possibilities already put the present media system under heavy pressure. Cheap access to the media might give way to a far more expensive market system in which parties are forced to buy (prime) time on the airwaves in order to reach the voters. It remains to be seen whether the "serene" atmosphere with regard to party finance will survive a breakdown of the remaining bastions of the pillarized society.

Notes

1 See Arend Lijphart, *The Politics of Accommodation, Pluralism and Democracy in the Netherlands* (Berkeley: University of California Press, 1968/75). This book has stimulated much of the discussion about this type of democracy. See also the special issue of *Acta Politica* (January, 1984), edited by Marinus P. C. M. van Schendelen, entitled "Consociationalism, pillarization and conflict-management in the Low Countries" and H. Daalder, "Consociationalism, center and periphery in the Netherlands," in Peter Torsik, ed., *Mobilization, Centerperiphery Structures and Nation-Building* (Bergen/Oslo: Universitets forlaget, 1981).

2 In 1956, with 100 seats in Parliament, seven parties were represented; in 1959, after the number of seats in Parliament had been raised to 150, eight parties were represented. After 1963 this number increased to fourteen in 1971 and 1972. In the elections of 1982 twelve parties succeeded in winning at least one seat; so did nine in 1986.

3 Unless otherwise specified, all data in this chapter stems from calculations by the author based on official party records. Here the audit of the PvdA from 1983/4 and the audits of the affiliated foundations from 1984 were used, as well as the Jaarverslagen (Annual reports) 1958–60, pp. 70–87.

4 *Proceedings of the Second Chamber* (Handelingen Tweede Kamer), 1968/9, pp. 249, 336, 337, and 371. Also see Douwe J. Elzinga, *De politieke partij en het constitutionele recht* (Nijmegen: Ars Aequi, 1982), p. 220.

5 Quoted in *Nieuwsblad van het Noorden*, August 28, 1985.

6 Some affiliated institutes of the PvdA receive monies every year (most received Dfl. 20,000, while one received Dfl. 30,000) from the insurance company "De Centrale," closely connected to the Federation of Dutch Trade Unions (FNV); the audits of the VVD-Research Institute are not available.

7 CDA and VVD had requested grants from the enterprise Daf-trucks, and received Dfl. 2500 (US $1175) each. The company made an offer to contribute the same sum to the PvdA, but the party refused the contribution. The affair was covered by most of the dailies on February 2, 1977. Elzinga states that the CDA received Dfl. 26,000 from business circles for the election campaign of 1977, see Douwe J. Elzinga, *De politieke partij en het constitutionele recht* (Nijmegen: Ars Aequi, 1982), p. 272. These contributions, however, constituted only 2 percent of the total campaign budget of Dfl. 1.2 million.

8 Khayyam Zev Paltiel, "Campaign Finance: Contrasting Practices and Reform," in David Butler, Howard R. Penniman and Austin Ranney, eds., *Democracy at the Polls: A Comparative Study of Competitive National Elections* (Washington/London: American Enterprise Institute for Public Policy Research, 1981), p. 151.

9 Ibid., p. 147.

10 See Kees Brants, Walther Kok and Philip van Praag Jr., *De strijd om de kiezersgunst: Verkiezingscampagnes in Nederland* (Amsterdam: Kobra, 1982), pp. 15–36, 99–108.

11 The term "foundation" refers to the official legal status of party-connected research and educational organizations. The term "institute" is a broader, non-legal, designation for the same organizations. To receive public funding in the Netherlands, all research and educational organizations must be "found-ations," but most of these call themselves "institutes."

12 Cabinet's decision, September 27, 1985; See *Proceedings of the Second Chamber* (Handelingen Tweede Kamer), 1985–6, No. 19.508.

13 *Trouw*, February 26, 1981.

14 *Proceedings of the Second Chamber* (Handelingen Tweede Kamer), 1971, No. 11.105.

15 Ruud A. Koole, "Politieke partijen: de leden en het geld," in *Jaarboek Documentatiecentrum Nederlandse Politieke Partijen* (DNPP) (Groningen: University of Groningen, 1982), p. 6.

16 The chairman of the liberal VVD, for instance, is not paid by his party, but the chairman of CDA and PvdA are. Usually the chairmen of the parties are not the same as the parliamentary leaders; the latter are considered to be the political leaders of the party, unless the party furnishes the (vice) prime minister, who then will probably be its political leaders.

17 Jacques Gielen, *Verkiezingscampagnes blijven een miljoenenaangelegenheid* (Leuven: Katholieke Universiteit, Dept. Politieke Wetenschappen, s.a.), pp. 25, 36.

18 Karl-Heinz Nassmacher, "Oeffentliche Rechenschaft und Parteifinanzierung: Erfahrungen in Deutschland, Kanada und in den Vereinigten Staaten," *Das Parlament*, B 14–15. April, 1982, p. 14.

19 We had at our disposal all 1980-data of D66, CDA and PvdA and used other financial reports of VVD, CPN, SGP, PSP and PPR which were not always complete. Based on these data, we estimated the total expenditures of all parties at the national level at about Dfl. 30 million. From 1977 to 1980 this would be about Dfl. 100 million (counting with the inflation rate) or DM 90.9 million. For the comparative approach, we relied on Karl-Heinz Nassmacher, "Oeffent-liche Rechenschaft und Parteifinanzierung: Erfahrungen in Deutschland, Kanada und in den Vereinigten Staaten," *Das Parlament*, B 14–15, April, 1982, pp. 3–18. Thus, the average "costs of democracy" during an entire election-cycle (1977–80) per person entitled to vote was: the Netherlands – DM 8.9; West-Germany – DM 34.5; Canada – DM 14.0; United states – DM 7.7 (DM 1.0 = US$ 0.444). Also see Ruud Koole, "Partijfinancien: lessen voor Neder-land uit de recente Westduitse praktijk?" *Beleid en Maatschappij*, June 1985, pp. 142–9.

20 Alexander Heard, *The Costs of Democracy* (Chapel Hill: University of North Carolina Press, 1960).
21 Herbert E. Alexander, *Financing Politics: Money, Elections and Political Reform*, 2nd Edition (Washington, D.C.: Congressional Quarterly Press, 1980), p. 2.
22 Karl-Heinz Nassmacher, "Oeffentliche Rechenschaft und Parteifinanzierung: Erfahrungen in Deutschland, Kanada und in den Vereinigten Staaten," Das Parlament, B 14–15, April, 1982, p. 14.
23 NRC/Handelsblad, May 17, 1985.

10

The new German system of party funding: the Presidential committee report of 1983 and its realization

HANS-PETER SCHNEIDER

In 1959, West Germany became one of the first nations to adopt a system of partial public financing of its political parties. As with any public policy experiment, public funding has been altered over the years with the intention of adjusting to the needs of the larger political system. As Karl-Heinz Nassmacher notes in his chapter in this volume, the German public financing system, like those of several other countries, has thus far undergone three developmental stages: a stage of early experimentation; a second period in which legislators, more sure of the approach, enlarged the scope of the system; and currently, a stage of adjustments to keep the system in line with the rate of inflation.

In 1959, an annual allowance of five million Deutschmarks was given to political parties for their political education activities. By 1966, the parties received a boost in public payments to DM 38 million for the purpose of carrying out their responsibilities under the Basic Law. In 1966, however, the public financing system came under challenge, and the program in operation was declared unconstitutional by the Constitutional Court. In 1967, a revised form of public funding emerged which involved moderate tax benefits for donations to political parties, substantial flat grants by the federation and all states for election expenses, and an annual allowance to political foundations for political activities. In 1979, public subsidies were extended to include a flat grant for election expenses relating to the European Parliament.

The system often has been subject to various criticism by interest and advocacy groups. For example, some critics of public financing in West Germany have argued that the system has created a reliance by the parties on the state, thereby diminishing important ties between the parties and the citizenry. Others argue that certain tax regulations of private donations have resulted in financial difficulties for the parties. Such difficulties, in turn, have forced the parties to seek to raise funds by operating at the edge of the law. Still other critics, alarmed by revelations that well-known political leaders from various parties had been accused of tax evasion in connection with party fund-raising activities, have called for an enlarged public financing system.

On March 4, 1982, the Federal President, Professor Dr. Karl Carstens, set up a committee of experts to study issues raised by the German system of party funding. The President was acting in response to a joint request by the chairmen of the four major parties – the Social Democratic Party (SDP), the Christian Democratic Union (CDU), the Christian Social Union (CSU), and the Free Democratic Party (FDP) – to form an independent commission on party finance. The committee was charged with drawing up, in complete autonomy, proposals for a future arrangement governing the system.[1] Its members included Professor Walter Furst (Chair), Dr. Hermann Maassen (Deputy Chair), Professor Heino Kaack, Professor Hans-Peter Schneider and Professor Horst Vogel.

The committee's conclusions were extensive. With due regard for constitutional requirements and limitations,[2] the committee elaborated an overall concept designed to ensure the funding of political parties in accordance with their functions, while at the same time shifting the emphasis of party funding away from the state and toward the individual citizen. The panel endorsed new regulations requiring greater transparency of party revenues and expenditures, proscription of foreign revenues to German parties, a stipulation for annual reports concerning party finance, adjustment of the tax laws to limit the need of parties to attempt to circumvent those laws in order to stay afloat, and several new mechanisms of public financing, such as a "citizen's premium" and an "Election and Donation Fund." The committee felt that if its proposals were adopted, and if the scope, organization and necessity of party funding were clearly recognizable by the average citizen, it would help create a fuller basis of trust between citizens and parties, an indispensable condition for the health of a parliamentary democracy.

This article will describe in detail the conclusions of the committee as well as the rationales upon which these conclusions were based. The implementation of the committee's recommendation by the Bundestag and the political repercussions of the proposals also will be discussed.

MANAGEMENT OF EXPENDITURE AND TRANSPARENCY

In its deliberations, the committee attached particular importance to measures that would ensure economical party funding, would permit the use of public funds to be audited according to budgetary principles, and thus would make party funding transparent to citizens. For example, the committee called on parties to review constantly their trend toward increased expenditures by exercising self-restraint in the performance of their functions. It recommended that a reasonable joint financial framework for election campaigns be established by means of binding agreements on the limitation of expenditures. Such agreements ought to be concluded early enough for election campaign plans to take account of them. They also should cover all expenditures and thus include party branches.

The committee also proposed that parties be induced to curb their expenditures by limiting their borrowing. Parties, it was argued, should limit their borrowing activity according to the following principles: borrowing in anticipation of future regular income would require the treasurer's consent; loans raised could exceed 20 percent of the branch's average income of the last four years for no longer than twelve months per legislative term; loans should be regarded as regular income; a sliding scale of adjustment should be applied for newly established parties.[3]

The committee considered transparency of party finances to be a central element of any endeavor to limit expenditures. Unlike the existing arrangement at the time of the committee's report, whereby parties are merely obliged to account publicly for their sources of funds, the committee recommended that, in the future, parties also should publicly account for their expenditures and for their assets.[4]

The committee advised that the duty of public disclosure should, in the future, be extended to include all regional and district party branches. In addition to the then-existing procedure in which accounts were examined by auditors, auditing by the Federal Audit Office ought to be introduced in conformity with the Budgetary Principles Act (Section 43 (1) 3). This should be carried out at the instance of the Speaker of the Bundestag if warranted by the results of the audit. Since parties should ensure that their accounts are comprehensive, that is, that all income and expenditures are included, "party expenditures," according to the law, ought to mean all expenditures – in cash or in kind – incurred by a party in connection with its activities.

It was the consensus of the committee that comprehensive accountability of party finances is dependent on a controllable flow of funds. Accordingly, several measures were put forth to prevent attempts by parties to raise additional funds by circumventing the tax laws.

1 Contributions to parliamentary groups in the Bundestag which had – until then – been allocated and paid on the basis of the budget, were recommended to be governed by a specific act. The task of checking

these funds to be certain that they are used in accordance with their intended purpose would be assigned to the President of the Federal Audit Office in conformity with the Budgetary Code. Parliamentary groups would be obliged to report annually to the Speaker of the Bundestag on the use of the funds. This report would be issued as a Bundestag publication.

2 Payments – in cash or in kind – by political foundations to political parties ought to be impermissible.[5] In addition, the use of funds by political foundations should be audited more intensively by audit offices and financial authorities. It should be required that the business reports of such foundations be published in the Federal Gazette. Further, parties and foundations should have separate chairmen and treasurers at the national level.[6]

3 There should be changes made in the laws regarding certain special corporate bodies in Germany which are given tax exemptions if they promote the public welfare. These corporations, should, in the future, be treated as non-profit bodies for tax purposes. The transfer of funds by such corporate bodies to political parties must be prohibited. In addition, financial authorities should ensure compliance with the ban by constantly auditing the use of funds by such organizations.

4 Tax exemptions for "political associations," which are party-related organizations such as the Wirtschaftsrat der CDU, the CDU-Sozialausschusse, the Heinemann-Initiative and the Fritz-Erler-Kreis of the SPD, should be repealed. Giving tax exemptions for donations to such associations gives the parties access to the funds which they may then misuse for political purposes, thereby circumventing the strict rules and limits on the tax-privileged donations given directly to the parties. The duty of disclosure applicable to large donors could be circumvented if an association, rather than the donor himself, acts as the contributor.

5 Professional associations such as trade unions and employer's associations should, in the future, no longer be entitled to transfer portions of their tax-privileged income from membership dues to political parties. Such transfers impair the equality of opportunity for political parties guaranteed by the German constitution.

6 To protect German parties against outside influence, foreign donations to parties – in cash or in kind – must be made illegal. This policy also would preclude domestic sources from diverting funds through foreign channels for the purpose of securing illegal tax advantages. Exemptions, however, would be established for German citizens who are living abroad.

In sum, contributions – in cash or in kind – which flow to parties through the aforementioned channels should be deemed illegal. Donations that are anonymous, and those which have not been duly disclosed or have clearly been granted with a view to obtaining a certain economic or political concession, also should be considered illegal.

To guarantee that the regulations on the limitation of expenditures and on accountability are complied with, the committee considered it indispensable to make provisions for adequate sanctions designed to ensure the proper financial conduct of political parties. Such sanctions should be incorporated into the Political Parties Act. Graded according to the nature and gravity of the infringement, these sanctions ought to entail the cancellation or reduction of the public funds due for the reimbursement of election campaign expenditures.

For example, if a party acquires funds through illegal means, a sum of ten times the amount of those funds should be deducted from its election campaign expenditure reimbursement. If a tax-privileged organization, such as a political association or a political foundation, is involved, it would forfeit its exemptions from corporation and property tax. If a party's loans exceed 20 percent of its average income for more than twelve months, public funds equivilant to the overdrawn amount would be withheld.

To help monitor compliance with the proposed regulations, the committee proposed that the President of the Bundestag report annually to the Bundestag on the development of party finances, especially on the accounts of parties. The Speaker also should examine whether parties have used public funds in accordance with their intended purpose: whether the principles governing borrowing have been observed; whether the proportion of public funds have exceeded the limit established by the Federal Constitutional Court, pursuant to which parties must not be financed predominantly by public funds;[7] whether parties have illegally acquired funds. If the speaker deems it necessary, he or she would be able to arrange for an audit by the Federal Audit Office and to enforce the proposed sanctions. The report by the Speaker would be issued and distributed as a Bundestag publication.

PARTY FUNDING : PRIVATE AND PUBLIC

The committee also devoted attention to the fundamental political issue of the relationship of political parties to the state. Since political parties are freely established, independent, citizen's associations, their participation in the formation of the political will of the people, committee members felt, includes the duty to raise through efforts of their own the funds needed for the performance of their tasks. The state, therefore, is neither obliged nor entitled to meet the financial requirements of parties, neither can it relieve them of the risk of the failure of their own financial efforts. Further, on no account should parties be wholly financed by public funds. Complete or predominant party funding by the state is contrary to the decisions of the Federal Constitutional Court.[8]

For these reasons, the committee decided to give support to the efforts undertaken by parties to raise funds from the citizenry by supporting private initiatives aimed at increasing party funds. It was acknowledged that this goal can be advanced in a constitutional manner only if equal opportunities for parties and the right of citizens to equal participation in political affairs are guaranteed. Private donations to political parties should be neither prohibited by law nor morally questionable. In fact, the committee agreed, they are constitutionally desirable and indispensable if parties are to remain independent of the state. By donating to a party, the citizens exercise their right of participation in political affairs.

The committee also did not see any reasons for denying corporate bodies, notably joint stock companies, the opportunity of making dona-tions.[9] In any case, such prohibitions could be circumvented with the aid of intermediaries. The only reasonable precaution against parties becom-ing politically dependent on large-scale donors was already in the Basic Law (Article 21, (1), Sentence 4), pursuant to which parties must publicly account for the sources of their funds. The committee attached great importance to this requirement and recommended in addition not only that the requirement in the Political Parties Act (Section 25) that all donation above DM 20,000 be disclosed, but also that more stringent sanctions be established against the violation of the duty of disclosure. In the future, they felt, the duty of disclosure also should cover all donations to political parties made to this amount from a single source in one calendar year, irrespective of whether they stem from taxed or untaxed income.

The committee recommended that political parties should fully exploit the opportunities for increased income from membership dues afforded by a flexible system of calculating and collecting membership dues. However, the committee suggested that special contributions by members of parliament or other office-holders should be prohibited as a source of income under the Political Parties Act (Section 24 (2,2)). These special contributions constitute a substantial portion of party income. In the committee's view, these contributions, which have, in some cases, been excessive, are questionable because they are likely to impair the indepen-dence of members of parliament. The possibility cannot be ruled out that these payments are taken into account when determining the emoluments of members of parliament. This type of party income is therefore constitutionally questionable.

SOLVING DILEMMAS CAUSED BY THE TAX LAWS

The committee believed that it is inappropriate for a free democracy to discriminate in terms of tax laws against political parties in relation to other organizations. Such laws force parties into a position where they either have to do without donations intended for them or, through circumvention, operate in a "grey area" on the fringes of legality.[10] For example, political parties have narrow limits for self-generated funds because of the existing tax arrangements according to which membership dues and donations to political parties are tax deductible only up to a maximum of DM 1,800/3,600. Private contributions to parties in excess of this amount must be made from taxed income. This is one of the causes of the poor financial straits of parties, which has repeatedly led to roundabout funding, which involves special forms and methods of party financing with the aim of circumventing the tax laws. Such roundabout funding has been assisted by the "gulf" existing between the generous tax-deduction arrangements for donations to bodies that are non-profit and serve public policy as against the limited tax-deduction arrangements for donations to political parties. If a democracy based on political parties is not to suffer damage in the long run, it is indispensable for constitutional reasons to prevent such circumvention. This can only be achieved effectively if the incentives no longer exist.

Therefore, the committee suggested that membership dues and donations to political parties be regarded as expenditures serving public policy within the meaning of the Income Tax Act (Section 10 b (1)) and the Corporation Tax Act (Section 9 (3)) and that they should be deducted from the basic tax liability as special expenditures not exceeding 5 percent of annual income.[11] Under the existing laws is was possible to deduct donations up to an amount of ". . . 2 thousands of the turnover and the wages and salaries paid in the calendar year." The committee recommended that these regulations should be repealed. Corporate bodies which have been recognized as "eligible for promotion for reasons of public policy" should be given the status of non-profit bodies. The relevant sections of the Income Tax Act (Section 10 b (2)) and the Corporation Tax Act (Section 9 (3) b), the committee argued, also should be repealed.

Further, these arrangements were considered to be compatible with the Basic Law only if additional measures were enacted to ensure the citizen's right to participate in political affairs on equal terms, as well as freedom of the political parties and equal opportunities for them.[12] The committee, therefore, considered it necessary to deal with the inequities among citizens and parties resulting from the effect of the progressive income tax on the tax deductibility of private contributions to parties. To this end, the committee proposed a scheme producing equal opportunities among parties and between parties and citizens. This would rectify the situation caused by the tax law in which citizens with greater financial capacity and the parties assisted by them are privileged in a manner contrary to the principle of equality.

This equal-opportunites scheme would have two components. First, membership dues and small donations to parties up to DM 1,200/2,400 would be deductible from tax liabilities at a rate of 50 percent. Higher amounts are tax-deductible under the conditions of the Income Tax Act (Section 10 b (1)). Secondly, the different levels of tax relief for parties, which have a favorable impact on their income from membership dues and donations, would be equalized.

This plan for the equalization of opportunities among parties would be calculated on the basis of the total annual income of a party from membership dues and donations. Assuming a tax rate of 40 percent, it could be determined which party obtained the largest tax relief in relation to the number of votes cast for it at the last Bundestag elections. The party favored most by the existing tax regulations would serve as the yardstick. The other parties would receive sums from public funds which would bring them up to the level of tax relief enjoyed by the aforementioned reference party, computed on the basis of the votes polled. This scheme would not serve to compensate for the different amounts of parties' self-generated funds, but would merely eliminate the disparities that were caused by tax arrangements and thus interfered with natural competition among parties. As a result, all parties would be operating as if their self-generated funds from membership dues and donations in relation to their political strength enjoyed equal tax relief.[13]

The equal-opportunities scheme would exist for all parties that polled at least 0.5 percent of the votes cast at the preceding Bundestag elections. To prevent large parties from gaining unreasonable advantages, only parties which polled at least 5 percent of the votes cast could be taken into consideration as a "reference party." Further minimum limitations were not envisaged by the committee.

The equal-opportunities scheme would be put into effect only at the federal level to avoid multiple advantages for particular parties. Since the compensatory payments are not a form of (impermissible) public funding of general party activities, but a fiscally and constitutionally necessary means of public compensation, they should not be considered part of public funding, the size of which is limited by the prohibition that parties must not be financed predominantly by public funds. The committee's proposals on the treatment of membership dues and donations for tax purposes and on equal opportunities thus forms an integrated whole that cannot to be broken apart without jeopardizing the constitutionality of the overall concept.[14]

PUBLIC FUNDING

The committee also turned its attention directly to the subject of public funding. The self-generated funding of parties is restricted to varying degrees by their ability to raise funds. Additional support for parties from public funds is therefore not only constitutionally permissible, but also necessary if the parties are otherwise unable to perform the functions assigned to them by the Basic Law. The governmental system of the Federal Republic of Germany would neither function nor survive without the activities of political parties. However, according to a decision handed down by the Federal Constitutional Court, "meeting all or most of the general financing requirements of parties through public funds" is incompatible with the function of parties.[15] The committee sought to gear its proposals to the Court-established principle that public reimbursement can only apply to the "necessary expenditure of a reasonable election campaign,"[16] so as not to commit parties to comprehensive public support and dependence on the state.

In its consideration of public funding of parties, the committee proceeded on the assumption that the existing level of campaign expenditure reimbursement should be preserved, adjusting only for inflation. The existing lump-sum reimbursement per voter was increased in 1974 from DM 2.50 to DM 3.50. Since then, considerable increases in costs had occurred. These could be taken into account by fixing the lump-sum at DM 5.00.

The committee recommended changes in the existing system governing the reimbursement of election campaign expenditures. It proposed a new model according to which parties were to be assigned a "basic sum" and a new "citizen's premium." Since preparations for an election campaign must be planned well in advance and continue throughout the entire legislative term, the committee considered it advisable to make a specific sum available to parties which would meet their basic expenditures. Approximately 20 percent of the overall volume of public funding per legislative term would be earmarked for this basic sum. The number of votes each party polled, however, would not serve as the sole criterion for determining the basic sum. Since preparations for election campaigns are governed by the overall size and importance of each party, the scale of distribution, therefore, must take into account the relative political importance of the various parties. This importance is reflective, *inter alia*, of their territorial scope and membership. Therefore, the committee suggested that – in addition to the same fundamental payment for all parties – an allowance would be paid for every constituency in which a party has a candidate. The aforementioned sums would be increased by 50 percent if a party has at least 400,000 members.

As the minimum requirement for a party to receive the basic sum, the committee suggested that at least 0.5 percent of the votes cast must be polled by the party. This is the same requirement which governs the reimbursement of election campaign expenditures. The basic sum should be granted separately for Bundestag elections and elections to the European Parliament and be paid out at the start of the respective election years.

As part of the endeavor to reduce the dependence of parties on the state, the committee proposed the introduction of an election campaign contribution from public funds which would be determined by the citizens themselves. This would be called the "citizen's premium." At all elections to the Bundestag – or to the European Parliament – citizens would be given the right to designate a certain sum from public funds to be given to the party that they considered worthy of support. In this way, citizens would be granted an opportunity for participation in the public funding process. The citizens' premium would be determined by the voters at the polling stations, thus eliminating costly allocation procedures and a permanent "campaign to secure funds." The size of the citizen's premium would be determined by parliamentary legislation, and geared to the size of the existing lump-sum paid per voter, taking inflation into account.

Parties would receive the funds based on these citizens's premiums in annual installments. As under the existing arrangement for the reimbursement of election campaign expenditures (cf. Section 18 (2) of the Political Parties Act), the citizen's premium would be available to all parties which poll a minimum of either 0.5 percent of the total votes cast or 10 percent of the votes cast in a single constituency.

The ultimate objective of these premiums would be to eliminate completely the existing method for the reimbursement of election campaign expenditures. However, since the proposal entailed certain risks, and since experience had first to be gained with it, the committee agreed that the existing reimbursement procedure should be retained for a transition period of approximately five years during which time there would still be funds left available for reimbursement purposes after the payment of the basic sum and the premium. These residual funds would be distributed according to the existing principles governing the reimbursement of election campaign expenditures, but only once per election, namely, in the year in which the election would take place. In any case, the committee members noted, any such program must fall under the limitation established by the Federal Constitutional Court that parties cannot be financed mainly by public funds. Any amounts received in excess of such limits could not be paid out or would have to be returned.

ELECTION AND DONATION FUND

Finally, the committee recommended the establishment of an election and donation fund under the auspices of the Speaker of the Bundestag. This fund would serve as a central collection and distribution point for all donations and contributions that citizens do not give directly to parties. In the committee's conception, the agency which would administer the election and donation fund would also be a body suitable for organizing the annual computations and payments under the equal-opportunities scheme, for carrying out the administrative work connected with the citizen's premiums and for forwarding the annual installments to the parties, for arranging the annual payment of the basic sum for the reimbursement of election campaign expenditures, and for organizing the distribution of residual funds.

Under the proposed system, all citizens would still be able to donate directly to any party. However, if they wished to present a receipt to the tax office which did not specify the party receiving their donation, they would be able to make a donation via the fund. Donors would have to specify in each case the party for which their donation is intended. Further, the origin of the donation must be clearly delineated. Anonymous donations would accrue to the fund as income for administrative purposes. Parties also would be obliged to forward to the fund any anonymous donations that they receive directly. The donations received by the fund would be remitted monthly to the individual parties. Like parties themselves, the fund would be under an obligation to disclose donations of more than DM 20,000 that are made in one year from a single source. Finally, the fund's financial report would be attached to the party's accounts.

CONCLUSIONS

Overall, the committee's proposals could only take effect if, after adoption of the new arrangements, all parties were faced with similar conditions relative to their political importance. This would mean eliminating the distortions and financial difficulties faced by political parties on account of past and present circumstances. Though this was not directly connected with the committee's mandate, the committee was convinced that the devaluation by inflation of the lump-sum government reimbursement for political parties has exacerbated the financial problems of parties. The current reimbursement rate, which has not been increased since 1974, is DM 3.50 per second vote cast. It could be said that there is a "pentup demand" for government funding which, in line with inflation, would amount to DM 1.00 for the 1980 Bundestag elections and DM 1.50 for the 1983 Bundestag elections. But it was not for the committee to decide how any debts might be reduced with the aid of government funding; this would be a matter for parliament to decide as it saw fit.

It will take several years before the effects of the committee's proposals are fully discernible. The obligatory reports can serve the purpose of monitoring the progress made. Although the reports are primarily intended to produce greater accountability, they also are suitable for detecting deficiencies and undesirable developments in the implementation of the new concept.

The committee recommended that the legislative bodies review the consequences of the proposals in the light of experience and on the basis of the annual reports by the Speaker of the Bundestag and make adjustments every five years where deemed necessary. Such adjustments also should be made in line with economic development.

In response to the proposals of the Presidential Committee, the German Bundestag enacted a new law on party finance in December, 1983, which went into force on January 1, 1984.[17] The law included much of the committee's proposals, including an amendment to the Basic Law (Section 21, par. 1) requiring the parties to publicly account for their use of funds and for their assets, and alterations to the Political Parties Act of 1967, and reforms of the Tax Laws. The alterations to the Political Parties Act and the reforms of the Tax Laws were the same as the committee had recommended, with one addition: the tax reduction for donations of more than DM 20,000 per year can only be claimed if the actual donor's full name and address were published in the account reports of the parties.

The legislature did not, however, adopt the committee's recommendations concerning either limitations on loans by parties or the general concept of the Election and Donation Fund. It reduced the recommended penalties for parties which acquire funds illegally from ten to two times the sum illegally acquired. It also rejected the system of the "Citizen's Premium" because it seemed to the parties too dangerous to give the people an additional "finance vote." The parties feared that the voters could split their votes and give their political vote to one party and their financial support to another. This, they argued, could make the Citizens's Premium completely uncalculable.

The first official Report of Account of the political parties since the new legislation has now been published.[18] The Report was delayed because the FDP did not declare a DM 6 million donation from Helmut Horten (a famous "department store king" in Germany), which had been revealed by the newspapers.[19] The most noteworthy aspect of the Report was that the Social Democrats, against all expectations, received the largest share of tax reductions on their donations and membership fees relative to the number of votes they received.

Response to the new laws has been mostly positive. Political parties were pleased by the increases in funding permitted under the new regimen. The business sector also was pleased, particularly by the fact that limits on tax-deductible political donations were removed. The main criticisms of the new legislation have been from constitutional lawyers who have argued that the new regulations regarding tax-deductible donations violate the equal protection clause of the German constitution. The system, they contend, favors parties such as the Christian Democratic Union (CDU), the Christian Social Union (CSU), and the Free Democratic Party (FDP), which tend to represent the wealthier social classes. Since higher income individuals are more able than less wealthy persons to take advantage of such tax deduction opportunities, the new laws favor the parties which are likely to be the beneficiary of a greater percentage of support from wealthy individuals.

In July 1986, the Federal Constitutional Court in Karlsruhe ruled on a suit against the new law brought by the Green Party, the only party which had argued against the original passage of the law. The main issue under consideration concerned the status of "equal opportunities" for parties and the citizen's right of equal participation in the political process. The case also arose out of a scandal involving donations to parties by the Flick group which allegedly resulted in tax concessions.

The Court struck down the provisions of the 1984 law which allowed donations to parties to be deductible up to 5 percent of the donor's income. The Court set its own limit on the tax-deductibility of donations; only donations of less than DM 100,000 will now be deductible. The Court, however, upheld other aspects of the law, including provisions for block grants from public funds to the party foundations. The Greens had charged that such grants were an indirect form of party financing, and as such discriminate against those parties without foundations.

Responding to the ruling, Christian Democratic officials expressed satisfaction with the DM 100,000 limit, while Social Democrats and Green party members felt that the limit had been set too high. The Greens also announced plans to establish their own party foundation.

It is still too soon to measure adequately the effects of the new party finance system resulting from the committee's deliberations. It is reasonable, however, to conclude that the parties have been strengthened by the increase in private funds caused by the easing of tax restrictions. Further, the broadening of the transparency and disclosure laws ought to be a comfort to those alarmed by recent financial scandals involving high-ranking West German government officials. While some critics have felt that the role of public financing should be expanded as a result of these scandals, it was the committee's position that the Basic Law – as interpreted by the Courts – discourages an overwhelming reliance by the parties on the state. Increased transparency and disclosure requirements will provide necessary safeguards against abuse as the German system of political finance shifts away from reliance on government funding toward a greater role for the private sector.

Notes

1 Cf. *Bericht zur Neuordnung der Parteienfinanzierung* Vorschlaege der vom Bundespraesidenten berufenen Sachverstaendigen-Kommission, Koeln 1983; Hans Herbert von Arnim, "Zur Neuorduung der Parteienfinanzierung. Bemerkungen zum Bericht der Sachverstaendigen-Kommission," *Die Oeffentliche Verwaltung*, Vol. 36, 1983, p. 486; Hans Herbert von Arnim, "Verfassungsfragen der Parteienfinanzierung," *Juristische Arbeitsblaetter*, Vol. 17, 1985, Part 1: p. 121; Part 2: p. 207.

2 See the leading cases in *BVerfGE 8*, 51, 56; *24*, 300; *52*, 63; *73*, 40.

3 Cf. Hans Herbert von Arnim, *Parteienfinanzierung: Eine verfassungsrechtliche Untersuchung*. Wiesbaden: Karl-Braeuer-Institute, 1982, p. 57 sq., 98 sq.

4 The new version of Article 21 (1), sentence 4 or the Basic Law runs as follows: "Sie (cf. die Parteien) muessen ueber die Herkunft *und Verwendung* ihrer Mittel *sowie ueber ihr Vermoegen* oeffentlich Rechenschaft geben." See Karl Heinz Nassmacher, "Oeffentliche Rechenschaft und Parteienfinanzierung: Erfahrungen in Deutschland, Kanada und den Vereinigten Staaten," *Aus Politik und Zeitgeschichte* B 14–15/82, p. 3; Karl Heinz Nassmacher, "Parteienfinanzierung im internationalen Vergleich," *Aus Politik und Zeitgeschichte*, B 8/84, p. 27.

5 For further explanation of political foundations, see Alexander in this volume, p. 20, Note No. 9.

6 Hans Herbert von Arnim, *Parteienfinanzierung* (note 1 supra), p. 114 sq.; Henning von Vieregge, *Parteistiftungen*. Baden-Baden: Nomos Verlag, 1977; Henning von Vieregge, "Globalzuschuesse fuer die parteinahen Stiftungen: Partei-enfinanzierung auf Umwegen?," *Zeitschrift fuer Parlamentsfragen*, Vol. 8, 1977, p. 51.

7 See *BVerfGE 20*, 56 (102); *52*, 68 (85).

8 See *BVerfGe 8*, 51 (65); *14*, 121 (134); *20*, 56 (100); *52*, 63 (82).

9 Cf. Walter Schmidt, "Politische Parteien und andere Vereinigungen," *Neue Juristische Wochenschrift*, Vol. 37, 1984, p. 762.

10 Cf. Karl Koch, *Die Vorschriften des Einkommensteuergesetzes und des Koerperschaftsteuergesetzes ueber den Spendenabzug sind reformbeduerftig*. Bonn: Institut "Finanzen und Steuern," 1983, Brief 223.

11 Cf. *Bericht* (note 1 supra), p. 197 sq. (199); see also the critique by Hans Herbert von Arnim, *Verfassungsfragen* (note 1 supra), p. 216 sq.

12 See *BVerfGE 8*, 51 (64); *24*, 300 (360); *52*, 63 (88 f.). Cf. Hans Herbert von Arnim, *Der strenge und formale Gleichheitssatz, Die Oeffentliche Verwaltung*, Vol. 37, 1984, p. 85.

13 Cf. Joern Ipsen, Steuerbeguenstigung und Chancenausgleich, *Juristenzeitung*, Vol. 39, 1984, p. 1060.

14 Confirmed by Karl Heinrich Friauf, "Parteienfinanzierung im Spannungsfeld von Buergergleichheit und staatlicher Neutralitaetspflicht: Bemerkungen zur Verfassungsmaessigkeit der neuen Spendenregelung," *Aus Politik und Zeitgeschichte* B 8/84, p. 3; Joachim Lang, "Steuermindernde Parteienfinanzierung," *Steuern und Wirtschaft*, Vol. 61, 1984, p. 15.

15 See *BVerfGE 52*, 63 (85).

16 See *BVerfGE 20*, 56 (115 sq.); *24*, 300 (337).

17 *Gesetz zur Aenderung des Parteiengesetzes und anderer Gesetze vom 22.* Dezember 1983 (BGBl. I S.1577).

18 *Bekanntmachung von Rechenschaftsberichten der Parteien 1983* vol *23*. October 1984 (Bundestagsdrucksache 10/2172); *Bericht des Prasidenten des Deutschen Bundestages nach P 23 Sect. 5 des Parteiengesetzes* vol *23*. April 1985 (Bundestagsdrucksache 10/3235).

19 Cf. *Ergaenzung der Bekanntmachung von Rechenschaftsberichten der Parteien 1983* vol *14*. November 1984 (Bundestagsdrucksache 10/2366).

Structure and impact of public subsidies to political parties in Europe: the examples of Austria, Italy, Sweden and West Germany

KARL-HEINZ NASSMACHER

Private sponsorship used to be the normal way of funding political activity in western democracies. Nowadays, however, public subsidies to political parties have become a necessity, for there is no other way to bridge the permanent gap between voluntary giving for political purposes and established functions of political parties. Experience with political corruption and unequal opportunities has contributed toward the proliferation of public subsidies.

Although public subsidies to political parties have already become a traditional feature of quite a few western democracies, important changes of regulation by law or agreement have been implemented recently. This chapter presents a comparison of party and campaign finance (including public subsidies, their legal framework and their impact) in four European countries. Resulting from comparative research in Austria, Italy, Sweden[1] and West Germany it tries to evaluate:

different techniques of subsidizing political parties with public funds;
effects of these subsidies on the internal structure of parties and on party competition;
controls of party income and expenditure by legal restriction or disclosure and reporting to the public;
procedures applied to keep public subsidies at pace with inflation.

PERSPECTIVES OF COMPARATIVE RESEARCH

Since Arnold Heidenheimer and Alexander Heard started cross-national research[2] on political finance, elaborate studies on campaign and party

236

finance (both national and comparative) have focused their attention on a particular set of countries.[3] With respect to political finance in the four countries covered by this chapter, there is more information available today than there was two decades ago; scientific studies have provided a lot of useful information and governmental regulations require periodic reporting on political money.

In 1963 Heidenheimer hinted at a traditional dilemma for comparative researchers: "Advances toward the more genuinely comparative study of political finance processes require on the one hand greater amounts of data and information, and on the other unifying concepts which will help relate structures peculiar to various systems in terms of realistically conceived common denominators."[4] This situation still prevails; data covering all the aspects of political finance are presently not available for any one country. Therefore, comparative work generally has to be postponed until more than one nation has been studied in depth. This chapter takes a middle-of-the-road line: attempting to compare the data available without waiting for other (relevant, but still unavailable) information.

In each of the four countries studied in this chapter, a cabinet form of government has contributed toward the development of disciplined party organizations, and some sort of devolution (decentralized government or federalism) has created rival power centers. The traditional party system consists of more than two parties, time and again under fire by newcomers. Voter registration is completely provided by public authorities; political parties maintain permanent field organizations staffed with full-time party agents; the electronic media are generally run by public agencies and provide free broadcasting time to parties; no other public authority (including the post office) provides any campaign service free of charge; primaries – as a nomination procedure for parliamentary candidates – are unknown; party activities are heavily subsidized by public funds.

For the campaign- and candidate-oriented political cultures of North America, political finance heavily connotes campaign finance pointing at money spent in order to influence the outcome of an election. In Europe, the term political finance can appropriately be used as a synonym for party finance.

Public subsidies in North America were introduced because the electronic media caused skyrocketing expenses which were regarded as necessary for successful campaigns. Spending limits have been one answer to this problem. None of the European countries in this study have introduced statutory spending limits or anything close to the regulations familiar in the United States and Canada. Although election campaigns have become more expensive in these countries as well, parties in Europe face a financial burden unknown to their North American counterparts: a permanent organization at the grass roots as well as a party press which is increasingly unable to break even in the newspaper market.

Further differences between European and North American countries result from different approaches toward public funding and the publicity of political money: in North America, disclosure of individual donors seems to be at the core of controlling political finance; in Europe, the emphasis (if any) is on reporting the major financial sources of the parties.

PUBLIC ROADS TO POLITICAL MONEY

Costa Rica (1954), Argentina (1955), Puerto Rico (1957), and West Germany (1959), pioneered new modes of access to political money, that is, direct subsidies taken from the public purse. Since then, almost all western democracies have taken a similar line. Public subsidies are expected to contribute to less corruption, more control of lobbying, more equal opportunities in party competition and some control of the cost explosion. When Austria introduced the direct subsidy system, political reasoning went along an almost classical line: "Parties had found that costs had been increasing, particularly in the field of communications, and existing sources of income were proving to be insufficient."[5] This reasoning is likely to be accepted also by politicians in Italy, Sweden and West Germany: In all European countries studied in this chapter, public subsidies were introduced when the parties felt that they were no longer able to get enough money from private donors or party members. Despite the fact that the roads taken to public subsidies reveal interesting differences, the present state of subsidization has passed through three structurally similar but overlapping stages of implementation.

In the first stage (1954 to 1974) all countries approached public subsidies rather tentatively. We will call this the "stage of experimentation" with West Germany setting out for new horizons in 1959, Austria and Sweden following in 1963 and 1965, respectively, and Italy coming last in 1974. Regarding the fact that public subsidies to political parties were spreading worldwide and the other nations had already entered the second stage when Italy introduced its first subsidy, it is not surprising to learn that this "late developer" did not pretend to be too cautious with the first step.

At that time West Germany, Austria and Sweden had already entered the second stage, which may be named the "stage of enlargement," and which lasted from 1967 to 1982. During this period, all countries in a stepwise procedure enlarged the parties' claim to public money by introducing new objects of subsidization. Again West Germany (due to a Constitutional Court decision) set the stage; the party subsidy was partly transformed into a grant toward party institutions for education and research (party foundations) and partly substituted by a "reimbursement" of campaign spending. Then, during the early seventies, subsidies given to parliamentary groups (caucusses) and party foundations were increased extremely.[6] Finally, in 1979, a "reimbursement" for elections to the European parliament was added. In 1967, Austria followed suit by supplementing the existing subsidy for parliamentary groups with a bonus of an extra of 90 percent designed to be spent on public relations work of party caucusses. Only a few years later, money was granted to party foundations in 1972 as well as general subsidies to parties and the press in 1975. In 1982, the members of the second chamber were included in the computation of the caucus subsidy. Sweden introduced party subsidies by all local authorities between 1969 and 1977, added press subsidies between 1969 and 1975 and legislated that an equal amount of money, a "basic grant," had to be given to each party which was entitled to receive a subsidy in 1972. Italy started with campaign and organization subsidies, then added a press subsidy in 1975 and a "reimbursement" for campaigns to the European parliament and all regional councils in 1980 and 1981, respectively.

Between 1974 and 1982, the four countries entered the third stage, the "stage of adjustment." The most urgent problem of public subsidies to political parties in this stage is: how to adjust the various types of party subsidies to inflation to make sure that the parties do not receive less and less in real money terms over time. Austria has been least concerned with this problem, because no law granting a subsidy to political parties set the amount of money to be received. Instead, an amount that seems politically appropriate is allocated by the annual budget and distributed according to rules stated by law. Specific sections of other laws even link the subsidies (for parliamentary groups and – more recently – also for party academies) to the regular pay of certain civil servants.[7] Adjustment to inflation is thus achieved automatically. The other countries probably made a mistake in putting definite money figures into their laws regulating party subsidies. Among those countries, the late developer (Italy) has gone through the political trouble of adjusting figures only twice – in 1981 for the annual allowance and in 1985 for the campaign expenses' grants. West Germany adjusted the amount of money to be "reimbursed" for each person entitled to vote twice (1974, 1983); the adjustment of grants to parliamentary groups and party foundations which both have no special legal basis can be effected by the annual budget. Inflation seems to have posed the most serious problems in Sweden: regulations of the party subsidy were adjusted five times (1974, 1975, 1977, 1982 and 1984).

CHANNELS OF SUBSIDIZATION

Accepting the necessity of adequate funds for political activity makes regulation of party and campaign finance a search for the optimum; the financial aspects of party competition still require constitutional innovation. Up to now no western democracy has been successful in combining the efficiency of the party system with:

permanent party organizations (i.e., a full-time staff);
rising costs due to inflation and an unlimited range of potential party
    activities;
independence and responsiveness of political parties; and
open collection of sufficient funds.

As a general rule in Western Europe, public broadcasting corporations provide radio and television time for campaign purposes free of expense.

In Austria, political parties – as well as important interest groups – are allocated free radio time even during off-campaign periods. In all four countries studied, paid political advertising is not permitted, but proportional to their previous voting strength all parties can use segments of free radio and TV time for their campaigns.[8] In Austria, Sweden and West Germany (this information is not available on Italy) youth and students' organizations (including those associated with political parties) also receive public grants for their activities. Such subsidies given to organizations linked to political parties may be regarded as additional subsidies to the parties.

Another indirect assistance to parties is a tax benefit provided by public law. Tax benefits for political contributions (to parties and/or candidates) by tax deduction or tax credit are familiar in the United States and Canada as well as in West Germany. Austria, Italy and Sweden do not provide similar benefits. A conservative estimate of the German tax benefit total received by those five parties currently represented in the national parliament for fiscal years 1968 thru 1983 would be approximately 400 million DM. The annual average of this is equivalent to 15 percent of all direct subsidies paid from federal funds in one year during the last decade. Due to urgent requests of the party treasurers and the recommendation of a Presidential Commission,[9] Germany considerably increased tax deductible donations and introduced a tax credit system (following the U.S. system repealed in 1986, not the Canadian model) both effective since 1984. Although there are a variety of indirect subsidies for party activity in western democracies, the term "public funding" is usually applied to direct subsidies only.

Following different national traditions, party activity is assisted by government in specific ways. Among these are direct subsidies from public funds given to parties' organizations, parliamentary groups, education and research institutions and party newspapers as well as indirect support to political parties and their activities.

Party press and party institutes

In all countries studied, a substantial segment of newspaper circulation was traditionally controlled by political parties. In West Germany, the bourgeois party press did not return after the Second World War; SPD papers returned to the market but have been steadily declining since. The country still does not pay a public subsidy to the press. Italy, by contrast, introduced legislation to increase the existing press subsidies recently. In both Sweden and Austria public subsidies to the press are closely linked to legislative action regarding parties and their funds. The Swedish party subsidy of 1965 was the substitute for a proposed press subsidy; nevertheless, a specific press subsidy was enacted a few years later. In Austria, legislation concerning the party subsidy and the press subsidy was passed jointly and even published in two consecutive chapters of the statute book.

The general principle of Swedish press policy is to support competition in the news market wherever possible. Among various press subsidies, a production grant is given to "low-coverage" newspapers, that is, those which sell less than 50 percent of the circulation in a regional market. Among the nation's dailies with the largest circulation in their relevant market, there is no party publication. All papers belonging to the Social Democratic Party or to the Trade Unions are eligible for a press subsidy, as well as some papers owned by the (previously agrarian) Centerpartiet. In the early 1970s, Social Democratic dailies received about 55 percent of the total subsidy provided for all daily party papers, thus adding a 225 bonus to Socialdemokraterna's share of the national party subsidy (See Table 1).[10]

Until 1984, the Austrian press subsidy – negotiated with the newspaper publishers' association before legislation – provided federal support for the basic production costs of every paper with a separate editorial board without applying criteria related to the newspaper market. Due to this general philosophy, a paper with the largest national circulation and the highest return on investment in that industry is entitled to receive almost the same amount of subsidy as a paper run by a regional party organization. Between 1975 and 1982, eight daily papers that were closely linked to the political parties – with less than one fifth of the total circulation – received about one third of the federal press subsidy. This amounted to a 40 percent supplement of the party organization subsidy.[11]

Table 1. *Party subsidies from the national (federal) treasury*
(in millions of national currency units: AS, LIT, SEK, DM)

	Party organization	Campaign reimbursement	Parliamentary groups	Party institutes	Total of national subsidies	National Subsidies (in U.S. $) divided by:	
						population	registered voters
Austria							
1974	—	—	17.80	28.95	46.75	0.37	0.53
1975	25.00	—	19.40	28.95	73.35	0.58	0.84
1976	64.00	—	22.35	36.95	123.30	0.98	1.41
1977	60.80	—	23.30	35.15	119.25	0.95	1.36
1978	60.80	—	25.00	35.15	120.95	0.96	1.38
1979	60.80	—	27.00	38.65	126.45	1.01	1.44
1980	70.00	—	28.08	44.00	142.08	1.13	1.62
1981	70.00	—	33.26	48.40	151.66	1.21	1.73
1982	77.00	—	35.03	44.00	156.03	1.24	1.78
1983	77.00	—	39.15	44.00	160.15	1.28	1.83
1984	82.90	—	39.55	47.20	169.65	1.35	1.87
1985	122.90	—	40.65	55.83	219.38	1.75	2.42
1974–85	771.20	—	350.57	487.23	1,609.00	12.81	17.71
Italy							
1974	42,750	—	2,250	—	45,000	0.58	0.76
1975	42,750	—	2,250	—	45,000	0.58	0.76
1976	42,750	15,000	2,250	—	60,000	0.77	1.02
1977	42,750	—	2,250	—	45,000	0.58	0.76
1978	42,750	—	2,250	—	45,000	0.58	0.76
1979	42,750	15,000	2,250	—	60,000	0.77	1.02

1980	68,998	30,000	3,632	—	102,630	1.31	1.76
1981	74,597	5,000	8,289	—	87,886	1.12	1.50
1982	74,597	—	8,289	—	82,886	1.06	1.42
1983	74,597	35,000	8,289	—	117,886	1.51	2.02
1984	74,597	30,000	8,289	—	112,886	1.45	1.93
1985	74,597	40,000	8,289	—	122,886	1.57	2.11
1974–85	698,483	170,000	58,577	—	927,060	11.88	15.82
Sweden							
1974	29.75	—	9.06	—	38.81	0.64	0.88
1975	27.93	—	8.77	—	36.70	0.61	0.83
1976	40.25	—	12.66	—	52.91	0.87	1.20
1977	40.25	—	12.58	—	52.83	0.87	1.19
1978	52.50	—	16.33	—	68.83	1.13	1.56
1979	52.35	—	16.85	—	69.20	1.14	1.55
1980	52.35	—	16.35	—	68.70	1.13	1.54
1981	52.50	—	16.35	—	68.85	1.14	1.54
1982	60.55	—	19.11	—	79.66	1.32	1.78
1983	60.38	—	18.94	—	79.32	1.31	1.77
1984	60.38	—	18.94	—	79.32	1.31	1.77
1985	72.60	—	22.73	—	95.33	1.57	2.14
1974–85	601.79	—	188.67	—	790.46	13.04	17.75

Table 1. (cont.)

Party organization	Campaign reimbursement	Parliamentary groups	Party institutes	Total of national subsidies	National Subsidies (in U.S. $) divided by:	
					population	registered voters
West Germany						
1974 —	26.3	26.3	35.0	87.6	0.60	0.85
1975 —	50.8	29.3	42.5	122.6	0.84	1.19
1976 —	59.0	30.5	42.2	131.7	0.90	1.28
1977 —	15.0	35.0	53.7	103.7	0.71	1.01
1978 —	22.1	38.6	61.6	122.3	0.84	1.19
1979 —	198.7	41.6	68.3	308.6	2.11	2.99
1980 —	63.8	44.6	74.3	182.7	1.25	1.77
1981 —	15.1	47.0	79.7	141.8	0.97	1.37
1982 —	52.6	48.4	83.3	184.3	1.26	1.78
1983 —	173.3	50.9	85.8	310.0	2.12	2.96
1984 —	175.3	56.6	85.8	317.7	2.17	3.07
1985 —	77.3	58.2	96.9	232.4	1.59	2.25
1974-83 —	676.7	392.2	626.4	1,695.3	11.60	16.39

Figures in U.S.-$ computed at exchange rates of December 31, 1982.
Note: Election years are in italics.
Sources: Data on subsidies from legal sources published in *Gazetta Ufficiale* and reprinted in Giorgio Pacifici, *Il costo della democrazia* (Roma: Cadmo editore, 1983), pp. 192–229; the Austrian and West German federal budgets of 1974 to 1985; Gullan M. Gidlund, *Partistod* (Umea: CWK Gleerup, 1983), pp. 240s. Population data from Statistisches Jahrbuch fur die Bundesrepublik Deutschland; registered voters from Keesing's Contemporary Archives.

In 1985, an additional subsidy for low-coverage papers was added. About one third of the total press subsidy for that year was distributed under this new provision. It is very likely that regional party papers will benefit especially from this most recent amendment. Finally, in addition to the federal benefits, the Austrian states distribute additional press subsidies of their own.

When West Germany introduced party subsidies through a block grant from the federal budget in 1959, the governing parties had claimed to perform activities in adult education by training people to participate in politics. The provision that a subsidy was given to foster civic education was dropped in 1963. In 1966, the Constitutional Court ruled that subsidies to political parties – for the whole range of their activities as well as for civic education – were unconstitutional. The Constitutional Court considered only a limited reimbursement of campaign expenses to be constitutional under the Basic Law. Beside legislating what they considered to be a campaign reimbursement, the parties remodeled the general party subsidy into a grant which was given to support civic education activities of separate institutions linked to established parties, namely the "political foundations." This turned out to be Germany's innovative contribution to political finance.

Activities of the German political foundations range from adult education in residential colleges, training courses at the grassroots, and grants to students or doctoral candidates to running institutes for policy research and historical documentation; they even reach out to development projects in third world countries.[12] Financial support for party foundations is provided by annual block grants from federal (See Table 1) and state budgets, and supplemented by special grants for specific activities.

When Austria implanted the institution in 1972, it avoided some of the problems in the German model. Both compulsory reporting for each fiscal year and auditing are required. Because their range of activity is limited (not including third world relations or scholarships), the Austrian "party academies" are closely defined as service institutions for their parties.[13] Austrian federal law provides for a "basic grant," that is, an equal amount of money is given to each "party academy." In addition, a specific grant is given to each party determined according to the number of parliamentary seats held by that party and the total allocation for parties in the federal budget (See Table 1). In 1984, the basic grant and the additional grant were tied to the salaries of public servants, especially university professors. Italy and Sweden do not have similar subsidies or institutions.

Parliamentary groups and campaign spending

In each of the four countries, a part of the public subsidy is distributed to parliamentary groups (i.e., caucusses – See Table 1). The four countries studied almost seem to be designed as examples of continuous scaling. The party subsidy in Italy is formally paid to the parliamentary groups. According to the law, the caucusses are allowed to keep a maximum of 10 percent for their own purposes, and they are legally obliged to transfer at least 90 percent of the grant to their party headquarters. Thus, in reality, the subsidy goes to the party organization. In Sweden, parliamentary groups receive a basic grant and supplement according to their respective size and status, with a 50 percent bonus given to the parties in opposition. This kind of subsidy is the smallest of all Swedish subsidies.

West Germany pays considerable subsidies to parliamentary groups with an opposition bonus of about 15 percent. This amount however, is neither based on legal provisions nor indexed to take care of inflation. Only in Austria do party caucusses receive the most sophisticated kind of subsidization. Provided by a special act, grants to parliamentary groups are computed according to the number of seats held and by the salaries of certain public servants, namely staff members with clerical and academic training. To this amount, a 90 percent bonus for publicity activities of the parliamentary groups is added.

Although the rising costs of political campaigns have stimulated the introduction of party subsidies, Sweden and Austria do not provide a special subsidy related to campaign expenditures. In both countries, parties polling a minimum of votes without gaining representation in the national parliament can be subsidized in election years only. This provision might be interpreted as a specific kind of campaign reimbursement for small – that is, unsuccessful – parties. In Italy, parties which are considered "serious competitors" on the national level receive a flat grant after the election of the national parliament, the European parliament and the regional councils as a subsidy to cover part of their campaign expenditures (See Table 1). According to the type of election, different modes of allocation and eligibility are applied, with some including a basic grant to all parties eligible for the subsidy.

In West Germany, the system of party subsidization works the other way around. Due to a Constitutional Court ruling that political parties may only receive compensation for a fair amount of necessary campaign expenditure from public funds,[14] the party subsidy was built on the fictitious principle that parties are to receive a "reimbursement" of campaign expenditure based on a fixed amount per vote and election. Between 1969 and 1983, the actual amount of campaign expenses was never published, calculated or controlled in any other way. Starting at DM 2.50 in 1967, the lump sum per registered voter was increased to DM 5.00 for the election of the European Parliament in 1984 and the federal election to be held in 1987. The states provide similar subsidies; state and federal subsidies work through a system of increasing installments which turns the "reimbursement" into an odd type of annual allowance (See Table 1).

Party organization

Subsidizing the operational costs of parties constitutes the Austrian, Italian and Swedish road of public subsidies (See Table 1). Political parties in Italy which are represented in the Chamber of Deputies or the Senate receive annual grants. The total amount of these subsidies as well as the mode of their distributors are fixed by law. In Austria, the national party headquarters receive subsidies allocated to the parties in the annual budget. These subsidies, however, are divided into a basic grant and a supplement paid according to the number of parliamentary seats held by members of each party. Distribution according to seats in the national legislature also applies to the Swedish subsidy, where a certain amount per seat is set by law. In order to account for changes in party strength caused by election results and to avoid marked differences in each party's claim to the subsidy, the distribution is based on a sliding scale which takes into account the number of seats held by each party in both the new and old parliaments.

Sweden's innovative contribution to public funding is a subsidy to regional and local party organizations provided by provincial and local authorities.[15] National legislation empowered provincial and local authorities in 1969 to subsidize parties represented in the provincial diet or the local council, respectively. Each council may decide on the amount of the subsidy and the mode of allocation, but each party must receive the same amount of money per seat in the council. By 1971, 90 percent of about 280 local authorities and all twenty-two provinces had introduced the subsidy; since 1977, all local authorities and provinces subsidize the parties represented in their councils. In 1980, the amount paid for each seat ranged between 500 SEK in a small rural authority and 75,000 SEK in Stockholm. The estimated total of local grants rose from 140 percent of the national subsidy in 1974 to 180 percent in 1977 and 220 percent in 1980; the most dynamic subsidy is the one paid by the provinces.[16]

EFFECTS OF PUBLIC SUBSIDIES

Empirical evaluation of the impact of public funding on political parties and party systems is related to scientific concepts such as participation, legitimacy, identification, centralization and bureaucratization. Some of the hypotheses put forward in scholarly research[17] and political debates can be evaluated with reference to the experience of the four European countries studied in this chapter.

Petrification of the party system

The term "petrification" refers to the absence of change in a party system. As far as political competition between parties is concerned public funding tends to favor bigger parties rather than smaller ones, and established parties over newcomers. Thus, there are two dimensions of the petrification issue: one refers to the strength of existing parties as compared to each other; the other dimension aims at the opportunity for new parties to enter the system.

Looking at the change of power positions within different political systems, Sweden and West Germany experienced an alternation of power (back and forth): in one country the bourgeois parties lost power to the Social Democrats and regained it, in the other, it was a governing socialist party that lost – and then regained – power. In Italy, the office of Prime Minister has been held by three different parties despite the fact that only one of them – the Christian Democratic party – is the dominant or ruling party. In Austria, after the election of 1983 the big Socialist party (SPO) was joined by a small bourgeois party (FPO) in forming a type of coalition government unknown to that country for more than fifty years. In all four countries, since the two main parties experienced marked losses and gains in popular support during the last decade, public funding was obviously a negligible factor in the fluctuations.

Looking at the entry of new parties into the system, Italy and West Germany offer some evidence. In each country, a new party – in both cases, of a "New Left" political orientation[18] – has successfully entered the party system by winning representation in the national parliament: The Partido Radicale in Italy and Die Grunen (The Green Party) in West Germany both exercised remarkable political influence on certain issues: Partido Radicale was successful in forcing all "parties of the constitutional arch" to defend party subsidies in a close referendum while the Green Party forced the main party of the left – the Social Democratic Party (SPD) – into alignment with the "Peace Movement" on the disarmament issue. The Green party also has been characterized as the first case of party building by public subsidies. This is partly due to technicalities of the German funding system. A threshold of 0.5 percent of the popular vote gives access to a "reimbursement" of campaign expenditures without winning a seat in parliament. By contrast, the threshold is 1 percent in Austria, 2 percent in Italy and 2.5 percent in Sweden. Entry into the party system is rather a

question of thresholds (for public subsidies and parliamentary representation) than of principle.

Alienation of supporters

When the financial resources of political parties are limited, the combined
risks of corruption, scandal and electoral defeat have served as important
checks on party activities designed to acquire more money. Statutory
control or pressure by public opinion on certain sources of income can limit
political spending and a reduction of party activity seems the inevitable
result.[19]

Public subsidies have removed this check on resources and the extension
of party activity. Parties develop a "help yourself" attitude toward public
money. Subsidies contribute to the professionalization of campaigns and
to a full-time party organization; both of these, in turn, lead to a "cost
explosion." The professionalization of political activity, catch-all parties
competing for political markets and electorates unwilling to contribute
personally may produce a cycle of alienation between parties and their
active supporters in western democracies. Regarding the financial links
between parties and their "faithful," evidence from the countries studied is
rather diverse:

> Bourgeois Parties in Sweden – due to the public subsidy and coalition
> pressures – have decided to refuse corporate donations. As a result,
> corporate money flows into single issue groups which carry out public
> relations work on behalf of conservative causes.

> In Italy and Austria membership fees have been traditionally low and
> the majority of donations used to come from public corporations
> (Italy)[20] or from kickbacks by government contractors (Austria).[21]
> There is some doubt that this flow of money has been stopped
> because of the introduction of public subsidies and legal restrictions.

> In Germany, party membership has increased during the 1970s while
> voluntary contributions – mostly from corporate money – have
> declined dramatically. According to party treasurers, these changes
> have resulted from the critical attitude of the media toward party
> donations combined with a lack of adequate opportunities for legal
> tax deductions. Recent amendments to federal law cope with the
> latter problem. The results of this new legislation will prove whether
> or not the party treasurers gave sound judgment.

The leaders of the right-of-center party in Austria (Oesterreichische
Volkspartei – OVP) and those of the left-of-center party in Germany (SPD)
advocating an increase of public subsidies indicate that their parties find it

more rewarding to weather the "political costs" of public funding than to bother their supporters for individual contributions. Private willingness to give appears to be waning. A referendum of OVP members in 1980 denied the party's leadership an additional levy of AS5 a month (i.e. less than $5 a year) by a 5 to 4 margin.[22] Even though the average monthly membership fee of a traditional mass-membership party such as the SPD, has been increased at the same rate as the industrial workers' hourly wage (186 percent from 1969 to 1983), party expenditures have outgrown the willingness of party supporters to give and the capabilities of party leaders to collect. Public subsidies are bridging the gap. National party organizations which rely heavily on this kind of funding seem to set the trend in political finance (See Table 2). Party leaders' reluctance either to cut their budgets or to stage fund-raising drives is an alarming aspect of this development.

Benefits to ruling circles

A party organization that relies on small donations and local income – as well as on voluntary activity – has to keep in touch with the active segments of its electorate. Public funding which is channeled through the national headquarters changes the character of political parties from voluntary associations to political institutions. Within each party, the balance of power shifts from party activists to full-time party workers, from local associations to the central apparatus, from changing coalitions of minorities to stable majorities. Although the new way of funding may have had a severe impact on the internal working of political parties, oligarchy is not a notion completely new to modern party organization following the "sin" of public funding: the "party boss" and the "power elite" antecede the party subsidy.

Any empirical evaluation of the impact of public funding would require detailed analysis of leadership selection, elite circulation and the techniques applied to govern a party organization. As long as different factions, cliques, groups or any other party sub-unit can independently use party resources for their own political purposes, a certain level of internal competition and democracy seem to be secured. Every system of subsidization, therefore, can be judged on this kind of impact.

The method of public financing which directs funds toward centralized party organizations, such as that practiced in Italy, deserves the highest degree of criticism. The mechanical operation of the Swedish scheme supplying public funds at all levels of government (and party organization) deserves an equal amount of praise; minorities ruling in the periphery get resources of their own from the provincial and local authorities, which are funding the grass roots of a party organization with even more money than the national administration pays to parties' headquarters.

West Germany and Austria – due to their federal systems with two levels of public funding – combine elements of the extremes. In both countries access to political money from the public purse is less centralized than in Italy, but more centralized than in Sweden. The outcomes in those countries look like a mixed blessing; they are positive as long as minorities within parties organize along regional cleavages, and negative as soon as the type of intra-party conflict approaches other patterns, for example, issue and leadership factionalism or cross-regional social cleavages respectively.

Procedures of control

With respect to party finance – "the least transparent chapter of party history"[23] – ideas of control and disclosure have time and again attracted curiosity and activity by scholars and reformers. Because political money has become an issue of public policy, it seems necessary to work out a precise line between the legitimate uses of political money, which has to be disclosed to the public, and the illegitimate transactions that ought to be subject to financial or legal sanctions.

Aims and scope of accountability

Controlling the flow of political funds can be achieved by administrative regulation or political competition. Whereas Canada and the United States have deliberately introduced spending and/or contribution limits as well as public agencies to enforce specific regulations of political finance, European countries have taken a more or less *laissez-faire* stand towards the control of party finance: there are neither spending nor contribution limits, there is incidental disclosure of large donors only, there are no independent controlling agencies and practically no sanctions. Just public access to annual reports (on party income and expenditures) and a certain form (model balance) for these reports is the European approach to the issue.

The general aim of financial accountability is to enable anyone to bring up matters of political finance for public debate.[24] By extension, the goal is to make parties raise and spend their funds in ways that are beyond reproof. The voting citizen is supposed to act as a referee if cases of financial misbehavior happen to occur. Disclosure of major political donors and press reports on political funds provide the information necessary for this judgment. News editors and competing parties act as advocates on behalf of the citizen's moral sensitivity to political finance. Making all this happen would require full disclosure of donations and

Table 2. *State funding of national party headquarters (organizations)*
(public subsidies as percentage of total income by year and party)

				Party				
Country year	Communists	New left	Social Democrats	Farmers	Liberals	Christian Democrats	Conservatives	Neofacists
Austria			SPO		FPO	OVP		
1975	—	—	14.3	—	19.0	25.9	—	—
1976	—	—	32.2	—	55.7	50.6	—	—
1977	—	—	28.0	—	45.4	48.2	—	—
1978	—	—	29.0	—	45.5	43.5	—	—
1979	—	—	16.6	—	26.2	23.8	—	—
1980	—	—	23.6	—	42.0	25.4	—	—
1981	—	—	25.1	—	46.8	38.6	—	—
1982	—	—	20.9	—	38.9	22.1	—	—
1983	—	—	—	—	31.8	38.0	—	—
1984	—	—	—	—	51.0	36.1	—	—
Italy	PCI	PR	PSI		PRI	DC		MSI
1974	44.8	—	58.2	—	95.4	75.7	—	79.8
1975	40.5	—	49.4	—	96.9	63.5	—	91.9
1976	40.0	61.8	50.3	—	96.4	64.5	—	92.7
1977	33.5	51.6	35.2	—	91.4	63.3	—	70.9
1978	27.9	79.8	31.9	—	91.3	50.1	—	83.5
1979	28.5	80.5	37.1	—	84.7	59.6	—	80.9
1980	30.8	87.9	48.6	—	92.6	61.0	—	86.3
1981	38.0	93.6	59.1	—	90.0	60.0	—	90.5
1982	30.7	90.0	42.3	—	82.7	66.4	—	85.4
1983	27.0	76.6	39.5	—	83.9	53.3	—	81.4
1984	23.7	64.3	36.5	—	82.6	58.6	—	83.5

Sweden	VPK	S	C	FPO	M
1966	45.0	58.7	80.5	41.6	38.3
1967	65.9	74.2	93.3	64.8	33.9
1968	61.7	54.6	94.5	47.3	24.6
1969	37.1	77.9	87.8	68.4	41.5
1970	25.0	49.8	82.3	54.4	35.0
1971	89.5	66.2	91.0	85.5	37.2
1972	.	64.0	.	.	36.0
1973	.	53.0	.	83.0	36.0
1974	.	72.0	.	.	37.0
1975	.	64.0	.	73.0	42.0
1976	.	54.0	.	.	38.0
1977	.	63.0	.	.	51.0
1978	.	61.0	.	70.0	55.9
1979	69.4	42.9	87.8	61.0	46.4
1980	77.9	54.2	82.0	62.9	55.7
1981	.	49.6	77.6	59.8	53.7
1982	67.4	40.0	69.4	61.3	49.9
1983	—	50.1	—	—	56.0
1984	—	51.8	—	—	58.3

Table 2. (cont.)

Country Year	Communists	New left GRUNE	Social Democrats SPD	Farmers	Liberals FDP	Christian Democrats CDU	Conservatives CSU	Neofacists
West Germany								
1968	—	—	77.5	—	94.0	78.2	65.7	—
1969	—	—	59.0	—	0.0	35.5	37.1	—
1970	—	—	31.0	—	20.5	21.6	32.1	—
1971	—	—	40.9	—	34.2	38.1	79.9	—
1972	—	—	63.5	—	56.6	50.7	57.6	—
1973	—	—	26.5	—	15.3	12.1	30.4	—
1974	—	—	51.4	—	38.1	33.7	57.7	—
1975	—	—	46.3	—	46.2	50.5	69.6	—
1976	—	—	41.3	—	34.9	40.5	39.7	—
1977	—	—	21.6	—	24.7	18.3	28.6	—
1978	—	—	28.1	—	36.4	26.6	30.6	—
1979	—	98.2	88.7	—	80.1	84.0	83.7	—
1980	—	88.0	30.7	—	65.3	34.9	27.7	—
1981	—	31.0	35.9	—	20.6	18.0	19.1	—
1982	—	78.0	50.7	—	65.2	52.3	42.9	—
1983	—	93.7	89.6	—	47.7	84.8	75.5	—
1984	—	92.5	74.0	—	86.7	75.5	63.4	—

Note: Election years have been italicized; abbreviation of party names according to national custom.
Explanation:
— = no member of this party family represented in the national parliament;
. = data not available.
Sources: Karl-Heinz Nassmacher, "Parteienfinanzierung im internationalen Vergleich," *Aus politik und zeigeschichte,* B 8/1984, p. 33. Data for 1983 and 1984 from additional information available for the four nations, mainly official reports.

reporting of all political money, neither of which any European country has yet implemented.

In West Germany, reporting includes financial transactions at all levels of the formal party organization. In this respect, Germany has always had the most advanced party finance regulation in Europe. On the other hand, regulation requiring parties to report their expenditures – common to other jurisdictions – was introduced only recently in the Federal Republic of Germany. Even after the 1983 amendment, the German reporting requirements do not include the financial situation of parliamentary groups, such as caucusses at the federal, state and local level, as well as the political foundations and incorporated enterprises, such as Konzentration GmbH and Union Betriebs-GmbH which are run as subsidiaries of political parties.

In Austria, Italy and Sweden, parties report their headquarters' finances only. Local and provincial organizations and commercial enterprises as well as the very powerful – and allegedly well-funded – internal factions of Italian parties (correnti) are not included in the reports. This leaves all financial transactions by local and provincial parties to their own discretion and prevents public curiosity from reaching out for party enterprises such as publishing firms, specific organizations or caucusses at all levels of the political system. Further, political academies and party headquarters in Austria publish their balance sheets separately, and there is no disclosure whatsoever of political funds administered by certain interest groups closely tied to specific parties, such as Kammern and Bunde.

Patterns of reporting

The 1983 amendment to reporting legislation in West Germany in one respect meant innovation for all western democracies. Far ahead of all European reporting schemes, parties in this country now have to publish a statement of their debts and assets annually. In adding the reporting of expenditures, German legislation in 1983 only caught up with that of other countries. An annual report of income and expenditures accessible to the public either on request (Sweden) or via mandatory publication in newspapers or parliamentary reports (Austria, Italy and West Germany) is a common feature of European regulation. According to an agreement between the national parties (Sweden), a decree by the Speaker of the Chamber of Deputies (Italy) or a special section of the Parties' Act (Austria and West Germany) the balance sheet of each party has to make use of a certain standardized form. Although details of the "model balances" vary there are many similarities.[25]

Neglecting national peculiarities such as lotteries in Sweden or international activity in Austria some relevant pieces of information for comparative research can be derived, at least at the national level. For example, membership dues, private donations and public subsidies as well as expenditures for staff and administration can be deduced. Important problems, however, remain unsolved. Kickbacks from the salaries of Members of Parliament – called the "party's tax" in Austria – are no longer listed separately in West Germany[26] and not mentioned in Italy; in Sweden, salaries are considered to be too low for collecting kickbacks. Transfers between different elements of a party organization as well as the development of reserves (set aside for certain purposes, e.g., election campaigns) and debts incurred to survive a shortage of funds are not discernable in a comparative manner.

Strategies of enforcement

Due to strong concern with the internal autonomy of political parties,[27] Sweden has not introduced any statutory control or restriction regarding party funds. An agreement between the five parties represented in parliament signed in 1980 covers only the reporting of income and expenditure to each other and public access to the information thus exchanged. The other European countries exercise different – although not very efficient – strategies in order to enforce public control of political money.

Subsidies to "party academies" in Austria and "political foundations" in West Germany are audited in detail by the Federal Audit Offices. In principle, the same applies to the funds provided for parliamentary groups. However, after decades of subsidization, auditors in West Germany only recently began this practice. The annual reports published by parties in three countries – not in Sweden, of course – are audited by chartered accountants. Austrian and German parties may hire chartered accountants at their own discretion; a financial report published officially must be countersigned by those who audited it. In Italy, the Speaker of the Chamber of Deputies performs his duty of checking the financial reports presented to his office – after publication in a daily newspaper with nationwide circulation – by asking three chartered accountants who are close to DC, PCI or PSI, respectively, to give a report. Procedures like these enforce little more than a minimum professional standard which is applied by political parties when preparing their financial reports. Since no regulation provides for cross-checking of details by an independent enforcing agency, other controlling effects cannot be expected.

The same applies to Austria's statutory control of campaign spending. Eight weeks before the election, parties present their campaign budget for the prior five weeks to a joint commission composed of party representatives and advertising professionals and chaired by the Minister of the Interior. After the election, parties report their actual expenditures. The commission compares budgets and reports, publishes the reports and issues a statement that each party has – or has not – kept spending within the preview budget. This procedure may help a party treasurer in turning down last minute efforts proposed by the campaign manager but it cannot be seriously considered a method to prevent cost explosion. In fact, campaign expenditures reported to – and by – the joint commission have remained almost constant over time whereas the annual financial reports for each election year show considerable leaps in overall spending. These two peices of information go together because Austrian parties spend more money in pre-campaign activities.[28]

Another feature of party finance control legislation in Italy and West Germany focuses on certain kinds of sponsorship. In Italy, for example, parties, members of parliament, regional and local councillors, candidates and factions (correnti) are not allowed to accept donations from public agencies and corporations owned by the state, whether totaly or partly, directly or indirectly. The legal sanction for both donor and recipient includes a penalty of twice the amount donated and a jail sentence. In West Germany, beginning in 1984, parties cannot receive donations from political foundations, charitable organizations and foreign or anonymous sources as well as money channeled through trade associations or donated with a certain purpose in mind. As a penalty a party caught in accepting any of these donations shall find its public subsidy reduced by twice the illegally accepted amount. This kind of regulation obviously intends to cushion emotions aroused in the general public by certain practices of the past that have come up for debate. Designed to prevent similar action in the future these rules look very much like paper tigers.

The preceding sections have probably posed more questions than they have provided answers. Therefore, it seems desirable to sum up a few persistent problems such as the accountability of political funds, the interrelation between disclosure and control, and inflation as a secular trend.

Regulation loopholes

The basic philosophy underlying the reporting of party income and expenditures has been to make the parties' accounts subject to public debate. After a decade since the enactment of European transparency legislation – more in West Germany, less in Sweden and almost that much in Italy – one question has to be asked: How much of the "costs of democracy"[29] caused by political parties is revealed by the prevailing reporting procedures? Any answer has to consider those parts of political activity that are not included in the financial reports and to relate the figures published to informed estimates of overall spending totals.

The only legitimate claim to be made for the West German situation, based on the information available, is that more than half of all political money is covered by reporting. Any other estimate of how much of a party's "combine" is revealed to the public would be premature. Italian parties prepare their balances within two or three weeks after the end of a fiscal year and publish their reports in daily newspapers with nationwide circulation. This is the quickest procedure in Europe. Following the initial rush, it takes more than a year to process the reports administratively and prepare an official publication. All of this reemphasizes Paltiel's advice that Italian reports "must be treated quizzically";[30] using only the annual reports published by the parties not even a promising guess on the total budget of party democracy in Italy could be made.

The situation in Sweden and Austria, although far from transparent, seems less obscure. In Sweden, by combining the amount of public money used to fund party headquarters' operations with informed estimates on the provincial and local subsidies and by assuming that the share of public money does not decrease on the lower levels of party organization, it can be estimated that the financial reports of Sweden's "big five" parties for 1980 disclosed only about one third of all political money spent in that country. Austrian political funds are even less open to public curiosity. According to scholarly estimates, published balances report 25 to 30 percent of the total spent on political activity.[31] Informed party workers go further to suggest that no more than 12 to 15 percent of all political money is reported. None of the four countries really seems to offer sufficient information for public debate on the issue.

Decision making after public debate of political issues is part of the essence of democracy. However, in many countries, most of the debate has been taken over by institutions acting on behalf of the general public, such as parties, pressure groups and mass media. As political money has become an issue of public policy some political systems have created public agents for the public interest, for example, the Federal Election Commission in the United States and the Chief Electoral Officers in Canada. The European countries studied have not provided anything similar; the public interest in this issue has to be safeguarded by public debate alone.

Such debate does occur whenever party finance legislation is the issue of the day. Although legislative action usually centers around details, public debate is either caused or accompanied by scandal or at least by a taste thereof. The media frequently breeds suspicion that the public purse is being exploited and opposes subsidization on principle. The parties, in turn, have invented devices to limit such criticisms. For example, legislation concerning political finance has been deprived of its partisan taste since many of the laws are passed with an inter-party consensus. This strategy forces minority parties into joint responsibility for the laws. It also leads to a situation in which all parties fall victim to scandalizing newscasts which arouse the political emotions of the mass public. The media, in turn, claims success as the only watchdog acting in the public interest.

In Sweden and West Germany this kind of ritual interplay does not seem to have produced significant results. In Austria, the parties, which have effective control of public broadcasting, managed to tranquilize independent newspapers by means of the press subsidy which was introduced at the same time as the party subsidy. For a couple of years both subsidies were increased at equal pace. In Italy, Partido Radicale and other critics in 1978 put a proposition on the ballot that would abolish public subsidies for political parties. The Christian Democratic (DC), Socialist (PSI), Republican (PRI), Social Democratic (PSDI) and Communist (PCI) parties all campaigned heavily to retain the law and almost suffered defeat.[32] The Austrian and Italian incidents make it rather hard to tell if the outcome meant victory or defeat for party democracy and public subsidies in principle. In both cases, the details of subsidization or the financial situation of individual parties were not part of the public debate.

COPING WITH INFLATION

An important issue for public funding programs is that of inflation. Inflation affects every recipient of a transfer payment; in the course of time, all subsidies have to be adjusted to rising prices. None of the subsidies to political parties studied in this article is formally indexed. The only grants which are adjusted automatically are received by the parliamentary groups and the party academies in Austria. All other subsidies in the countries studied require individual adjustments by formal legislation, either within the annual budget or by amendment to the law. Both kinds of adjustments cause "political costs" to the parties which argue for them.

During the "stage of enlargement," the parties did not feel the effects of inflation severely because they invented new kinds of subsidies and discovered items that could be included when calculating the amount of a subsidy. This direction of legislative action postponed necessary adjustments and enabled the parties to participate in economic growth (or even extend their share of the GNP). Currently, inflation is hitting parties harder

Table 3. *Party subsidies and economic indicators*
(growth and inflation)

Country	Subsidy Recipient	Type	1974	1975	1976	1977	1978	1979	1980	1981	1982	1983	1984	1985
Austria	party organizations	b	—	100	128	122	122	122	140	140	154	154	166	246
	parliamentary groups	a	92	100	115	120	129	139	145	171	181	202	204	210
	party institutes	b/a	100	100	128	121	121	134	152	167	152	152	163	193
	total of national subsidies	—	98	100	125	121	123	129	144	154	159	163	172	223
	(gross domestic product)	—	94	100	110	121	128	141	152	161	173	184	196	206
	(consumer prices)	—	92	100	107	113	117	122	129	138	146	150	159	
Italy	party organizations	1	100	100	100	100	100	100	161	184	184	184	184	184
	campaign reimbursements	1	100	100	133	100	100	300	300	333	333	333	533	600
	total of national subsidies	—	100	100	125	152	177	133	228	195	184	262	251	273
	(gross domestic product)	—	88	100	117	137	153	215	269	318	376	427	488	542
	(consumer prices)	—	86	100	117	137	153	176	213	251	293	335	372	.
Sweden	party organizations	1	107	100	144	144	188	188	188	188	217	216	216	260
	parliamentary groups	1	103	100	144	143	186	192	186	186	217	216	216	260
	total of national subsidies	—	106	100	144	144	188	189	187	188	217	216	216	260
	(gross domestic product)	—	87	100	113	123	136	153	173	190	209	234	261	.
	(consumer prices)	—	91	100	110	123	135	145	165	185	200	218	236	.
West Germany	campaign reimbursements	1	71	100	100	100	100	200	200	200	200	214	286	286
	parliamentary groups	b	90	100	104	119	132	142	152	160	165	174	193	199
	party institutes	b	82	100	99	126	145	161	175	187	196	202	202	228
	total of national subsidies	—	71	100	107	85	100	252	149	116	150	253	259	189
	(gross domestic product)	—	96	100	109	116	124	135	144	149	156	163	170	178
	(consumer prices)	—	94	100	104	108	111	116	122	129	136	141	144	

Note: Figures for gross domestic product at current prices. Explanation for type of subsidy: a = total amount adjusted automatically; b = total amount set by annual budget; 1 = amount set by separate law.
Sources: Data on subsidies from Table 1; economic indicators: Statistisches Jahrbuch für die Bundesrepublik Deutschland.

than before. As a result, the adjustment of the subsidies has become an increasingly important issue.

Figures for more than a decade (1974 to 1985; See Table 3), indicate that in the smaller democracies of Austria and Sweden, where parties have participated in the economic development of their nation, they have experienced growth as well as inflation. The two larger countries have undergone different trends: West German subsidies have significantly run ahead of economic indicators; in Italy, subsidies are considerably lagging behind. While German parties were able to increase their share of the gross domestic product, Italian parties, probably because of the subsidies referendum as well as continuing opposition from Partido Radicals, did not even dare to defend their initial share of funding. Thus they did not even secure adjustments for the loss of buying power caused by inflation.

One final note of caution is necessary. The general comparative perspective for these four systems may be somewhat distorted due to the absence of certain relevant information. For example, because the press subsidy is not included in the figures given here, the general impression may be misleading as far as Italy is concerned. This might also affect the leading position of West Germany among the countries studied. There may be further changes if all sub-national funds were included: state subsidies in Austria and local subsidies in Sweden are notoriously more dynamic than their national counterparts.[33] Where adjustment to inflation is decided upon by a number of separate bodies, this does not multiply the "political costs." Decisions on political money at the state or provincial level obviously are equally far away from the national and the local media.

CONCLUSION

Although the purposes and recipients of party subsidies vary depending on the specific structure of political systems, this paper has demonstrated that in the countries studied public funding provides considerable support for party activity: Italy seems to subsidize national parties only; Sweden provides subsidies at all levels of public administration; in Austria and West Germany, this is true for the federation and the states. The bulk of public subsidies in West Germany comes from the federation, in Austria from the states, and in Sweden from the local authorities. Information regarding Italy that reaches below the national level has not been found.

Neither the total amount of party subsidies for all levels of a political system nor the share of the public purse involved in party and campaign finance for the countries studied can be estimated adequately from the data available at present. Nevertheless, a general remark should be made regarding the overall situation. Looking at the subsidies of the four countries on a per capita basis shows that the range of difference between the rates of subsidization is fairly small (See Table 1). West German parties receive more than those of Austria and Sweden while Italy lags behind the others in the total value of subsidies received from national funds. Information available on the per capita total does not include either subsidies given to the party press, tax benefits, indirect support by any public institution, such as the broadcasting system, corporations in public ownership or quasi-public institutions like the Austrian Kammern, or direct subsidies provided by state, provincial or local authorities. After more sophisticated research, the overall picture of political funding may turn out to be rather different from the evidence presented here.

Regarding the effects of subsidization, only a tentative evaluation is appropriate. In all four countries, the bulk of public subsidies is paid to established parties – including the main opposition party. The "petrification" of party systems in Austria, Italy, Sweden and West Germany has neither kept the governing party in power nor excluded new parties from successfully competing for parliamentary representation. Open access to the national parliament as well as to public subsidies depends on specific thresholds set by law. Among the countries studied, West Germany stands out as the most open system of regulation in this respect. The distribution of power within each party system seems to depend more on political issues and social change and less on public funding.

Because public subsidies are bridging the gap between party supporters' willingness to provide and party leaders' capability to collect political money, evidence from Europe seems to hint at growing problems in the relationship between parties and citizens. Direct public subsidies to political parties are less likely to contribute toward a solution than tax incentives for individual political donations, such as a tax credit. In this respect, the European countries should learn a lesson from the Canadian experience.

Another problem posed by public subsidies is its effect on democracy within each competing party. Although public funding generally fosters centralization of power and bureaucratization of parties, some financial support for internal minorities can be provided by a multiplicity of subsidies and recipients. Federal systems of government and decentralized political finance seem to produce more favorable effects in this respect.

Disclosure and reporting of political funds have not been emphasized by any European government. Neither the reporting procedures applied, attempts towards disclosure of political donors, legal controls of campaign spending nor restrictions on certain kinds of donations really promise financial accountability of political parties in any one of the countries studied. As compared with the United States, the only European advantage had been to avoid overregulation of political finance. This should not, however, suggest that the obvious underregulation of the issue prevalent in Western Europe is the optimum for public policy.

Notes

1 The Deutsche Forschungsgemeinschaft (DFG) provided a travel grant for my field research in Austria, Italy and Sweden. The field work was turned into a success by those who provided written material and granted interviews. For their kind and useful help I am most obliged to Gote Ekstrom, Leif Gustafson, Goran Lennmarker, Bo Malmqvist, Christer Nilsson and Brigitta Tennander (Stockholm), Horst Bachmann, Bruno Peloso, Dr. de Stefano and Guiseppe Tonnuti (Rome), Karl Blecha, Friedhelm Frischenschlager, Anton Kofler, Peter Kostelka, Wolfgang Muller, Heinrich Neisser, Werner Obermayer, Erich Reiter, Robert Sedlaczek, Alfred Stirnemann, Stefan Swoboda (Vienna). Although details of the information received are not acknowledged I want to apologize for any misinterpretation that I have added. Annegret Morell (Rome), the Ministry of Finance (Vienna) and Brigitte Hetzel (Heidelberg) contributed considerably to the tedious updating process. I gratefully acknowledge their contribution.
2 Cf. Herbert E. Alexander, ed., *Political Finance* (Beverly Hills: Sage Publications, 1979); Klaus von Beyme, *Parteien in westlichen Demokratien* (Muenchen: R. Piper and Co. Verlag, 1982), pp. 241–61; Alexander Heard, *The Costs of Democracy* (Chapel Hill, North Carolina: University of North Carolina Press, 1960); Alexander Heard, "Political Financing," in *International Encyclopedia of the Social Sciences*, Vol. 12 (New York: The Free Press, 1968), pp. 235–41; Khayyam Z. Paltiel, "Campaign Finance: Contrasting Practices and Reforms," in David Butler, Howard R. Penniman, and Austin Ranney, eds., *Democracy at the Polls*, (Washington, D.C.: American Enterprise Institute, 1981), pp. 138–72.
3 Among these are the European countries discussed in this chapter as well as the United States, the United Kingdom and Canada. Recent works on these countries include: Herbert E. Alexander and Brian A. Haggerty, *Financing the 1984 Election* (Lexington, Mass.: Lexington Books, 1987); Michael Pinto-Duschinsky, *British Political Finance* (Washington: American Enterprise Institute, 1981); Leslie Seidle and Khayyam Z. Paltiel, "Party Finance, the Election Expenses Act, and Campaign Spending in 1979 and 1980," Howard R. Penniman, eds., *Canada at the Polls, 1979 and 1980* (Washington, D.C.: American Enterprise Institute, 1981), pp. 226–79.
4 Arnold J. Heidenheimer, "Comparative Party Finance: Notes On Practices And Towards A Theory," *The Journal of Politics*, Vol. 25, No. 3, 1963, p. 790.

264

5 Lord Houghton of Sowerby (Chairman), *Report of the Committee on Financial Aid to Political Parties* (Houghton Report), Cmnd. 6601, (London: Her Majesty's Stationary Office, 1976), p. 321.

6 Hans Herbert von Arnim, *Parteienfinanzierung* (Wiesbaden: Karl-Brauer-Institut, 1982), pp. 27, 31.

7 Wolfgang C. Mueller and Martin Hartmann, "Finanzen im Dunkeln – Aspekte der Parteienfinanzierung," in Peter Gerlich and Wolfgang C. Mueller, eds., *Zwischen Koalition und Konkurrenz: Oesterreichs Parteien seit 1945* (Wien: Wilhelm Braumuller, 1983), p. 254. Barbara Wicha, "Nehmen und Schaemen," *Oesterreichische Monatshefte*, Vol. 36, N. 9, 1980, p. 23.

8 Anthony Smith, "Mass Communications," in David Butler, Howard R. Penniman, and Austin Ranney, eds., *Democracy at the Polls* (Washington, D.C.: American Enterprise Institute, 1981), p. 174s.

9 Bericht zur Neuordnung der Parteienfinanzierung, *Vorschlaege der vom Bundespraesidenten berufenen Sachverstaendigen-Kommission* (Koeln: Bundesanzeiger, 1983). See Schneider in this volume for details of the Presidential Commission's deliberations.

10 Karl Erik Gustafson and Stig Hadenius, *Swedish Press Policy* (Stockholm: The Swedish Institute, 1976), pp. 103, 105.

11 Institut fuer Publizistik und Kommunikationstheorie der Universitaet Salzburg, ed., *Massenmedien in Oesterreich* (Wien: Internationale Publikationen, 1977), p. 22; Institut fuer Publizistik und Kommunikationstheorie der Universitaet Salzburg, ed., *Massenmedien in Oesterreich* (Wien: Internationale Publikationen, 1983), p. 99s.

12 Cf. Henning von Vieregge, *Parteistiftungen* (Baden-Baden: Nomos Verlag, 1977).

13 Herbert Dachs, "Ueber die politischen Akademien in Oesterreich," *Oesterreichische Zeitschrift fuer Politikwissenschaft*, Vol. 5, No. 3, 1976, pp. 391–405; Rupert Haberson and Csaba Szkely, "Die politischen Akademien – eine Zwischenbilanz," *Oesterreichisches Jahrbuch fuer Politik*, 1979, pp. 337–59.

14 For an evaluation of the ruling, see Karl-Heinz Nassmacher, "Parteienfinanzierung im internationalen Vergleich," *aus politik und zeitgeschichte*, B 8/1984, pp. 28, 31; Uwe Schleth, *Parteifinanzen* (Meisenheim: Verlag Anton Hain), 1973, pp. 265–85.

15 Harry Forsell, "Det kommunala partistoedet," *Statens offentliga udredningar* (SOU) 1972: 52, pp. 37–68; Harry Forsell, "Some Aspects of the Communal Party Subsidy in Sweden," paper delivered to the International Political Science Association, 1983, Montreal, 1973 (Los Angeles: Citizens' Research Foundation, 1983).

16 Gullan M. Gidlund, *Partistoed* (Umea: CWK Gleerup, 1983), pp. 240s, 277s.

17 See Heino Kaack, "Die Finanzen der Bundestagsparteien von 1968 bis 1975," in Heino and U. Kaack, eds., *Parteien-Jahrbuch 1975* (Meisenheim: Verlag Anton Hain, 1978), pp. 296. Dick Leonard, "Contrasts in Selected Western Democracies – Germany, Sweden, Britain," in Alexander, 1979, pp. 51, 63. Khayyam Z. Paltiel, "The Impact of Election Expenses Legislation in Canada, Western Europe and Israel," in Alexander, 1979, pp. 26, 28, 33, 35, 37.

18 The term is used as a common denominator for the two parties. Whereas

Partido Radicale is clearly "New Left," Die Gruenen (like Alternative Liste Oesterreichs and Miljopartiet) more precisely should be labelled "Environmentalists."

19 Lord Houghton of Sowerby (Chairman), *Report of the Committee on Financial Aid to Political Parties* (Houghton Report), Cmnd. 6601 (London: Her Majesty's Stationery Office, 1976), p. 53s.

20 Stefano Passigli, "Italy," *The Journal of Politics*, Vol. 25, No. 3, 1963, pp. 730s.

21 Anton Kofler, "Parteienfinanzierung und deren Auswirkungen auf innerparteiliche Strukturen," *Oesterreichisches Jahrbuch fur Politik*, 1980, p. 380.

22 Anton Pelinka, "Die Oesterreichische Volkspartei (OEVP)," in Hans-Joachim Veen, ed., *Christlich-demokratische und konservative Parteien in Westeuropa I* (Paderborn: Ferdinand Schoningh-UTB, 1983), p. 209.

23 Max Weber, *Wirtschaft und Gesellschaft*, 2nd. ed. (Tubingen: J. C. B. Mohr, 1925), p. 169.

24 Bericht zur Neuordnung der Parteienfinanzierung, *Vorschlaege der vom Bundespraesidenten berufenen Sachverstaendigen-Kommission* (Koeln: Bundes- anzeiger, 1983), p. 181.

25 Cf. Karl-Heinz Nassmacher, "Parteienfinanzierung im internationalen Ver- gleich," *aus politik und zeitgeschichte*, B 8/1984, p. 43s.

26 Hans Herbert von Arnim, "Zur Neuordnung der Parteienfinanzierung," *Die oeffentliche Verwaltung*, Vol. 36, No. 12, 1983, p. 488; Hans Herbert von Arnim, "Verfassungsrechtliche Aspekte der Neuregelung der Parteienfinanzierung 1984," *aus politik und zeitgeschichte*, B 8/1984, p. 21s; Bericht zur Neuordnung der Parteienfinanzierung, *Vorschlaege der vom Bundespraesidenten berufenen Sachverstaendigen-Kommission* (Koeln: Bundesanzeiger, 1983), p. 188.

27 Cf. Statens offentliga utredningar (SOU), Om offentlig redovisning av den politiska propagandans finansiering, SOU 1951, p. 56; Hannfried Walter, "Staatliche Parteienfinanzierung in Schweden seit dem Reichstagsbeschluss vom 15.12, 1965," *Zeitschrift fuer auslaendisches oeffentliches Recht und Voelkerrecht*, vol. 26, No. 2, 1966, pp. 399–401.

28 Anton Kofler, *Parteien im Umbruch*, Dissertation, Innsbruck 1983, pp. 146, 160s.

29 Alexander Heard, *The Costs of Democracy* (Chapel Hill, North Carolina: University of North Carolina Press, 1960). Giorgio Pacific, *Il costo della democrazia* (Roma: Cadmo editore, 1983).

30 Khayyam Z. Paltiel, "The Impact of Election Expenses Legislation in Canada, Western Europe and Israel," in Alexander, 1979, p. 35.

31 Anton Kofler, "Parteienfinanzierung und deren Auswirkungen auf innerparteiliche Strukturen," *Oesterreichisches Jahrbuch fur Politik*, 1980, pp. 381, 383; Wolfgang C. Mueller and Martin Hartmann, "Finanzen im Dunklen – Aspekte der Parteienfinanzierung," in P. Gerlich, W. C. Mueller, ed., *Zwischen Koalition und Konkurrenz: Oesterreichs Parteien seit 1949* (Wien: Wilhelm Braumuller, 1983), pp. 264–70.

32 Angelo Panebianco, "L'ultimo referendum?," *Il Mulino*, Vol. 27, No. 258, 1978, pp. 503–73; Arturo Parisi and Maurizio Rossi, "Le relazioni elettori-partiti: quale lezione?," *Il Mulino*, Vol. 27, No. 258, 1978, pp. 503–47; Gianfranco

Pasquino, "Con i partiti, oltre i partiti," *Il Mulino*, Vol. 27, No. 258, 1978, pp. 548–65.

33 Gullan M. Gidlund, *Partistoed* (Umea: CWK Gleerup, 1983), pp. 240s, 277s; Anton Kofler, "Parteienfinanzierung und deren Auswirkungen auf innerparteiliche Strukturen," *Oesterreichisches Jahrbuch for Politik*, 1980, p. 372s.

Index

accountability of political parties: and
   public funding, 251–5, 257–8, 262–3
advertising, political: in Australia, 88, 89;
   in Britain, 28, 33, 36, 38–9, 39–41; in
   Canada, 67; in European countries, 240;
   in Israel, 136; in Spain, 182–3, 184
agency, doctrine of: in Canada, 53, 54, 55,
   57–9
Aims of Industry, 38–9, 46
Alberta: election expenses legislation, 56,
   57–8, 66–7
Alianza Popular (AP), Spain, 173, 174,
   175, 177, 178, 180, 187, 188, 191–2, 193,
   195
Alliance Party (Liberal and Social
   Democrats, Britain), 25, 36, 38, 39, 48
ALP (Australian Labor Party), 3, 76, 77,
   80, 81, 82, 83, 85, 86, 87, 88–9, 90
America, *see* North America; United
   States
Americans for Responsible Government,
   113
Anderson, John, 4, 106, 107, 115, 116
anonymous donations: in West Germany,
   230, 257
Anti-Revolutionary Party (ARP),
   Netherlands, 201, 202
Argentina: public funding, 12, 14, 238
Armstrong, Ian, 80
Australia, public funding in, 12, 14, 15; of
   elections, 3–4, 76–94
Australian Democrats, 77, 81, 82, 83, 86,
   87, 88, 89
Australian Electoral Commission, 83, 84,
   86
Austria, public subsidies in, 12, 14, 15,
   247, 251, 262; adjustments to, 259;
   corporate donations, 249; and inflation,

259, 260, 261; in *laender*, 15;
   parliamentary groups, 246; party income
   from, 252; party subsidies, 238, 239,
   242, 245; political power changes, 248;
   press subsidies, 241, 245, 259; radio
   advertising, 240; reports on party
   finance, 255, 256, 258

balance sheets of political parties: in Italy,
   5–6, 155–6, 167–8
Barbeau Committee on Election Expenses
   (1964), 54–5, 56, 65
Basque National Party (PNV), 173, 174,
   175, 186
Bavarian Social Christian Union (CSU),
   192
Beauharnois Scandal, 52
Belgium: election costs, 212–14
Ben Gurion, David, 124
Bender, Paul, 61
Berg, Larry, 61
Bertoldi, Luigi, 153
Bill C-169 (Canada), 3, 59, 64–6
Brazil: public funding, 12, 14
Britain: political funding, 2–3, 24–50
Brown, Colin, 59
bureaucracies, political parties: in the
   Netherlands, 211–14
Bush, George, 4, 99, 103, 106, 110, 111,
   116
businesses, donations from, *see* corporate
   donations

Call to Australia, 81, 82
campaign expenditure: in the American
   presidential elections, 8, 14, 95–123; in
   Britain, 28, 29, 30, 31, 33, 36–41; in
   Israel, 132–6, 142–6; in Italy, 166–7,

168, 169; in the Netherlands, 211–14; party subsidies for, 246–7; in West Germany, 228–30; *see also* elections; expenditure limits

campaign reimbursement: in Italy, 242–3; thresholds, 248–9; in West Germany, 244, 245

Canada: election costs, 3, 51–75, 214; public funding, 12, 14, 15, 237

Canadian Charter of Rights and Freedoms, 60, 61, 62, 63

candidates, parliamentary: in Britain, 24, 25, 30

Cariglia, Antonio, 154

Carrick, John, 85

Carstens, Karl, 221

Carter, Jimmy, 4, 106, 116

Catalonian Nationalists (CiU), 173, 174, 175, 186

Catholic People's Party (KVP), Netherlands, 201, 202, 203, 205, 207

Center Democratic Union (Spain), 175, 178, 179, 188

Center for Responsive Politics, 113

CFA (Committee for the Future of America), 103, 104, 118

Chamber of Deputies (Italy), 154–5, 156, 255, 256

Christian Democratic Appeal (Netherlands, CDA), 202, 204, 205, 206, 207, 210, 211, 212, 213

Christian Democratic Union (West Germany, CDU), 221, 232, 233

Christian Democrats (Italy, DC), 153, 158, 160, 161, 162, 163, 164, 165, 166, 167, 252, 259

Christian Democrats (Spain, PDP), 175

Christian Historical Union (Netherlands, CHU), 201, 202

Christian Social Union (West Germany, CSU), 221, 232

Christian Voice Moral Government Fund, 114

citizens' premium: in West Germany, 221, 228, 229–30, 232

Clancy, James, 64

Committee for the Future of America, 118

Communist Party (Italy, PCI), 158, 159, 160, 161, 162, 163, 164, 165, 166, 167, 252, 259

Communist Party (Netherlands), 207, 208

Communist Party, Spain, *see* Spanish Communist Party

Companies Act (1967), 44, 46

company donations, *see* corporate donations

Connally, John, 103, 117–18

Conservative Party (Britain), 24; and the 1983 general election, 28, 30, 33, 38, 39, 40, 41; company donations to, 44–6, 47; expenditure in general elections, 26, 27, 28, 40, 42; finances, 25–30, 33–4; fund raising, 25, 48; staff at Central Office, 26; trade union legislation, 47; trade union votes for, 41

Constituency Fund (Australia), 78, 79, 80

contributions, *see* donations, political

corporate donations: in Austria, 249; in Britain, 41, 44–6, 47; in Israel, 147; in Italy, 155; in the Netherlands, 206; in Sweden, 249; in West Germany, 17–18, 223

Coporation Tax Act (West Germany), 226

Costa Rica: public funding, 12, 14, 238

Country Party (Australia), *see* National Party

Cranston, Alan, 100

Curti, Aurelio, 153

d'Hondt formula: in Spanish elections, 173, 184

D66 (Democrats, Netherlands), 202, 204, 205, 206, 207, 212, 213

DC, *see* Christian Democrats (Italy)

debate, public: and party finance legislation, 258–9

Decree-Law (Spain), 172, 173

democracy, effects of subsidies on, 262

Democratic Center Union (UCD), Spain, 173, 174, 175, 177, 186, 187, 195

Democratic Party (United States), 48, 101–2, 117

Denmark: public funding, 12, 14

Diefenbaker, John, 54

direct mail solicitations, 3, 48; in the American presidential campaigns, 101–2; by the SDP (Britain), 34, 48

disclosure of political donations: European countries, 251; in Spain, 181–2; in West Germany, 222, 223, 225, 230, 231, 233

DNC (Democratic National Committee), 110, 112, 115

Dole, Robert, 103

Dominion Elections Act (Canada, 1874), 52

Dominion Elections Act (Canada, 1908), 52

donations, political, 9, 251; in Australia, 76, 84, 85; by British companies, 41, 44–6, 47; in Israel, 138–9, 140, 147; in Italy, 153, 155, 156; legal restrictions, 257; in the Netherlands, 206–8, 215, 216; and public financing, 16, 17; in Spain, 179–80, 194; in the United States, 95, 96, 101–2, 147; in West Gemany, 222–4, 225, 226, 227, 230, 231–2; *see also* corporate donations; individual donations

Duplessis, Maurice, 53

educational institutes, subventions to: in the Netherlands, 205, 210

Election and Donation Fund: in West Germany, 221, 230, 232

elections: in Australia, public funding of, 3–4, 76–94; British general election (1983), 38–41; expense legislation in Canada, 3, 51–75; frivolous candidates in (Britain), 25; in the Netherlands, 202; and public financing, 13; in Spain, 176–84; *see also* campaign expenditure; campaign reimbursement

entertainers, and benefit concerts: in the American presidential campaigns, 102, 116–17

equality of opportunity: Israeli political parties, 132, 136–7; in the Netherlands, 206; and public funding, 10, 17–18; West German tax laws, 227–8, 232

Etzioni, A., 128

European parliamentary elections, 12, 155; in Italy, 154, 155, 239; in the Netherlands, 208, 210; in West Germany, 220, 229, 247

Ewing, K.D., 41

expenditure limits: in the American presidential elections, 96, 97, 98–101; in Australia, 77; on candidates or parties, 19; in Israel, 132–3, 138–9; in Spain, 180–1; in West Germany, 222; *see also* campaign expenditure

extra-parliamentary political parties: in Spain, 18, 176–8

FCM (Fund for a Conservative Majority), 114, 115

FEC (Federal Election Commission), 100, 104, 105, 106, 108, 115, 118, 120, 258

FECA (Federal Election Campaign Act, 1971), 95, 96–8, 100, 106, 107, 108–9, 111, 113, 118; Amendments, 95, 101, 107, 108–9, 111, 115

Federal Election Commission, 100

Federal Republic of Germany, *see* West Germany

Ferraro, Geraldine, 112, 114

Finland: public funding, 12, 14

Flick case, 180, 186, 191, 232

foreign political donations: in Spain, 179–80; in West Germany, 223, 237

Fraga, Manuel, 192

France: public funding, 12, 14, 15

Free Democratic Party (West Germany, FDP), 221, 232

fund raising: in the American presidential campaigns, 101–2; and the British Conservative Party, 25, 48; and public financing, 13

Furst, Walter, 221

Germany, *see* West Germany

Glenn, John, 100–1

Gordon, Walter, 54

Gorman, Joseph, 61

government: and political funding, 9, 10, 12–20

GPV (Netherlands), *see* Reformed Political League

Grant, Wyn, 46

Green Party (West Germany), 8, 17–18, 232–3, 248

Guttman, E., 124

Hamel, Jean-Marc, 61

Hans Seidel (German foundation), 192

Hart, Gary, 4, 99, 105, 116

Heard, Alexander, 214, 236

Heidenheimer, Arnold, 159, 236, 237

Histadrut (Trade Union Confederation, Israel), 124, 129–32, 139

Honors (Prevention of Abuses) Act (1925), 45

Houghton Committee, 28

House of Representatives (Australia), 77

Hughes, Colin, 77

Hunt, .R.J., 85

income tax, *see* taxation

Income Tax Act (West Germany), 226

individual donations: in the American presidential campaigns, 101; in Austria and West Germany, 250; in North America, 238

inflation: and public funding, 239, 259–61

interest groups: advertising by, in Britain, 38–41

Irvine, William, 52

Israel: party financing, 5, 124–52; public
  funding, 12, 14, 17
Italian Social Movement-National Right
  (MSI-DN), 159, 160, 162, 163, 164, 165,
  166, 167, 252
Italy, public funding in, 12, 14, 15, 247,
  250, 262; attempts to abolish, 259;
  corporate donations, 249, 257; and
  inflation, 260, 261; party income from,
  6, 252; party subsidies, 238, 239, 242–3,
  246; political power changes, 248; press
  subsidies, 241; reports on party finance,
  255, 256, 258

Jackson, Henry M., 106
Jackson, Jesse, 4, 100, 116
Japan: public funding, 12, 14
Jones, Leonard, of Moncton, 58
Joseph Rowntree Social Services Trust
  Ltd, 34, 36–8

Kaack, Heino, 221
Kennedy, Edward, 103
Kirscheimer, Otto, 13
Klugman, R.E., 83
Knesset (Israeli parliament), 124, 125, 128,
  130, 137, 138, 141, 142, 143, 144, 149

KVP (Netherlands), *see* Catholic People's
  Party

Labor Party (Australia), *see* ALP
  (Australian Labor Party)
Labor Party (Britain): and the 1983
  general election, 38, 39, 40, 41, 42;
  expenditure on general elections, 40, 42;
  finances, 30–4; membership, 33; political
  funding, 24, 25; staff at Head Office, 26;
  trade union affiliation fees, 2, 30–2,
  41–4, 46–8
Labor Party (Israel), 124, 131, 135
Labor Party (PvdA), Netherlands, 201,
  203, 204, 205, 206, 207, 209, 210, 211,
  212, 213, 216
Labor Research Department, 44, 45
labour unions: in Spain, 190, 194; *see also*
  trade unions
Labour Party, *see* Labor Party (Britain)
Law for the Elections to the Knesset and
  Local Authorities (1969), 5, 125, 132–6,
  138, 141, 142
Law for the Financing of Parties (1973),
  136–41
legal cases: *Buckley vs. Valeo*, 19, 61, 102,

115; *Green Party vs. the German
  Budestag*, 17–18, 232–3
Lesage, Jean, 53
Liberal Party (Australia), 76, 77–8, 79, 80,
  81, 82, 84, 85, 86, 87, 88, 89
Liberal Party (Britain), 34–6, 38, 40, 41
Liberal Party (Canada), 52, 54, 55, 56, 65,
  67, 68, 69, 70, 71, 72
Liberal Party (Italy, PLI), 159, 160, 162,
  164, 165, 166, 167, 168
Liberal Party (Netherlands), 211
Liberal "society": in the Netherlands, 200,
  201, 211, 215
local authorities: in Sweden, 261
local elections: in Spain, 183–4
Lubbers, Rund, 202

Maassen, Hermann, 221
Macdonald, John A., 52
Mackenzie, Alexander, 52
Mackenzie King, W.L., 52
Maassen, Hermann, 221
Mariotti, Luigi, 154
Mason, John, 79
matching funds, public: and the American
  presidential elections, 4, 95, 98, 106, 116,
  117; in the Netherlands, 209
McMullan, Bob, 89
media: and party finance legislation, 259;
  in the Netherlands, 216; *see also*
  newspapers; radio; television
membership of political parties: in Austria,
  249; in Britain, 33; in Israel, 129, 146; in
  Italy, 158–9, 249; in the Netherlands,
  203–6; in Palestine, 127; in Spain, 175,
  186–8, 188–9, 190, 191, 193, 194, 195; in
  West Germany, 223, 225, 226, 232, 249,
  250
Mexico: public funding, 12, 14
minor parties, 20; in the United States, 95,
  107, 109, 115
Mondale, Walter: presidential campaign,
  98–9, 100, 101–2, 103–5, 110, 111, 112,
  114–15, 118
money: and politics, 2, 9–23
Montero, J.R., 186, 187
multicandidate committees, *see* PACs
  (Political Action Committees)

NALGO (National Association of Local
  Government Officers), 39, 47
National Party (Australia), 76, 77–8, 79,
  80, 81, 82, 84, 85, 86, 87, 88, 89, 90
National Right to Work Committee, 105

NCC (National Citizens' Coalition,
Canada): constitutional challenge by,
59–64
NCPAC (National Conservative Political
Action Committee), 114, 115
Neibenzal, Itzhak, 138
Netherlands: contributions, 206–8;
expenditure of parties, 211–14;
membership dues, 205–6; party finance,
7, 200–19; party membership, 203–5;
pillarization of society in, 7, 200–3, 205,
209, 215–16; public funding, 12, 14,
208–11
New Democratic Party (NDP, Canada),
54, 55, 56, 65, 68, 69, 70, 71, 72
new political parties, 262; in Israel, 132,
146; in Italy and West Germany, 248
New South Wales: public funding, 12, 15,
77–80, 89–90
newspapers: Australian, 77–8, 88, 89;
European political parties, 238; Italian
political parties, 165–6; Netherlands
political parties, 208; press subsidies,
241, 245, 261
North America: public subsidies, 8; *see
also* Canada; United States
Norway: public funding, 12, 14
Nova Scotia: election expense legislation,
51, 56, 57, 66, 67, 69
Nuclear Disarmament Party (Australia),
86, 87, 88, 89

Ontario: election expenses legislation, 3,
56, 57–8, 66–7, 69, 70
opposition parties: and public funding, 18,
262

Pacific Scandal (1873), 52
Pacifist Socialist Party (PSP), Netherlands,
201, 204, 207, 213
PACs (Political Action Committees), 61,
216; and the American presidential
elections, 99, 102, 103–5, 112, 114, 118,
120
Palestine: Zionist parties in, 126–9; *see also*
Israel
Paltiel, Khayyam Z., 16, 18
parliament (Italian): laws on public
financing, 153–4
parliamentary groups: public subsidies to,
246–7
Patten, David, 80
payroll costs: Italian political parties,
163–4

PCI, *see* Communist Party, Italy
PDUP (Party of Proletarian Unity for
Communism), Italy, 159
Pearson, Lester, 54
people: and political power, 11
People's Party for Freedom and
Democracy (VVD), Netherlands, 201,
204, 205, 206, 207, 210, 211, 212, 213
Piccoli, Flaminio, 154
Pinto-Duschinsky, Michael, 16, 17
Political Parties Act (West Germany), 224,
225, 229, 231
Political Parties Law 1978 (Spain), 184–6
Political Reformed Party (SGP),
Netherlands, 201, 203, 204, 205, 208,
211, 212, 213
power, political: and money, 9, 10, 11
prenomination campaigns: in the
American presidential elections, 14, 95,
96–8, 116–17
Presidential Committee of Experts on
Party Funding (West Germany), 7–8,
220–35
Presidential Election Campaign Fund, 115,
121
presidential elections: in the United States,
4, 95–123
press subsidies, 241, 245, 261; *see also*
newspapers
Progressive Conservative Party (Canada),
54, 58, 59, 65, 68, 69, 70, 71, 72
Proletarian Democracy (PU), Italy, 159,
160
propaganda, electoral: in Italy, 165–6
proportional representation: in the
Netherlands, 201, 208–11
PSDI, *see* Social Democratic Party, Italy
PSI, *see* Socialist Party, Italy
Puerto Rico: public funding, 12, 15, 238
PvdA (Netherlands), *see* Labor Party

Quebec: election expenses legislation, 55,
56, 57, 69, 70
Quebec Election Act (1963), 53–4
Quinn, Ernie, 78

Radical Party (PR), Italy, 159, 160, 162,
163, 164, 166, 167, 168, 248, 252, 259,
261
radio advertising: in Australia, 88, 89; in
Austria, 240; in the Netherlands, 208–9;
in Spain, 183, 184
Rae, Douglas, 184
Raffi Party (Israel), 124, 129

Reagan, Ronald: presidential campaign, 99, 102–3, 107, 110, 111, 113, 114, 118, 120, 121
Reale, Oronzo, 154
Rees, W.M., 41
referendum campaigns, costs of: in Italy, 167
Reformed Political League (GPV), Netherlands, 201, 203, 204, 212, 213
regional elections: in Italy, 239; in Spain, 183–4
religious institutions: in Israel, 5, 148–9
Republican Party (Italy, PRI), 154, 159, 160, 163, 164, 166, 167–8, 252, 259
Republican Party (United States): direct mail solicitations, 48; and the presidential campaigns, 111–12, 112–13
research institutes, subventions to, 211; in the Netherlands, 205, 210
Revenue Act (1971), 95, 108–9
Richardson, G.R., 83, 85–6
RNC (Republican National Convention), 110, 111, 112, 113
Rose, Richard, 38

Sainsbury, David, 34, 36
Saskatchewan Election Act, 68
Schmelzer, Norbert, 205
SDP, *see* Social Democratic Party (Britain)
Senate (Australia): candidates' expenditure limits, 77
Senate (Italy): election funds, 154–5, 156
SGP (Netherlands), *see* Political Reformed Party
small political parties, *see* minor parties
Social Democratic Center (CDS), Spain, 174, 179
Social Democratic Party (Britain, SDP), 34, 36, 37, 38, 48
Social Democratic Party (Italy, PSDI), 154, 159, 160, 162, 163, 164, 165, 166, 167, 259
Social Democratic Party (West Germany, SPD), 221, 232, 233, 241, 248, 250
social organizations: and political power, 11
Socialist Party, Italy (PSI), 153, 158, 159–60, 162, 165–6, 166, 167
Socialist Workers Party (Canada), 72
Spain: equal opportunity, 18; party funding, 6–7, 172–99; public funding, 12, 14, 15, 18
Spanish Communist Party (PCE), 173, 174, 175, 177, 178, 180, 186, 187, 192–5

Spanish Socialist Workers Party (PSOE), 173, 174, 175, 177, 178, 180, 186, 187, 188–91, 195
SPD, *see* Social Democratic Party (West Germany)
St Laurent, Louis, 53
Stanfield, Robert, 58
Suarez, Adolfo, 172
subsidies "in kind": in Spain, 182–3
Sweden, public subsidies in, 12, 14, 15, 247, 250–1, 262; corporate donations, 249; and inflation, 260, 261; parliamentary groups, 246; party income from, 253; party subsidies, 238, 239, 243; political power changes, 248; press subsidies, 241; reports on party finance, 255, 258; youth organizations, 240

Tarte, Israel, 52
Tasmania: public funding of elections, 77, 86, 87
taxation, and political funding, 8, 262; in Canada, 55, 69, 70–2, 262; in Israel, 130–2; in the Netherlands, 206, 208; in the United States, 13, 14, 15, 95–6, 120, 121, 240; in West Germany, 8, 220–1, 223, 226–8, 231, 232, 233, 240
Tebbit, Norman, 46
television advertising: in the American presidential campaigns, 99; in Australia, 88, 89; in the Netherlands, 208–9; in Spain, 182–3, 184
Trade Union Act (1913), 46
Trade Union Act (1984), 24–5, 47
trade unions: Israel (Histadrut), 124, 129–32, 139; in the Netherlands, 216; in West Germany, 223; political levy funds (Britain), 2, 24–5, 30–2, 41–4, 46–8; *see also* labor unions
Transport and General Workers' Union, 32, 44, 48
Trudeau, Pierre-Elliott, 55
Turkey: public funding, 12, 14

United States: direct mail solicitations, 48, 101–2; election costs, 214; political donations, 95, 96, 101–2, 147; presidential elections, 4, 95–123; public funding, 12–13, 15, 17, 263, 237; taxation, 13, 14, 15, 95–6, 120, 121, 240

Venezuela: public funding, 12, 14
Vogel, Horst, 221

voter registration drives: in the American
  presidential campaigns, 113–14
VVD (Netherlands), *see* People's Party for
  Freedom and Democracy

Weimer Republic (Germany), 17
West Germany, public funding in, 12, 14,
  15, 17–18, 245, 251, 262; contribution
  laws, 257; corporate donations, 249;
  election campaigns, 13, 202, 214; Green
  Party, 8, 17–18, 232–3, 248; and
  inflation, 260, 261; in *laender*, 15;
  parliamentary groups, 246; party

financing, 7–8, 214–15, 220–35, 238–9,
  244, 246–7; party income from, 254;
  political power changes, 248; press
  subsidies, 241; reports on party finance,
  255, 256, 258; youth organizations, 240
Woodsworth, J.S., 52
Wran, Neville, 78

youth organizations, subventions to, 240;
  in the Netherlands, 205, 210

Zamir, Itzhak, 148
Zionist political parties, 126–9